# VOICES
## FROM THE
# TRENCHES

# VOICES FROM THE TRENCHES

## LETTERS TO HOME

## NOEL CARTHEW

NEW HOLLAND

First published in Australia in 2002 by
New Holland Publishers (Australia) Pty Ltd
Sydney • Auckland • London • Cape Town

14 Aquatic Drive Frenchs Forest NSW 2086 Australia
218 Lake Road Northcote Auckland New Zealand
86 Edgware Road London W2 2EA United Kingdom
80 McKenzie Street Cape Town 8001 South Africa

National Library of Australia Cataloguing-in-Publication Data:

Carthew, Noel.
Voices from the trenches: letters to home.

ISBN 1 86436 744 X.

1. World War, 1914–1918 – Personal narratives, Australian.
2. Soldiers – Australia – Correspondence. I. Title.

940.48194

Publishing Manager: Anouska Good
Project Editor: Sophie Church
Designer: Nanette Backhouse
Cartographer: Ian Faulkner
Production Manager: Janelle Treloar
Printer: Mcpherson's Printing Group

This book is typeset in Scala LF 10pt.

10 9 8 7 6 5 4 3 2 1

---

## ACKNOWLEDGMENTS

p. 182: *The Letter*, from *The Poems of Wilfred Owen* edited by Jon Stallworthy,
published by Chatto & Windus. Reprinted by permission of The Random
House Group Ltd; p. 234: *Everyone Sang*; and p.238: four lines from *Aftermath*,
copyright Siegfried Sassoon, by kind permission of George Sassoon; p. 243:
three verses from *For the Fallen* (September 1914), by permission of The Society
of Authors on behalf of the Laurence Binyon Estate; front cover (bottom):
Australian War Memorial E00833.

---

## PUBLISHER'S NOTE

Although certain descriptions are fictious, this book is based entirely on fact.
The letters are reproduced exactly as they were written and there are no
fictional characters, places or events.

For my father, JAMES HOLMAN CARTHEW, his brothers
CHARLES and FRED CARTHEW, my father-in-law
WELLWOOD T. SMITH, and their Australian and
New Zealand comrades of the First World War;
and for their sons and daughters—including my
husband, ANTONY WELLWOOD SMITH—to whom
we owe our freedom.

*Greater love hath no man than this,*
*that a man lay down his*
*life for his friends.*
JOHN 15:13

# → Contents ←

# The Carthew Family

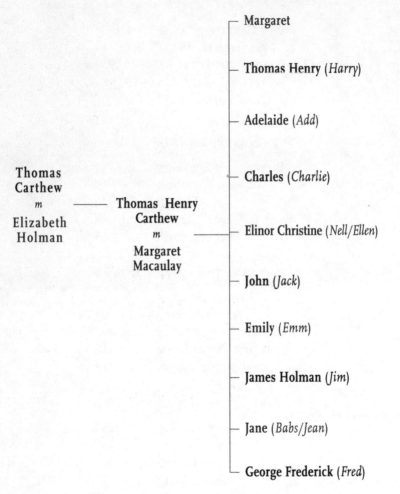

Thomas
Carthew
*m*
Elizabeth
Holman

Thomas Henry
Carthew
*m*
Margaret
Macaulay

Margaret

**Thomas Henry** (*Harry*)

Adelaide (*Add*)

**Charles** (*Charlie*)

Elinor Christine (*Nell/Ellen*)

**John** (*Jack*)

Emily (*Emm*)

**James Holman** (*Jim*)

Jane (*Babs/Jean*)

**George Frederick** (*Fred*)

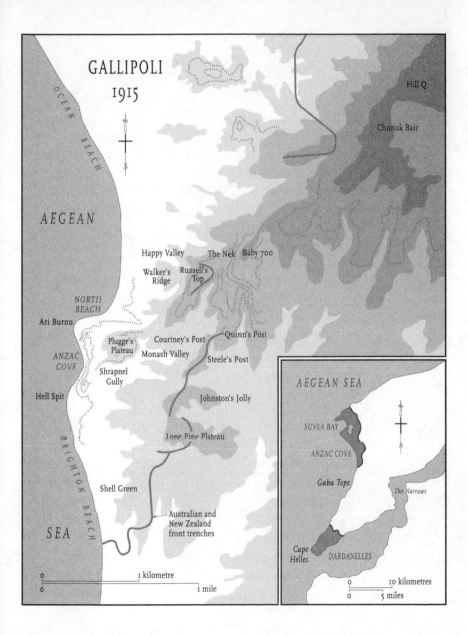

GALLIPOLI
1915

OCEAN BEACH

AEGEAN

NORTH BEACH

Ari Burnu

ANZAC COVE

Hell Spit

BRIGHTON BEACH

SEA

Happy Valley

Walker's Ridge

Plugge's Plateau

Shrapnel Gully

The Nek    Baby 700

Russell's Top

Courtney's Post    Quinn's Post

Monash Valley    Steele's Post

Johnston's Jolly

Lone Pine Plateau

Shell Green

Australian and
New Zealand
front trenches

Hill Q

Chunuk Bair

0  1 kilometre
0  1 mile

AEGEAN SEA

SUVLA BAY

ANZAC COVE

Gaba Tepe    The Narrows

Cape Helles    DARDANELLES

0  10 kilometres
0  5 miles

TURKEY

MEDITERRANEAN

SEA

Tripoli

○ Damascus

SEA OF GALILEE

Jaffa ○
Jerusalem ○
Gaza ○  PALESTINE
Rafa ○
  ○ Beersheba  DEAD SEA

Alexandria ○
Port Said ○
Romani ○
Ismailia ○
SUEZ CANAL
Heliopolis ○
Cairo ○ Suez

Nile River

EGYPT

SINAI

RED SEA

R. Jordan

**SINAI AND PALESTINE
1914 – 1919**

160 kilometres
100 miles

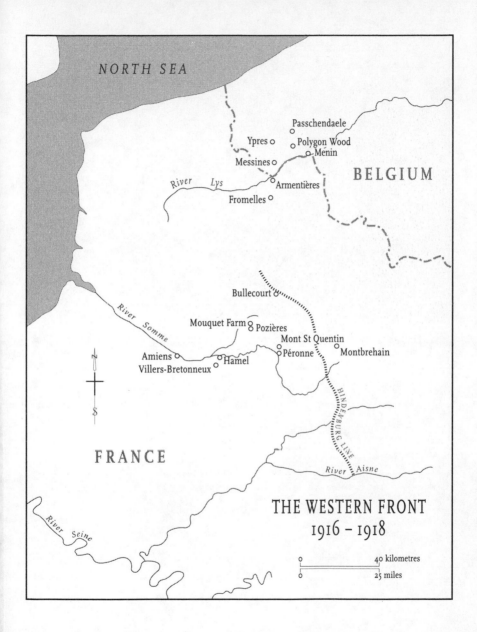

NORTH SEA

BELGIUM

Passchendaele
Ypres
Polygon Wood
Menin
Messines
River Lys
Armentières
Fromelles

Bullecourt
Mouquet Farm
PoN Pozières
Mont St Quentin
River Somme
Péronne
Montbrehain
Amiens
Hamel
Villers-Bretonneux

HINDENBURG LINE

FRANCE

River Aisne

THE WESTERN FRONT
1916 – 1918

River Seine

40 kilometres
25 miles

# → Prologue ←

THE SMALL PARAGRAPH in the *Myrtleford Mail* early in July 1914, reporting the assassination of an Austrian archduke and his wife in Sarajevo, an obscure European town in Serbia, raised scarcely a ripple of interest among its readers. The Victorian farming community was far more deeply concerned by the continuing drought, which had ravished the countryside, causing a glut in livestock, with prices plummeting and an astronomical rise in the cost of fodder. Things had never been so bad, they told each other gloomily, as they vainly scanned the heavens for signs of life-saving rain.

Among those hardest hit was the Carthew family of Happy Valley, who had farmed their land for more than fifty years, carving out a holding from virgin bush and adding to it, from time to time, as land was opened up for selection. Thomas Carthew had emigrated in 1857 from the family farm, Treggojerran in Cornwall, hoping, like thousands of others, to make his fortune on the Victorian goldfields. He never found his El Dorado, but he did save enough money to bring his wife and family of nine children out to Australia within the next few years, and to buy a smallholding near Myrtleford in order to establish a cattle run with his eldest son, Thomas Henry.

'Young Thomas', aged thirty-two, brought his timid, eighteen-year-old bride home to his autocratic mother, Elizabeth, in 1872. Young wives were expected to work hard in the nineteenth century, and Margaret Macaulay was no exception. A tiny woman, only five feet tall and of slight build, she was required to rise well before dawn, often in freezing weather, to help milk the cows and feed the stock, and to labour alongside her husband, digging post holes in the hard, clay soil, splitting rails and chopping wood, and lifting back-breaking sacks of grain. She paused only to wash, iron, scrub and cook for her ever-increasing family, often until midnight, while her husband and his mother took their ease on either side of the fireplace. Her only respite came when she was too unwieldy in pregnancy and for the two weeks following her lying-in. This was in no way a concession to her recovery, but to ensure a good supply of milk for the infant.

Margaret bore five sons and five daughters, all of them healthy except her first-born. The baby was brought into the world after a protracted and very difficult birth aided by her mother-in-law, Elizabeth, who at first pronounced the child stillborn. Although eventually resuscitated, the girl, Margaret, was severely brain damaged. Thereafter, as each healthy child was born, Elizabeth would summon the minister and have the baby christened after each of her own nine children: Thomas Henry, Adelaide, Charles, Elinor Christine, John, Emily, James Holman, Jane and George Frederick. In all likelihood, their mother Margaret was not even consulted.

To do her justice, Elizabeth was not idle. She sewed for the whole family, using an ancient sewing machine, and supervised the smaller children, instilling in each from an early age her own rigid code of English gentility (once even scolding Jane for not bowing when a neighbouring farmer came to visit), making no concession to the primitive conditions in which they lived.

At intervals, Elizabeth would receive letters from her family, the Holmans, who owned iron and steel mills in Cornwall, sometimes enclosing a money order for five pounds. On receipt of this bounty she would ask Thomas to harness the horses and secure her platform rocker to the dray floor for her regal procession into Myrtleford. There she would purchase an entire bolt of turkey twill—a dark red, serviceable material with which she would clothe almost the entire family. The children detested this fabric, but wear it they did for most of their childhood. The arrogant old woman died at the ripe age of eighty-six, surviving her son Thomas by several years, and ruling the roost until the last.

After she was widowed at the age of forty-six, Margaret continued to run the farm as her husband Thomas would have wished, aided by her son Charles, while at the same time rearing the seven younger children and caring for her eldest daughter Margaret. Her eldest son, Thomas Henry, or Harry as he was always called, had left home after an argument with his father and gone to Western Australia to make his way in the world.

———— • ————

Even when it was reported, a couple of weeks after Serbian student Gavrilo Princip's assassination of Archduke Franz Ferdinand, that Austria was making impossibly harsh demands on Serbia as a pretext for war, there was little interest among the country folk of Australia. After all, Europe was half a world away. Charles Carthew, however— now aged thirty-two—read the paragraph closely.

Four years before, he had helped organise the formation of the district's light horse troop, and as its commanding officer he attended the annual training camp at Broadmeadows. The program not only encompassed manoeuvres, drill, weapons training and equestrian skills, but also lectures on military tactics and strategy, world history and politics. From these lectures, Charles was aware that Europe, and particularly the Balkans, had been a smouldering powder keg for years—a powder keg waiting for the spark struck by a consumptive Serbian student that was to set the entire world ablaze.

Unless Charles was much mistaken, it was now almost inevitable that France, still smarting over the loss of her rich territory, Alsace-Lorraine, during the Franco–Prussian war, would seize the opportunity to attack Germany, and Britain would have no choice but to join France. The colonies would be asked for support, and the Australian High Command would call for volunteers to aid the mother country as they had done in the past, and would doubtless do so in the future. But Charles said nothing of this to the family; time enough for that later.

He was not mistaken in his predictions. When Serbia failed to meet Austria's demands, and also refused to allow Austrian police to investigate the assassinations, Austria declared war on Serbia. All European powers were mobilised, and Germany, who had initially professed to be determined to maintain peace, joined Austria in declaring war on Serbia. Germany then sent an ultimatum to Russia and France, who had each sided with Serbia, and declared war on both, before announcing its intention of marching through Belgium 'for security reasons'—a threat which Germany then proceeded to carry out. This of course could not be tolerated, and Britain sent an ultimatum to Germany to withdraw its troops from Belgium by midnight of 4 August 1914. When the deadline passed with no action taken by Germany, Britain announced immediately that their two countries were at war.

The British went wild with euphoria. There was not the slightest doubt in their minds that Britain—the greatest and most powerful nation on earth, with her limitless dominions, her empire on which the sun never set, her vast resources and enormous wealth accumulated over the relatively peaceful years of Victoria's and Edward's reigns—would be victorious. And of course, one Englishman was worth a dozen Germans.

Above all, the British Navy indubitably ruled the waves, comprising nearly eighty destroyers, ten armoured and ten battle cruisers, a dozen or so light cruisers and more than twenty battleships. Their very names were redolent of the glory of past victories: *Revenge, Agincourt, Iron Duke, Marlborough, Conqueror, Collossus, Hercules* and *Monarch*, to name but a few. With such an enormous armada, and scores of armed merchantmen to guard their shores and blockade Germany, most people believed the war would certainly be over by Christmas.

One of the few who did not share this optimistic view was the eminent statesman Sir Edward Grey—a man of great vision and wide knowledge. He was only too aware of the burning ambition of Germany, the Fatherland, for a great, united teutonic state encompassing the whole of Europe, and its greed to acquire the rich resources of Russia, the Low Countries and France—an ambition that would engender limitless power. He also knew that the jingoistic Prussian generals commanded an army of superbly trained and disciplined troops, and held the resources necessary to mount a long and aggressively fought campaign. 'The lamps are going out all over Europe—we shall not see them lit again in our lifetime,' wrote Sir Edward, sadly.

The British people, however, responded with patriotic fervour. Brass bands playing martial music led parades of volunteers, and lorries equipped with loudhailers challenged young men to join the march to enlistment and make their sweethearts proud to be soldiers' girls. Little boys dressed in sailor suits and military jackets waved Union Jacks, and Lord Kitchener, the Boer War hero, glared hypnotically from billboards, pointing at every passer-by declaiming 'I want you!' Thousands responded—hundreds of thousands, in fact. Students from universities and colleges, the youth of whole neighbourhoods, entire villages, factories and mines, not to be outdone by their comrades, sometimes enlisted en masse and marched off together to the 'great adventure'.

Within a day or so of the declaration of war, Britain had requested aid from her colonies, and the Australian Government had immediately cabled a pledge of 20 000 troops, seventy field artillery guns and the necessary ships to transport them to Europe. Britain accepted gratefully.

Margaret Carthew heard the news from a passing neighbour with a sinking heart. She had no doubt at all that her son Charles would consider it his duty to enlist, although, as a farmer, he would not be expected to do so.

Charles's feelings were ambivalent. On the one hand, he had been trained since 1910 for just such a contingency, and his duty was clear. Furthermore, the adventure of a lifetime beckoned, although he knew the dangers it entailed, and the prospect of journeying to the other end of the earth was infinitely exciting. On the other hand, he would be leaving his ageing mother and his sisters to shoulder the running of the farm, with only Old Dave, the cowman, to help (his younger brother Jack was no longer living at home). And there was Ethel, his sweetheart, who was dreaming of a June wedding, after which they would live happily ever after.

One week later, the Australian Imperial Force (AIF), comprising infantry, artillery and light horse, was formed. It called for volunteers, and overnight the whole country went wild with patriotism. In Melbourne, long, ragged queues of men representing every stratum of society besieged Victoria Barracks, waiting patiently to enlist. Eager-faced schoolboys in straw boaters or cadet uniforms listened respectfully to medalled Boer War veterans' reminiscences. Bowler-hatted office workers leaning on furled umbrellas, some nattily attired in spats, brushed shoulders with apprentices and farmers' sons, and swapped yarns with middle-aged men, the spirit of adventure still strong in their veins. An infectious mood of euphoria and camaraderie pervaded the motley crowd. To further whip up patriotism, a brass band played martial music and popular songs of the Boer War: 'Soldiers of the Queen' and 'Goodbye Dolly Gray'. Well-dressed matrons, eager to do their patriotic bit, dispensed mugs of hot, sweet tea to the volunteers.

Not all were motivated by patriotism, however. The unemployed saw enlistment as the promise of a steady income to feed their families; shabby, unshaven hoboes hoped to salvage their self-respect and earn an honest shilling. Chronically dissatisfied workers grasped at the prospect of an exciting lifestyle, and others trapped in a loveless marriage sought to escape from a nagging spouse and demanding offspring. But one and all looked forward to adventure and travel to far-off places, the glamour of a uniform and the respect it engendered.

In late October 1914, less than three months after the Australian Government responded to the British call for aid, the AIF of 20 000 men, in twenty-six transports, made rendezvous in the magnificent King George Sound in Albany, Western Australia, along with ten ships carrying New Zealand's expeditionary force of 10 000 troops. (These men of the Australian and New Zealand Army Corps were soon to be universally known as 'Anzacs'.) The vessels also carried the promised seventy field artillery guns and 7477 horses, the largest contingent ever to leave Australia. (A total of 160 000 Australian horses were sent overseas during the course of the conflict, and only one was ever to return.)

At dawn on 1 November, the Australian and New Zealand transports, escorted by four cruisers—HMAS *Melbourne*, HMAS *Sydney*, HMS *Minotaur* and the Japanese cruiser *Ibuki*—steamed majestically out to sea, their tall funnels belching smoke, bound for Egypt and the Dardanelles. Tragically for many of their complement, Albany was to be their last view of their native land.

Day by day, Margaret waited for her son's decision with a heavy heart. It was almost a relief when Charles told her that he was going into town to enlist in the 8th Light Horse. She made no demur. He would do his duty as he saw it, as he had always done, and she would not add to his burden by pointing out that he was needed at home.

Young Fred Carthew (Margaret's youngest son, nineteen-year-old George Frederick), had already followed his eldest brother Harry to Western Australia, and, as his enlistment number, twelve, testifies, lost no time in joining the AIF in Perth. Having been a trooper in his brother Charles's Light Horse Militia in Victoria, he had no trouble at all being accepted by the Western Australian 10th Light Horse. Like the 8th Light Horse, the 10th recruited only those who could pass the most stringent tests of health and fitness, and as a result was almost exclusively made up of station hands and farmers' and squatters' sons, who could ride anything on four legs and shoot the eye out of a needle. Fred fitted admirably into this category.

Kitted out in his uniform, wearing his polished leather leggings and his slouch hat at a jaunty angle, Fred swaggered up Wellington Street to his brother James Holman's boarding house, where he was greeted with something less than enthusiasm. It appeared that James had also opted for the light horse and had presented himself at the Barracks Recruiting Office at the top of St George's Terrace, confident that he would be accepted. Of medium height, he looked taller than he was, and appeared very fit, with his broad shoulders and narrow hips, his hair as black as a raven's wing, his dark eyes and a bronzed complexion.

The interview went well, and after passing the riding test with flying colours he went along to the medical officer who, on checking his chest, regretfully told him that he had severe asthma, probably as a result of horseriding, and that because he would be in constant contact with horses he could not be passed. James was well aware of his asthma, having suffered acutely from it all his life on the farm, but doctors had never connected it with the horses he rode each day to school. Since coming to Western Australia he had been reasonably free of the severe attacks which had sent him to hospital frequently as a child. Bitterly disappointed, he resolved to try again at a later date.

On Christmas Eve, Margaret was both overjoyed and saddened by a surprise visit from Fred, accompanied by his mate Jack Regan. She was happy to learn that he and Jack would be spending Christmas with the family, but appalled at the possibility of losing both Charles and Fred in a faraway war which she saw as having nothing to do with Australia. However, she stifled her worry and made every effort to ensure that the Christmas celebration was a happy occasion. Charles and his friend Lieutenant Henry had also been able to get leave, and, apart from Harry and James, the entire family was present.

Would these carefree youngsters have hesitated for even a moment, one wonders, had they the slightest inkling of the horror and tragedy that was to follow? I think not.

→ PART ONE ←

# Charles

# ⇢ Farewell, Happy Valley ⇠

AFTER HIRING A LAD to help Old Dave with the heavier farm work and visiting a lawyer to make his will, Charles and his two horses, Silver and Buller, reported for duty at Broadmeadows, which had been the chief training camp for Victorian military personnel since the Boer War.

Charles had found it almost as painful to take leave of his cattle dog, Black, as it had been to farewell his fiancée, Ethel. Ethel understood that he felt it was his duty to volunteer, but Black did not—and would certainly not have approved anyway.

Charles had reared Black from a tiny puppy when his mother died, and from then on the two were inseparable. Margaret often wondered whether there was some mystic link between the dog and her son. It was always necessary to tie Black up whenever Charles left the farm, otherwise he would simply materialise wherever his master happened to be, whether in town on business, or drilling his light horse troop, or, as on one memorable occasion, in church. Black had arrived in the middle of 'Onward Christian Soldiers' and joined in, howling and yelping joyously, just as he always did at home when the family gathered around the piano on winter evenings. Charles, scarlet with embarrassment and suppressed laughter, had had to drag Black out by the collar!

Sensing Margaret's distress, Black had viewed the preparations for his master's departure with foreboding. He watched anxiously as the big wood and canvas cabin trunk was loaded into the boot of the buggy, just as he had watched on other occasions when Charles had departed for the annual training camp, but he seemed to know instinctively that this time was different. Attuned as he was to his master's every mood, Black was well aware of Charles's sadness, and gazed pleadingly up at his master as he sat down on the front steps and took the dog's head lovingly between his hands.

'Black, I have to go away, perhaps for a long, long time, and I want you to look after Mother for me while I'm gone.' Charles could not go on, but pulled the dog's ears gently, then sprang to his feet. 'Hold him, Nell,' he said gruffly to his sister Elinor as he turned away and climbed into the buggy where Old Dave waited holding the reins. One last wave, and then he was gone.

---

8th Light Horse Reg. A.I.F.
Broadmeadows

Dear Nell,

*I suppose you think it is about time I reported myself. I been expecting a letter from home but as none has come to hand I had better write one myself. Well I have droped back to my old self again feeling tip top. Mother and Em was here this evening.*

*As I believe we are off on about the 20th for sure so we wont be long now the sooner the better. The first contingent are landed in Egypt so they will have it fairly warm. It will do me.*

*We have the most of the horses in now they are not much of a mob.*

*Well how are things progressing up home has Dave got that crop in. Ill drop him a line or two — has Jack taken those grunters [pigs] away yet and has he got his sheep shorn. Did Dave do any buss with those sheep men with regards to Freds top paddock.*

*Has there been any more rain up there it was a bit wet here this morning.*

*What do you think Sir Henniker Heaton, Bart. claims to be a cousin of mine. Says his mother's G.dad or something like that was Thomas Carthew and came from Pensance what do you think of that. A Sir in the family ... better let Jinnie know. Dont think there is anything in it though Ill investigate further. Oh send me the Holmans address if I get Home I may dig up our ancestors.*

*Well goodnight. C.C.*

DEAR JANEY,

*I sposed you'll be surprised to get this but I have nothing better to do as our lecture was called off. Old Conner is in the tent here writing to his intended as usual, dont know what he writes about as hes at it all the time. We have been out bivoucking* [military-style camping] *all day. We have most of the horses in now, they are not much of a mob. I'm glad I decided to bring Silver and Buller they run rings around the rest. Another inspection tomorrow by the Gov. Gen. damn him, more work for us. Have just been up to see my lot — they are all hard at work with the kiwi* [boot polish], *there seems to be no end to inspections. I hope Mother is quite recovered now. Was told last night I'm likely to get another star when we embark, hope so.*

*Well goodnight old girl. C.C.*

*P.S. Fred writes that he and Jim are thinking of joining the Light Horse in Perth. Mother will be rather cut up if they do.*

As the embarkation date for the 8th Light Horse drew nearer, Charles received letters from the parents of the men in his troop, among them Mr Cox, entrusting their sons to his care and wishing them godspeed.

MINYUP
FEB. 8TH 1915

DEAR SIR,

*I beg to tender to you and your troop (of which I was pleased to get a photo from my boy Fred) my best wishes for your welfare and success. I am also very pleased to know the respect and confidence which my son places in you. In a sense I must commend him to your care. I don't expect you to think him 'the white haired boy' his mother does, but I think you can depend on him to do his bit, and rely on him at a pinch. It's hard to part with him but I'd sooner do it than own a 'Midgley'. That you will both do your duty I do not doubt, and trust you will have your wishes gratified and return to us with honour and promotion is the wishes of Mrs. Cox and myself.*

*With our sincerest wishes for your welfare,*

*I remain, Yours truly, A.E. Cox.*

Church of England Mision Tent
8th Light Horse
24.2.'15

Dear Nell,

*I'm just back from seeing one of my boys who has had the bad luck to get the measels — he is almost broken hearted to think he is to be left behind. Ethel is coming down to try and see me off tomorrow morning but I'm afraid there is no chance, they are dam strick [sic] about it and wont leave anyone off or anyone on the warfe. You are right when you said she is a jolly girl. She is more, she is all thats good. I'm making no mistake this time old Girl. In fact I wonder why she has taken to an old roughian [sic] like me. Well Nell we are sleeping under service conditions tonight, no blankets or anything, greatcoat on the hard ground with the stars for a roof. Keep an eye on Black and dont let him sit on his heel too much. Well old Girl its getting late so will ring off and check the fellows and have a bit of sleep before we move off — havent had too much this last night or two. Nell, look after Mother for me. Goodnight hope to get home again some day when this affair is over.*

*Your Affect Bro Charlie.*

As Charles had written, the public were not allowed on the wharf as the 8th Light Horse, plus a further detachment of infantry, embarked on the *Star of Victoria* in the cold, misty, grey dawn of 25 February 1915.

Ethel Seymour, Margaret and her four daughters joined the milling throng of relatives and friends who pressed against the iron railings, hoping to catch one last glimpse of their menfolk. It was quite impossible to distinguish any one person among the sea of faces that lined the ship's rails. After they had waited for nearly two hours among the packed crowds, the ship's horn blew several times before the small tugs eased the great, grey vessel away from the wharf, a military band playing martial music all the while.

On board, the prevailing mood was sombre as the men craned to catch one final glimpse of their loved ones and to gaze at what would be their last sight of home for a long while—and for some, ever. Those on land watched, with mingled pride and heartbreak, as the ship carried husbands, sons, sweethearts and fathers away, perhaps forever, to fight for King and Country. They strained to see through tear-blurred eyes as the troop ship turned and headed for the open sea.

It was a sad, silent little group who boarded the train home to Myrtleford that fateful February day that was to change their lives forever.

---

DEAR MOTHER,

*We have had a very fair trip so far and are now anchored in Port and are to stay a day or two. I am in charge of the squadron horses, not the best job in the world but I dont mind, the smell is the worst as it gets very stuffy below. We've only lost one horse so far. Well Mother I hope you are keeping in good health, you want to look after yourself and dont go doing too much work. I suppose Jack is in camp now with my troop. I'd very much like to know how they turned out under their new leader. They are a very poor crowd altogether, only four out of thirtyfive volunteered, I am very much disappointed with them. Hoping this finds you all in the best of health.*

*Your Affect. son C. Carthew.*

---

LIEUT. C CARTHEW, AT SEA
WENSDAY MAR. 17TH '15

MY DEAR MOTHER,

*I must wish you many Happy returns of this day before I go any further and I hope you are keeping in the best of health. We are keeping fairly busy, I have 159 horses to look after besides signalling classes, sword exercises and lectures, and every officer has to give a lecture, but it is not all work. We have sports of different kinds, boxing tournaments, tug of war and other events. I was introduced to Father Neptune yesterday — it was great fun. The barber shaves you in a very rough and ready way with a bucket of white paint and a two foot wooden razor and then one is ducked several times. We have been inoculated twice and vacinated — we ought to be nearly bullet proof by the time we reach our destination. We have been fortunate as regards sickness in this Regt. we left two behind at our last port* one of Dip and the other Typhoid, nothing further. We are all to get leave tomorrow and may be able to get a good drink of that beverage we are all so fond of.

When you see the Bank Manager just ask him if my three pounds ten shillings a week is being put into your account. I may as well tell you Mother that I made my will out in your favour, as what you get out of the estate wont be much. But there is one thing I'd like you to do Mother if anything happens to me — one never knows when one is out on a job like this — and that is to send My Dear Girl one hundred pounds out of my place. It is not much but I do think I should do something in that way. Dont let this worry you Mother, I dont think for one moment I wont come back. All the same I like to be on the safe side and Ethel is a grand girl and I want you to invite her over and look after her for my sake. I think you will think nearly as much of her as I do. Well Mother we are going ashore today at Colombo and I shall post this and miss the censor. We have been rather fortunate with our horses, only 8 has gone over the side, 2 from our 'C' Sqdrn. My horses are doing tip top, better now than when they left, especially old Silver who takes everything as a matter of course — he's a grand old horse and Buller is looking grand too. I hope the drought has broken by this. Well Mother remember me to all enquiring friends, trusting you are all in the best of health.

From your Affectionate son Charlie.

---

LIEUT. C. CARTHEW, 'C' COY
8TH LIGHT HORSE, MENA CAMP
15TH APRIL, '15

DEAR MOTHER,

We arrived here last Sunday after a splendid trip across, disembarking at Suez and train to Cairo and walked here leading our horses the 10 miles and were a weary crowd when we got into camp. We were better off than any of the Regts that came before us as Cpt. McLaurin and his advance party had horse lines and tents fixed up for us. We are very comfortable here, much more so than at Broadmeadows — the only thing I dont like is our mess which is run by Egyptians. We pay three shillings and sixpence a day and I havent relished a meal since being here with these smelle natives waiting on one. Imagination may have something to do with it but a fellow hears such tales of filth about these people that you carnt help it.

The men are more comfortable too, they have two big tents per troop to sleep in and each Sqdrn has big mess sheds with tables and forms for the men to have their meals in.

The old historic buildings in Cairo are wonderful and the population is nearly double that of Melbourne, and such a mixture of all the breeds under the sun.

Well Mother I suppose the Summer is over with you now and I hope the drought — I heard one of the officers in camp got a cable saying there had been good rain all over Aust. but there is nothing in the latest papers about it. How is everything at home. Those stock of mine should sell well judging by the price of chaff. I was a member of the Board of Enquiry today and we got through early so I am writing this before lunch. I wrote from every Port so its time I got an answer. The mail has just come and all my mates are sitting around reading letters and none for me has turned up yet. We get no news and in fact one hears more in Aust. of what is going on at the front than we do here. The natives run around every day selling a thing they call a paper but it is not worth reading. At daylight you hear them selling goods and everything is very good very nice.

We are only about three days from the fighting but there doesnt seem much use for mounted men at present. Fred is here and looks tiptop, roaring like one thing because he has not got a letter from home since being here. We are leaving here for Heliopolis Camp 15 miles away as the water here is bad. The weather is beautiful but Summer is just starting — the worst thing we have to put up with is sandstorms, one can scarcely open your eyes then.

All the Infantry has left and one Sqdrn of Light Horse we have a good idea of where they have gone but must not say.

I seen most of the Myrtleford boys — they marched out the night we came in. We cannot ride our horses yet but I am dead lucky — Cptn. McLaurin has lent me one of his horses until mine are fit. Old Buller has had bad luck. I landed him in better condition than at Broad-meadows and now he must get kicked in both front and hind legs.

*Am pleased to say I landed all my men and horse but have 4 men at present in Mena Hospital — two of them have been very bad, influenza I think. Well Mother I have to attend a lecture in 10 minutes, I wouldn't mind if we learnt anything but we dont. Tell those girls to write and I like to know how my stock is getting on.*

*Will close now, From your Affect. son Charlie.*

# ✦ The First Bloodbath ✦

*B*Y THE BEGINNING OF 1915, the Allied and German armies in France had reached a stalemate. Not only was there dissention among the French and English Generals regarding strategy, but the Chief of the German General Staff, von Falkenhayn, who wished to deliver a decisive blow to the Allies on the Western Front, was frustrated by the Kaiser and Generals Hindenburg and Ludendorff, who favoured demolishing Russia on the Eastern Front first. Although the Germans had come within 20 miles (32 kilometres) of Paris during the early stages of the war, they were weakened by the decisive Battle of the Marne in September and the transfer of troops to the Eastern Front, which was in need of reinforcement against Russia.

With the entry of Turkey into the war, on the side of Germany, Russia found herself geographically cut off from her allies. To aid Russia, Winston Churchill, the First Lord of the British Admiralty, conceived the daring idea of using the French and British navies to attack the strong Turkish forts guarding the narrow Straits of the Dardanelles. This was the gateway between Europe and Asia, and the vital passage to the Black Sea and Russia. If the straits could be taken, the way to Constantinople would be clear, the Turks could be dealt with, and Russia could then concentrate her forces on the Western Front. It was a brilliant concept but was undermined by bad planning and the use of old, slow, unreliable ships, resulting in complete failure.

The decision was then made to land troops on the Gallipoli Peninsula instead and to try to conquer the forts by land. By 15 April an armada of more than 200 vessels had assembled off Lemnos Island, 80 kilometres from the Dardanelles, with a complement of 75 000

British, French and Anzac troops. The 85 000 Turks who lay in wait had had knowledge of the coming invasion for months and had prepared their defences accordingly.

On the evening of 24 April the fleet of ships sailed from Lemnos past the island of Imbros, 15 miles (24 kilometres) off the Turkish Peninsula. At a point just out of range of enemy guns they anchored for the night, and the troops were ordered to take what rest they could in preparation for a dawn assault.

In an atmosphere so charged with excitement, anticipation and apprehension, it was impossible to sleep. As the endless night dragged on, the men smoked incessantly, and although cautioned against showing a light, forgetfully struck matches to light pipes and cigarettes. Speaking in low voices, as if the enemy could hear, they talked of home, their families and what they hoped to do when the war was over. The land they had left with such high hopes of adventure suddenly seemed the most desirable place on earth as they lay on the decks and gazed up at the alien stars. (Some were mere children—Western Australian Len Hall was sixteen years old when he was accepted as a bugler, Lance Corporal John Harris was only fifteen when he was killed on 6 August 1915, and Private Jim Martin was still only fourteen when he died of typhoid on 25 October 1915.) Many spent the time writing what might well be their last letters to loved ones, and not a few silently prayed.

As the first rays of light stole across a cloudless sky and the destroyers and lighters glided into position, the thousands of men lining the ships' rails saw, for the first time—oblivious to the tens of thousands of hidden eyes that watched them—the high line of hills covered with dense scrub that was to be their objective in the next few hours. Steep and forbidding, the frowning cliffs and deep ravines made a daunting sight to the young, untried warriors, but there was no reluctance as they swarmed over the side and into the waiting vessels that were to ferry them ashore.

Soon they were within firing distance and shells began to scream overhead, bursting in all directions to shower their lethal burden of shrapnel over the defenceless boats, and from the heights the Turks sprayed the troops with murderous machine-gun fire. Many were wounded or killed even before the boats grounded, and those uninjured were forced to wade as much as 30 yards (27 metres) through breast-high surf, holding their weapons and ammunition above their heads. Some even drowned, dragged under by their heavy back-packs as they tried to struggle ashore. Others were saved by the heroism of their mates.

In the shallows, the water turned to crimson as the bodies of the dead gently eddied to and fro with the waves, gazing sightlessly up at the blue sky. For them, the war was over almost before it had begun. Few of the young men frantically striking for the beach had ever seen a dead body, but there was no time to pause to mourn a friend, or even a brother, as they fought to gain a foothold on the soft sand and to reach the comparative safety of the overhanging cliffs they would have to scale.

*The Daily Telegraph*'s correspondent at Gallipoli, Ellis Ashmead-Bartlett, filed the following report.

> All the boats towed had almost reached the beach when a party of Turks entrenched on the shore opened up a terrible fusillade of rifles and machine guns, and many men were hit as they huddled forty to fifty to a boat.
>
> The Australian volunteers rose as a man to the occasion. They waited neither for orders from the boats to reach the beach, but leaped out into the sea and waded ashore, rushing straight at the flashes of the Turk's guns.
>
> Their magazines were not even charged, and they just went in with cold steel, and I believe I am right in saying that the first Ottoman Turk since the last Crusade received an Anglo-Saxon bayonet in him not five minutes after 5 a.m. on April 25th.

The Australians had been ordered to land at Gaba Tepe, 13 miles (21 kilometres) north of Cape Helles where the British were landing. However, in the first of a series of calamitous errors that was to doom the campaign from the start, they were carried almost 2 miles (3.2 kilo-metres) north of Gaba Tepe. Their landfall, later dubbed Anzac Cove, was between steep slopes and precipices some 300 feet (91 metres) high, covered with raw sand, holly and dense scrub. In between, deep gullies afforded some cover from the rifle and machine-gun fire from the heights of Gaba Tepe and, against all odds, some 8000 Australian soldiers of the Australian 3rd Brigade, carrying heavy 55 lb (25 kilo-gram) packs, gained and took three ridges, the furthest the Allies were to advance in the entire eight months of the campaign. The enemy were difficult to distinguish from their own men, as they also wore khaki, and their snipers were expert marksmen, trained and com-manded mostly by German officers. It was soon evident to the invaders that there would be no easy victory, as anticipated, over the despised Turks. They were, it seemed, a formidable foe.

General Sir Ian Hamilton, the British commander of the opera-tion, instructed the Australians to 'dig in and stick it out'. As the day wore on, the men followed orders and began digging in with their entrenching tools in the ravines and cliff faces, using whatever cover they could, eventually establishing a system of connecting trenches. The legend of the 'Digger' was born.

Of the 10 000 Anzacs who landed that fateful day, more than 2000 were killed or wounded before darkness fell. The injured were first attended to at a dressing station on the beach, before being ferried out to the hospital ships lying offshore where lights blazed throughout the night. Even those bearing quite superficial wounds were sent, because of the high risk of infection, and were treated at Lemnos Island. Only the more serious cases were relayed to Alexandria and Cairo.

A lieutenant in the Army Service Corps, 1st Australian Division, wrote later that night (quoted in *The Age*, 25 August 1915):

> It has all been so terrible that I can hardly write what I
> have seen today. We who were still on the ships—only
> the Infantry had gone—were able to watch the opera-
> tions. Shall I ever forget it, it was hell let loose. Guns
> boomed from everywhere and it was an awfully anxious
> time for us watching every lot of our boat parties get-

ting ashore, and though shots and shells were coming
out to us we funked it more for those trying to land.
 It wasn't very long before boatloads of wounded
were being brought back onto the hospital ships, and
they had to pass through our lines. I'll never forget it—
I felt sick and had to turn away.

In the days that followed it became of paramount importance to
secure a good supply of fresh water, because although spring water flowed
from the hills, this quickly became fouled by the dead bodies from both
sides which fell, or were thrown, into the ravines. Later, water was
pumped via a hose from barges into receptacles on the beach, and carried
by mules up the slopes on panniers, two kerosene tins each side.

Owing to the difficulty of landing sufficient stores on Gallipoli,
four pontoon bridges were established, but ammunition was always in
short supply. It galled the troops that their howitzers (a type of short-
barrelled cannon used for shelling at a steep angle) were limited to two
shots per day by GHQ, and field guns to a mere four, and that as a
result they were compelled to watch the enemy building a road to their
forward trenches unhindered by gunfire.

When Turkish prisoners began to trickle in, they were regarded
with distrust by the Australians because of rumours of mutilation of
Allied prisoners, which later proved to have little foundation.
Consequently, the Australians took few prisoners initially. As time
went by, however, the Australians became quite friendly with the Turks
and would offer them cigarettes.

LIEUT. C. CARTHEW. 8TH LIGHT HORSE
HELIOPOLIS CAMP
MAY 1ST. 1915

DEAR MOTHER,
 *We left Mena last Thursday and I was glad to get away, it was an
unhealthy place, in fact if we hadnt left half our men would be in
hospital. We are camped on the racecourse right near the town.
There are some very fine buildings here, the Heliopolis Hotel is the
largest in the world and is now turned into a hospital.*

No doubt you will have heard what our boys have been doing before this reaches you. By jove, they got into a hot corner in the Dardanelles and no mistake. The hospital has over a thousand wounded men there now, there is something like 3,000 casualties of Aus. and N.Z. I visited Capt. Daley in the hospital who was in the last school with me — he got hit on the knee, only a flesh wound, I could get very little information on the Myrtleford boys. One lad in the 7th. Batt. who was shot in the back and the bullet came out in front through the stomach, he was walking about and it didnt seem to hurt him much. Tom Patton was his Corporal and he thought he was O.K. and Bushy Fern he thought escaped. Poor old Cpt. Sergent our old Ajunt of the 16th. was killed poor fellow.

By the way Mother one of our lads is playing the acordon [sic] — some of those old Waltz tunes we used to kick up to in our old kitchen. In fact I fancy I can see old Dave sitting in the corner dragging out the time now. How it brings back old memory.

I may state Mother that we are all dead anxious to get to the Turks after what our boys have done, but its not up to us — if we had our way every man Jack would be off tomorrow.

I went with a party of Brigade Officers to Luxor last week, we left camp Friday and got back Monday for breakfast — it was tip top — 450 miles up the Nile — travelled all night both ways, had sleeping berths and dinner on the train. Cost about a fiver all told. Twenty pounds would do it in the case of a private person. I sent you a book of views. I still havent had a letter what the duce is up, and Fred hasnt had one letter either except from Harry in W.A. — he volunteered but his teeth failed him, and just as well with a wife and young kiddie.

Hoping this finds you as well as Fred and I,
Your Affect Son Charlie.

---

LIEUT. C. CARTHEW,
'C' SQDRN. 8TH LIGHT HORSE, 3RD BRIG. A.S.F.
13.5.'15

DEAR MOTHER AND ALL AT HOME,
Just a line to let you know that we are off to the Front on Saturday next, and am sorry to say are going as dismounted L.H.

*We are not very much cut up about it despite all the work and training we've had with them because we are all anxious to be doing something in the real business.*

*One thing Mother, we are fitted out well as regards clothing — the trouble is carrying it. Us Officers are fitted out just like the men — Bandolier, Rifle and Bayonet, clothing and all issued with helmets — the reason is we carnt be picked out from the men — gives us a better chance.*

*Well Mother it wont be long now until our old Home will have to be broke up* [there had been little relief from the crippling drought and Margaret, from whom Charles had now received a letter, had made the painful decision to try and sell the farm] *and as I dont suppose Ill have any chance of buying the Home place I would like to have Phillips as it joins my other property — that is if I'm still in the land of the living at that time. I am writing this now as I may not have a chance to write again for some time. But I want you to call a sale and get things squared up as its time everyone got their due.*

*One more thing I would like you to do and that is to buy in for me old Bally and her foals. I wouldent part with her for the world.*

*Its nearly three months since we left Aus. and I have only received one letter from home. You ought to be here and see mail after mail come in and no letters and papers from home and then you would know what it is like. Fred has been here longer and he has only received one also. I have received four from one other Person whom I need not name so you have no excuse.*

*Dont forget that hundred Mother which I mentioned in another letter if anything should happen.*

*In concluding I would ask you not to worry about Fred or I as every man who gets wounded is looked after tip top.*

*And Dear Old Mother, if we should go under feel proud of the fact that you reared two sons who will do their job and who are not afraid to die for their country, like a lot we knew who stopped at home who should be here as its every mans duty who has no home ties.*

*Well Goodnight —*

*Hoping you are all as well as Fred and I.*

*Love from Charlie.*

# ⇥ Life and Death ⇤

SOON AFTER HIS ARRIVAL at Gallipoli, Charles observed that although Anzac Cove was now more or less secure, all Allied aircraft—Sopwiths, Nieuports and seaplanes—which had covered the landing were withdrawn, leaving only a small observation balloon at Gaba Tepe a mile or so to the south. On the other hand, German planes—Taubes and Rumplers—roamed at will, reconnoitring the Australian and New Zealand dispositions. Most artillery was also deployed at the southern (British) end of the Peninsula, and reinforcements sorely needed at Anzac were sent elsewhere, leaving the area undermanned.

In spite of this, when the Turks attacked at 3am on 19 May, without any of the usual covering fire, they were decisively beaten with an estimated 10 000 casualties, while Australian casualties totalled 160 dead and 468 wounded. No doubt the fact that the Moslem Turks heralded their approach by wailing and screaming 'Allah, Allah' as they advanced (to ensure their souls would go straight to Paradise) gave the defenders fair warning and had much to do with the victory.

The official news correspondent Charles Bean, while describing the New Zealanders as 'excellent and trustworthy soldiers', reserved his highest praise for the Australians, writing that 'they have the devil in them—the wild, independent pastoral life makes wild and superb soldiers'.

---

LIEUT. C. CARTHEW. 8TH L.H., A.I.F
1.6.'15

DEAR MOTHER,
*Just a line to let you know that I am tip top — never was better in*

*my life although life in the trenches is not the most comfortable in the world. Have not seen Fred for over a week altho he is only half a mile away. But one carnt wander about here.*

*Hope you are quite well Mother, also all at Home. Charlie.*

---

JUNE 4TH, 1915

DEAR MOTHER,

*Haven't had any mail for ages. I am still in the land of the living and are still in the trenches.*

*I have only had two of my Boys wounded so far. The enemy are very quite [sic] just at present but I don't suppose it will last long. Havent seen Fred for a fortnight.*

*Charlie.*

Charles's trench was close to the narrow neck of land between two valleys known as the Nek—only about 30 yards (27 metres) from the Turkish trenches situated on the hillside of Baby 700. The close proximity of the enemy trenches was almost irresistible to the fun-loving Australians, who would often call out good-natured insults and even toss gifts of condensed milk or bully beef to the Turks. Some 'gifts', like the maggoty, rancid bacon bone tossed over, were less well received than others (with pig being an abomination to the Moslem, this was a mortal insult and brought forth a response like a disturbed nest of angry bull ants). On another occasion one wag yelled out, 'Hey, Jacko, how many are you?' and on receiving the answer, 'Thousands,' then responded, 'Well, share this among you,' and, pulling out the pin, hurled a grenade.

On the whole, however, the Australians and the Turks learned to respect each other. On 24 May an armistice was declared in order for both sides to bury their respective dead, and the two armies mingled freely and cordially, exchanging names and cigarettes, shaking hands and enjoying the break in hostilities. Of course, both sides made good use of the amnesty to reconnoitre each other's positions and retrieve weapons, and instead of burying their dead the Turks merely threw the corpses down ravines, there being too many to dispose of otherwise.

To Charles, the sight of so many dead men, friend or foe, in their prime—brave, youthful, magnificent specimens of manhood—affected him greatly. He cared deeply for his men, and the loss of one of them was almost like losing a brother. Conscious of his heavy responsibilities, their welfare was of the utmost importance to him and he never spared himself on their behalf. In return, Charles's men gave him their total devotion.

In a climate of conflict and acute danger, where men depended upon each other to the exclusion of all others, even family, mateship was paramount, a closeness never experienced before or indeed ever after in their lives. Where peril was ever present, men would gladly lay down their lives for a friend, and in fact often did, without fanfare or recognition. It was commonplace for a soldier to risk his life to bring in a wounded mate under fire and to think nothing of it. (Sometimes they even rescued wounded Turks who might have died without treatment.) John Simpson Kirkpatrick, a familiar figure with his donkey named Duffy, carried wounded soldiers down the perilous slopes to the first-aid post on the beach. Day after day he cheated death, often in full view of the enemy, but one day, as he must have known would happen, there came a bullet with his name on it—he was killed in Shrapnel Gully by a sniper in May, a scant month after the fateful landing on Gallipoli.

There were to be no more armistices and thereafter the dead remained where they fell, hosts to the maggots and flies that tormented the men and laid them low in their thousands with dysentery, typhoid and gastric illnesses. The troops sometimes complained that the flies were worse than the Turks and, in fact, probably caused more casualties.

The stench emanating from the bloated cadavers, lying only metres from their trenches, remained in the men's nostrils for months, and at mealtimes their food was blanketed by swarms of shining, black flies. It was usually magoty anyway before it reached their mouths. Fresh food was very scarce and had to be carried up from the beach in donkey or mule panniers. The bread was stale and mouldy, and the biscuits, rumoured to have been left over from the Boer War fifteen years before, or even the Crimean War, were so old and hard it was necessary to soak them in water before they could be eaten. The men often tossed them in the air to use as target practice.

One Turkish corpse, sitting in an upright position almost as though he were alive, was a familiar sight to Charles and his men. They called him Jacko (their slang name for the Turks), and would often include him in their conversations as though he could answer back. Macabre humour was commonplace among the troops, probably as a means to hide their true feelings and to relieve the tension.

The Australians found much to laugh about in many situations, and they often played practical jokes on each other or the enemy. A favourite pastime was to place a hat on a stick and raise it cautiously just above the trench, drawing a hail of fire from the opposite trenches to the great delight and noisy derision of the Anzacs. Sometimes they would lob a tin of jam close to the Turkish lines and when one reached out to retrieve it, open fire on the luckless soldier. It was a red-letter day when a shell landed on the dentist's dugout, showering the hillside with porcelain and vulcanite false teeth. Suddenly, everyone was sporting extra-wide grins, and even the enemy were thrown a few sets, much to their mystification. They were more convinced than ever that the Anzac devils were quite mad.

---

C. CARTHEW. 8TH L.H.
DUGOUT VILLA,
JUNE 11TH '15

DEAR MOTHER,

*Just a line to let you know that Fred and I are both tip top. We are now behind the firing line haveing a spell after a fortnight in the trenches.*

*We dont do much but eat and sleep, also have a swim daily which we appreciate but it wont last long as we will have to releave* [sic] *some other unit.*

*Fred has a fairly safe job here — he is on the phone most of his time. I have lost three of my fellows.*

*All the Myrtleford Lads were wonderful lucky considering what they have gone through — only three wounded. I saw Patton and Fern on Wensday. Patton is an S.M. now and probably wont be long before he gets a star. Bushy is still the same old stick, says he has had all the fighting he wants and is quite prepared to shake*

*hands with the Turks and cry quits. He doesnt know anyone who*
*would be likely to want more fight but there is no doubt they have*
*gone through some hard fighting, and the more one looks at the*
*place where they landed the more one marvels. Our landing was in*
*much more comfortable conditions — a couple of shells burst over*
*our boat just after we left but they did no damage.*

*Well Mother you know much more of what is going on at the*
*Front in Europe at any rate than we do here. We get all sorts of*
*rumours but very little facts. Wish they would send our mail along*
*its a beggar.*

*Well Dear Mother hope everything is going on all right at home*
*and everyone in the best of health.*

*From your Affect. son Charlie.*

Apart from sleeping, letter writing was the main occupation for those
at the rest camp behind the lines, as mail from home was their chief
joy. It would be impossible to overestimate the anxious anticipation
among the troops on mail day, and the painful disappointment when
there was no letter from home.

It was Charles's job to censor his men's letters, loath though he was
to intrude on their privacy, and the outpouring of love and longing in
these sometimes ill-spelled epistles often brought tears to his eyes.
One and all made light of the dangers and discomforts of their day-to-
day life, assuring their families of their wellbeing and safety.

It was also Charles's melancholy duty to write letters of condolence
to the bereaved wives and families of his men killed in action. Never a
good correspondent, he found it difficult and pitifully inadequate to
try to express his own grief and anger at the loss of a precious young
life by means of cold, impersonal pencil and paper. He was too deeply
involved with his men—their problems, hopes and fears—to view
them, as most of the senior officers did, as expendable and
replaceable—necessary pawns in the traditional game of war. Despite
this, Charles fiercely believed in doing his duty and was fully prepared
to lay down his own life for King and Country, if necessary.

C. CARTHEW
ANZAC BAY
JUNE 15TH '15

*Dear Add,*

*I received your two very welcome letters and two lots of papers dated 22nd March so they took nearly three months to get here. There must be other letters as you say you wrote every week which was very good of you. A fellow appreciates letters I can assure you.*

*Am writing this while on Piquet* [a posting to watch for enemy approach] *24 hours and while writing two of our aeroplanes are flying around recconoitring and its very funny to see the Turks shelling them, their shells bursting about a couple of hundred yards away—the plane takes no notice of them whatever. Well Add we are in the same position as when I wrote Mother lust week—its rather motonous this Infantry work, I wish we had our horses.*

*Bye the way I was rung up on the Phone yesterday and told that Fred has been sent to Lembros Island with Influenza. About 3 or 4 hours sail from here. I saw him on Saturday night and wanted him to come to my place and get some Eucalyptus but he said it was nothing only a bit of a cold. So dont worry. They dont take any chance here with anyone who is not well — pack him off at once to Lembros as this is no place for anyone who is not fit and quite right too. No doubt he has wrote to Mother himself. I dont know why anyone should get colds here as the weather is beautiful. Dont know what the Cockeys think of it in that neighbourhood, expect they are growling. Can see one in the distance ploughing with his two bullocks and suppose wooden plough.*

*Well things do not seem to be too bright at home — cattle dieing so soon but you did not state how my stock was faring. Am glad Mother sold those of hers even if she did not make anything she did not lose.*

*So Black has turned me down, he did not seem to be much good on his own. I hope Jack sees that the rabbits are kept down as I dont want them to get a holt again. It seems to me he sold that chaff in too big a hurry — and I dont want any of my cattle sold if*

*they can be kept alive at all. What did those veilers* [young calves]
*make — they should have been good.*

*I carnt get over Jean Mac getting hooked up to that scoundrel.
Suppose Jean was tired of working and wanted a change — no doubt
she'll get it.*

*How are the Robinsons getting on I sent them a book of P.C. in
Egypt. And Mrs. Matthews — remember me to them all. I carnt
write them as there is a famine in writing material. I have to
censor my troops letters and you should see the makeshifts some of
them invent. No more paper so must ring off. Am very glad Mother
is keeping well — tell her not to worry about Fred he is alright and
having a holiday.*

*Love to all, Charlie.*

As Charles suspected, his dog Black wasn't any good on his own.
Where once he had shadowed Charles, joyfully leaping around him in
a frenzy of barking, his eyes sparkling and tongue lolling, he now trot-
ted obediently and without enthusiasm behind Nell, if she called to
him. He would, however, always accompany Margaret when she was
out of doors, mindful of Charles's last words to him. He spent most of
his day dozing down by the creek, no doubt pretending Charles was
there with him, fishing and talking to the dog of family matters or farm
problems, while he stood guard over his beloved master, alert for the
tiger snakes that also enjoyed basking in the sun on the creek bank.

THE TRENCHES
JUNE 25TH '15

Dear Mother,

*Just a line to say I am still going strong. I got a letter from Add
and another from Babs. Am pleased to hear you are all keeping
well. Suppose its nice and cold at home now, we are in mid
summer here and the weather is great, in fact could not be better
for the life we lead. A fellow is going night and day here. We have
to stand to arms early in the night and also before daybreak. I
should not like to put in a winter at this game though. I have lost
half a dozen of my troops so far, mainly wounded I'm glad to say.*

*I have not heard anything of Fred since he went away, but
I have no doubt he will be alright. You'll be sure to get a letter
from him.*

*Young Croucher of Dederang got badly wounded last week —
how badly I dont know as when a man leaves here its the last we
here of him. Ted Croucher is away also — influenza I believe.
Jack must be busy indeed if he carnt spare time to write a letter to
a fellow, as one has not come to light. Glad he has done so well
with his deals.*

*So he got that wild old buck up there at last, he ought to be alright
for rabbiting and scrubbing though.*

*Captn McLaurin has left us and has been promoted O.C., A
SQDRN. We are all sorry to lose him and have in his place an
Old Bird called Captn. Hore — come from Tassie — hes not worth
a d—. Tell Add Ill answer her letter next week — not much I can
write about, one day is much like the next, shot and shell flying
around and so on.*

*Well Mother take good care of yourself and dont worry about us
as we are alright.*

*From your loving son, Charlie.*

*P.S. This is our local paper so you see what information we get.
Your Myrtleford Mails are very acceptable.*

Paper was always in short supply and letters were often written on the
backs of envelopes, pages torn from diaries, or the reverse side of the
*Peninsula Press*—a single page of mainly British and French news of
no interest at all to the Anzacs except for the results of bomb-throwing
and target-shooting competitions. The *Peninsula Press* of 17 June 1915,
on which Charles wrote his letter of 25 June, announced the following:

## Bomb Throwing Competition

The following is the programme of a competi-
tion at Anzac:—

Commencing at 3 p.m.

CONDITIONS:—Each company will enter

8 teams of 3 men. The two trained N.C.O.s of each company to take 4 teams each and to act as observers with periscopes.

POINTS:—Hits (i.e. inside enemy's trench). 2 points for each direct hit, 1 point for each hit inside a space of 3ft. either in front or rear of enemy's trench.

PRIZES:—1st Prize. 20 packets of cigarettes and 1 tin Marmalade; 2nd Prize. 16 packets cigarettes and 1 tin Marmalade; 3rd Prize. 12 packets cigarettes.

---

C. CARTHEW, 'C' COY. 3RD L.H. BRIG.
ANZAC
JUNE 29TH '15

MY DEAR MOTHER,

*Just a line to let you know that I am still going strong — had a rather lively week in the trenches this time. Am sorry to say that Major Gregory and Captn Crowl were both killed the other morning. A shell lobed in my dugout and burst and destroyed most of my goods — am pleased to say I was not in at the time.*

*Fred is nearly alright I hear but he had not the manners to write and let me know.*

*Captn McLaurin is our Sqdrn Leader know [sic] — Major Weeble is 2nd in Command of the Regt. Are there any more men joined the Force in our part of the world — Ive never heard of any. Cold footed lot of beggars they are, dont know how men can stop away.*

*Well Mother our cook is yelling for me to come to tea and what do you think — eggs are on the board, or ground I should say. We get fresh bread twice a week now I am pleased to say.*

*Well Dear Mother take care of yourself — more news next time if I can get some paper.*

*From your loving son, Charlie.*

Since the early days of the war, a group of self-righteous servicemen's wives had taken it upon themselves to stand on busy street corners and hand out white feathers, the emblem of cowardice, to any young man not in uniform—no matter that they were ill or unfit, supporting a large family or engaged in essential services. For this reason, every man who had volunteered and been rejected was given a special badge. However, there were many able-bodied men with no home ties who did not volunteer, and the men at the front became increasingly resentful of these 'cold footers', as they were known, especially when they received letters telling of sweethearts, fiancées and even wives who had been seen in their company.

## ME BROTHER WOT STAYED AT 'OME.
*(Dedicated to my cold footed cobbers.)*

I'm pullin' orf me colours, I've chucked me web away,
I'm goin' back to Cairo, ter draw me bloomin' pay.
I'm fed up with bein' a soldier, so 'elp me bob I am,
Chewin' mouldy biscuits, an' eatin' bread an' jam.
I'm sick er fightin' Mr. Turk out on me bleedin' own,
When I thinks of 'im in 'Stralia, me brother wot stayed at 'ome.

I'll bet 'es walkin' up the street, 'is chest puffed out with pride,
A skitin' to 'is bloomin' cobbers, of 'ow 'es saved 'is 'ide.
And 'eres me in this blimy trench, where I carn't even straight me 'ead,
For fear a bally sniper 'll plug it up with lead.
But 'e 'olds 'is 'ead 'igh enough, when up the street 'ell roam,
But there ain't no bullets over there, me brother wot stayed at 'ome.

'E reads the 'Mornin' 'erald, an' sees the Turks is on the run,
Then 'e brags about Australia, an' wot 'er boys 'ave done.
'E shines before the barmaids, 'es good at beery skitin',
But round the corner of the street, is where 'e does 'is fightin'.
'Is dugouts in the taproom, the bar's 'is firin' zone,
An' the billiard cue the rifle, of me brother wot stayed at 'ome.

'Es not a bad shot in the field, when 'e gets on a bunny's track,
An' there ain't no bloomin' danger, cos a bunny can't shoot back.
But its different 'ere with Mr. Turk, lor lummy 'e ain't arf slick,
If 'e gets 'is peepers on yer first, my oath 'e'll make yer sick.
But 'e won't risk 'is bloomin' 'ide, why, 'is 'eart's a frigid zone,
An' 'is feet are bloomin' icebergs, me brother wot stayed at 'ome.

I'm pullin' orf me colours, I've chucked me web away,
An' I'm layin' down me rifle, I don't cares wot they say.
If 'e can shirk 'is duty, ses 'e won't go to drill,
Well two can play the same game, then in comes Kaiser Bill.
I'm not afraid 'er bullets, I'd 'ave died without a groan,
But 'e's put the Kybosh on it all, me brother wot stayed at 'ome.

Now when I ses to Mother, I've volunteered to fight,
She ses "Gawd Bless yer Laddie, an' bring yer back alright."
But 'im 'e called me a chocolate soldier, an' a bloomin' six bob tourist too,
'E ses "Ye'll never see the bloomin' firin' line, not even git a view."
'E ses "ye'll have a fine trip, across the oceans foam."
But still 'e wouldn't come 'imself, me brother wot stayed at 'ome.

'E's playin' golf an' football, an' many another game,
An' 'ere's me scrappin' for the bloomin' flag, ter keep Australia's name,
While 'e waltzes round the ballroom, for 'e thinks 'es used 'is wit,
Then 'e tries to pinch me tabby, What oh! its time ter quit.
But when the war is over, 'e'll reap just wot 'es sown,
An' we'll brand 'im a bleedin' coward, me brother wot stayed at 'ome.

I'd like to 'ave 'im over 'ere, just to show 'im 'ow things are,
For it ain't all beer an' skittles, an' there ain't no bloomin' bar.
We're in these bally trenches, eight days out of ten,
We carn't git a bloomin' spell, cos we 'aven't got the men.
For Mr. Turk is wily, 'e ain't no lazy drone,
An' 'e's twenty times as brave, as me brother wot stayed at 'ome.

I've picked up me old Lee-Enfield, an' I've buckled me web about,
For I'm only a bloomin' private, an' I've got ter see it out;
An' though 'e shames 'is manhood, an' stains 'is pedigree,
Thank God there's some of us old uns left, an we'll fight until we're free;
But should the foe o'erpower us, an we gits overthrown,
Then 'e'll know 'e 'elped ter kill me, me brother wot stayed at 'ome.

Sig. T. Skeyhill
8th Batt. A.I.F.

---

Anzac Cove
July 5th '15

Dear Add,

*Just a few lines in answer to your letters — On Saturday, I got one from Em, one from Winnie and 2 from Ethel so you see I am not doing to bad. Since my card to Mother we have had a rattle with the Turks.*

*The position we, the Eighth hold is about the worst on our front; the trenches being only about 25 to 30 yards apart, my 'C' Sqdrn holding this part.*

*On Wensday night last at 12.15 a.m. I had just been relieved from the firing line where my Troop, (or what is left of them — three killed and thirteen wounded and several sick up to date) was on duty. I had not gone far when I could hear 'Allah Allah' this cry went right along the Turk trenches. Needless to say I did not wait for any more but got back to the firing line as quick as I could get.*

*The beggars were charging our trenches in their hundreds — some of them got into our saps — they kept coming at us until just on daylight when they had to retire.*

*On about 50 yards of our front they left between 250 and 300 dead — we mowed them down in heaps.*

*You may read an account in the papers of what was done by the 8th and 9th L.H. but I can tell you the attack was mainly repulsed by 'C' Sqdrn.*

*Our losses were very slight — three of my Troop were killed and some wounded. Serg. Sweetland and Trooper Oats who were killed had just been allotted to my troop — they were in 'D' Troop.*

*We are back in the rest camp again now after a fortnight in the trenches and are glad to get back as everybody is done up. No sleep being the main trouble.*

*A young fellow called on me this morning — he had just returned from Lemnos — he saw Fred just before he was sent to Alexandria — he said he was not too bad atall [sic] — he was got early and sent to where he could be looked after properly. But no doubt it will be some time before he will come back here. Just as well perhaps as this is not the safetist place in the world to be in. I am pleased to say I have had know [sic] occasion for a Dr. as yet. Only to get some disinfectant after getting dead Turks out of our trenches which I can tell you was not a pleasant job, but its wonderful how callous a man becomes at this game. I would have run a mile without looking back from a dead man over there but one doesn't take any more notice than he would if they were rabbits.*

*I won't be sorry when we get out of this and back to our horses if we ever do.*

*I see Cpt. Shannon is coming with our reinforcements — will be pleased to see him.*

*How is the L.H. getting on over there — I have been looking at a photo in Punch of our old Sqdrn but dont recognise many.*

*I am pleased to hear from Em that Mother was never better for years than she is at present. May she keep on so. Tell Nell I will write her next week as all my writing material got blown up so I have to scratch for paper.*

*I wonder how my estate is getting on. I hope my stock is not dying.*

*Ethel sent me an Argus and I see there was over three inches of rain at Myrtleford, so if it dont freeze too much the Winter wont be too bad.*

*Jack has not come to light with a letter — mean dog.*

*This is our local paper, some of it refers to a place called Achi Babi about twelve or fourteen miles down the coast. My old Sergt Mullins had a narrow escape — a shell lobed on his dugout — he is now in hospital with concussion of the brain and several other hurts — dont think hell [sic] come back.*

*My other Sergt Mulder had two or three narow escapes — he is*

Q.m.s. now. Charlie Dale is Adjutant and Old McLaurin our Sqdrn Leader. Cpl Daniels is the only Non Com I have left now.

Well Add hope to get a letter soon from Mother. So long for the pressent.

Love to all at home. Charlie.

---

LIEUT. C. CARTHEW.
THE TRENCHES.

DEAR NELL,

Letters just came to hand — great rejoicing in camp. I got two of yours and two from Add, one from Jean and the most important of all from Ethel. Oh, and Jack's bit of a note at last. Good heavens what next will he be buying — a motor car, that licks everything. You shouldn't let him sell that buggie though. I am very thankful to him for fixing up my stock as he done alright rotten luck with the veilers though. And I am very thankful to you old Girl for the trouble you are taking in my interest. I wont forget it if I escape out of this hole. I hope all the starving stock is over by this time. Judging by Add's letter the drought has played old Harry with stock. I hope all my blooming cattle are not dead but its no use growling I suppose.

I went around to see some of the 4th LH. they have not been in the firing line yet. Old Ewart is now R.Q.M., a nice safe job, gave me 2 tins of tobacco and some jam, rather a windfall as our issue is rather light on those commodities. Glad you liked the P.C. I'll send more when we get to Constantanople. While in the Rest Camp we practise hill climbing twice a day, scaling the cliffs to get in training to chase the Turks I suppose.

Did Dave bring the timber for the shed on my block down from the mill as I asked. Well old Girl this is my last envelope so will have to start like some of the men and sow up envelopes. Hope all are well at home as this leaves me. Charlie.

P.S. This map may give you a bit of an idea of how we are situated — there is only about 30 yards separating the trenches on the Left Flank — that is where the 8th L.H. Reg. is at present. [See picture section.]

DEAR ADD,

Things are quite [sic] as far as the Turks are concerned. Am pleased to say I got a letter from Fred in Heliopolis this morning — he thought he would be back by this, but its very hard to get back here from Egypt and no doubt they will keep him for some time and I hope they do. Ted Croucher is over there with him. I heard, though not official that the Dederang Croucher died, poor fellow. Did I tell you that Dr. Colin Campbell died, poor fellow — he had both legs blown off with a shell. We miss him sorely — he was a splendid fellow — nothing was too much trouble, and he was one of my closest friends.

We are still in the rest camp but have fatigue party and Piquets going night and day so you see we dont have a great deal of rest. We stand to arms every second morning when out of the trenches from three till four in the morning which spoils the best part of a mans sleep. I generally go down and have a dip in the sea after stand to arms — its great. I am pleased to say the Eighth Regt. is free from what we call the Scotch Greys [lice] — you may guess what I mean — I dont know how we escape — all the other units seem to be worried by the pest. One sees men sitting along the beach like monkeys picking the pest off their clothes.

Well Add I am sitting in our Mess just after having tea — Bully Beef and biscuits and cocoa — we managed to score a tin and its very nice for a change. Our mess, if I can call it such a thing is a biscuit box for a table set in the middle of a bit of level ground cut out of the side of the Hill — we sit on the ground or anything thats handy. Mess tins is the extent of our crockery. Its rather hot in the daytime but the nights are fine — it dont require any blankets. We never undress and seldom take off our boots or equipment. Always ready you see. It tells on some of the fellows nerves, am pleased to say my nerves are all right and was never better in health in my life. All our Sqdrn Officers are tip top but not so the other Sqdrns.

Jean [Babs] seems to have a good time, Im glad she goes out. I got the papers alright thanks. I see old Kneebone got tied up. Better if he

*came over here and done his duty. Well Old Girl I'll have to close*
*now. Hope Mother is not worrying about us and that you are all in*
*the best of health.*
  *Goodbye, Charlie.*

Charles was more than thankful when he heard from Fred that he was
not yet fully recovered from his illness, and that he was not hopeful of
getting back to the Peninsula in the near future. There had been
rumours of plans for a big concerted push by the Allies, and he hoped
that his brother would remain in Egypt safely out of the firing line,
because this would be no ordinary foray.

Besides that, conditions at the Front were not good. There had
been a good deal of dissention among the top brass since the death of
General Bridges following a severe wound from a sniper. Most of the
younger officers were discouraged by the blatant mismanagement,
orders and counterorders, and the fact that in three months no worth-
while gains had been made.

Ammunition was always in short supply, a fact of which the enemy
was well aware, and every unit was undermanned, due not only to
casualties but also to the high rate of illness caused mainly by the
swarms of flies which bred in the thousands of rotting corpses and the
latrines. Those men that survived were sent to Lemnos Island, Cairo
or Alexandria, and even to England, and often did not return for many
months, if at all. Those who wished to return to the Front were often
refused, and the many others who wished to remain safely in Egypt
were allowed to do so.

Consequently, morale among the Allied troops was at a low ebb,
and, weakened by dysentery and malnutrition, nerves frayed by lack of
sleep and constant danger, the men bore little resemblance to the fit,
confident and eager warriors who disembarked in such high spirits a
scant three months before.

The awful conditions did not go unnoticed by onlookers. Charles
Bean noted that 'men were sacrificed needlessly by conflicting orders
and gross mismanagement by Officialdom', and British correspondent Ashmead-Bartlett was so sickened by the unnecessary carnage
that he courageously wrote to the British Prime Minister about the

true state of affairs on the peninsula. His letter was intercepted, and he was sent home in disgrace. Reporting the truth was not an easy task. All news correspondents at Gallipoli had to submit their communiqués to the authorities before sending them off and their reports were often discredited. To make matters worse, any Anzac victory or daring exploit was invariably credited in the papers to 'British Units'.

---

CHAS. CARTHEW
DARDANELLES
26.7.'15

DEAR GIRLS,

*Dont know what I'd do for paper if it wasn't for the local press. Young Calcutt was away sick and when he came back he brought me tobacco and envelopes — very good of him wasent it. Poor little beggar had to go away again though — came back before he was right.*

*I am at present sitting in a hole in the side of the cliff with Major McLaurin, Higgins and two other officers. We have just had lunch and feel contented although the Bill of Fare was nothing to write home about. B.F. spuds and biscuits and jam. Spuds are a luxurie I assure you, we very seldom get them. We are on a 24 hour job Inlying Piquet — that is we are to support the Firing line if the Turks attack — of course we dont know what moment they may come along. Well we have been here nine months now and I dont care how soon we move on. Same old thing every day, shells flying about. I am pleased to say I have missed all unpleasant things that are flying about — sickness included.*

*You will no doubt know about all our losses before this reaches you.*

*I was awful cut up about Major Gregory and Capt. Campbell. Old Simmie — you know who I mean — has gone back to Aus. where he should never have left, useless old boy. Our Sqdrn is the only one whose officers are still going strong — we havent stoped anything nor got sick.*

*We were issued with a DAMN Infantry equipment the other day so it looks blue our chance of getting our horses — its enough to break a fellows heart, but I suppose its all in the game and its no use growling.*

*I have heard nothing from Fred lately and the longer he stops over there the better Ill be pleased, but he wont stop any longer than he can help. Its very hard to get back once one goes to Egypt. In fact a fellow can stop there as long as he likes and some of the beggars take full advantage of it too.*

*We have been fortunate as regards the weather, but in another six weeks we may have a different tale to tell, the winter is very severe were [sic] we are camped and there will be six or eight inches of snow by that time. I dont think we will be here then at least I hope not. But one carnt say today were he'll be tomorrow on a job like this.*

*We run the risk of being knocked over every day but no one seems to worry in fact its no use worrying. Of course I dont put that in Mothers or Ethels letters.*

*Im very glad Jean you go out to Craigieburn* [the Seymour's farm] *occasionally. Ethel tells me shes so glad you do, no doubt you get all the news from her. Am writing this on my notebook — all my stationary got blown up with a shell. You may notice the corner of this paper is all crushed — this book was picked up about fifty yards from my dugout and just as well for me I did not go to sleep that morning or I would not be here now. I had only turned in about a half hour too, but when the Turks started to shoot like blazes I got back in the firing line as quick as I could. As it is I was knocked down twice that morning with concussion of bursting shells but luckily missed any of the fragments.*

*These shells are awful and they are screaming overhead at present. Well girls, I carnt say much. I censor all my troops letters and I have to scratch out a lot. Some of them are very shy about letting me read there love letters and they have my sympathy and therefore I just glance at them here and there. I shouldent like anyone to read my letters.*

*Old Hayden is over here. I venture to say he was never more fincial [sic] in his life — he is RQMS — about fourteen shillings a day its worth and carnt spend it.*

*So Em is to train for a nurse — you may be able to get a job over here. Glad everyone is well and Mother is enjoying good health. Suppose the old home will be broke up before long — I should like to have had the old place.*

*As for me I was never better in my life. The last letter from Fred in Egypt took three weeks getting here. Well goodbye for the present, Charlie.*

---

DARDANELLES
JULY 27TH 1915

MY DEAR MOTHER,

*Just a line to let you know that I am in the best of health and have escaped the Turks bullets up to date. We go back into the trenches in a few days again and I would rather be there than here, that is if we are up to strength, its rough on the men when we are not doing double shifts. Bert Talbot Woods lobed here during the night with 70 reinforcements so we wont be to bad now although we want a lot more men to build up to our proper strength.*

*You would hardly believe the wastage of war Mother. The last of my old Non Coms [noncommissioned officers] went away to the hospital last night. One or two of them might come back.*

*Our old Regt. that fine body of men that marched through town a short time ago would make a very poor show now — that is if we had only those that are left of the original crowd. Dont think I have ten men of my old crowd and not one Non Com. I'd give something to have them here today.*

*I havent heard from Fred but am not at all anxious about him now as he will be better off there than here.*

*Jack Regan went over there last week to get his ear attended to — I told him to try to dig Fred up and let me know. So you need not worry about him Mother he will be all right. I havent had any mail from home for some time, it must get delayed in Egypt, the beggars get it over there first and are in no hurry to send it on.*

*Bob Henry brought over reinforcements for the 4th L.H. today. One of the lads who came over tells me my old horse Buller was shot — he got kicked in the knee before I left. Its rotten luck isnt it. But goodness knows if it will make any difference to me, we were issued with Infantry equipment this week so it looks bad does it not.*

*Well Mother the winter will be over by the time you get this, I hope you have a good Spring.*

*I told Jack to put another man with old Jimmie to scrub my block,
but I think it would be better to call for tenders for scrubbing 300 acres
of it and leave Jimmie to deal with the rabbits and other things.
Kind remembrances to old friends, Your loving son, Charlie.*

Yes, Charles well remembered the day they marched through the streets of Melbourne, the euphoria and the carnival atmosphere as the military band played stirring marches, the sun glittering on their brass instruments. Even the horses, their satin coats groomed to perfection, seemed to sense the pageantry of the occasion and pranced and curvetted like the destriers of old as they proudly carried their riders.

He remembered the children lining the route, fervently waving Australian and British flags, and the deafening cheers from the thousands of people craning to get a view of the pride of Victoria, the 8th Light Horse. He would never forget his own overwhelming pride in his troop of superb horsemen whom he had led in the parade, his back ramrod straight, his head held high that sunny day, an aeon ago.

Where were they now, those debonair, bronzed warriors, the matchless flower of Australian chivalry, with their high spirits and their deathless courage? Some were shattered wrecks, blinded, maimed and broken in body or mind; and many, many were dead, lying quietly for all eternity in their shallow graves under foreign soil, marked by makeshift wooden crosses, or in no grave at all. Where was it now, the Glory and the Dream?

When at the rest camp behind the lines, Charles would spend time visiting the graves of his troopers and his friends—those that had graves, anyway—and he was always surprised by the large number of men sharing that sad pilgrimage. Bareheaded, they knelt to pray, to place a posy of oleander or of poppies on the final resting place of a brother or a cobber, or perhaps simply to talk to him. Most wiped tears from their eyes as they communed with their mates, and Charles was no exception.

It was commonplace to see men who had not darkened a church door in years laboriously reading a Bible by the dim light of a candle stub, taking comfort in the ancient words that recalled their secure childhood. With mortality a daily, grim reality, most men turned to God as the only sure refuge from the terrors of war.

## HALT! THY TREAD IS ON A HERO'S GRAVE

Halt! Thy tread is on a hero's grave, Australian lads lie sleeping below,
Just rough wooden crosses at their heads, to let their comrades know.
They'd sleep no better for marble ones, or monuments so grand,
They sleep in tranquil contentment, in that far off Turkish land.

The wildflowers are growing o'er them, the white heath blooms nearby,
The crickets chirp around, above, the wild birds fly.
Wild poppies thrive beside, their bloom is scarlet born,
Scarlet poppies—symmetrical emblems, of that blood red April morn.

The blue Mediterranean sighs, in the morning air so clear,
Grieving o'er the fallen brave, who knew no fear.
A Lonesome pine stands just beside, a grim sentinel it stands,
Guarding the last resting place, of that gallant little band.

I've often passed those little mounds, when the deadly bullets meow,
And the air is full of shrapnel, 'tis called Shrapnel Gully now.
Whilst coming from the trenches, and glancing over there,
I've oft seen many a khaki form, kneeling in silent prayer.

Kneeling o'er their fallen comrades, perhaps a boyhood chum,
Felled by the shrieking shrapnel, or the deadly sniper's gun.
They were only rough Australians, fiends in the bayonet charge,
But there with their fallen comrades, their hearts were very large.

Their back is to the firing line, the only time they've shown it to the foe,
Their heads were bent in stricken grief, down their cheeks the salt
    tears flow.
Hoarsely they murmur a broken prayer, what's in their hearts, why,
    who can tell,
They lay their hand upon the grave in fond caress, and say their
    last farewell.

There's many a loving mother, home in Australia dear,
Who's weeping brokenhearted, o'er their loved son's lonely bier,
There's many a true Australian girl, stricken with sudden pain,
Mourning for her fallen sweetheart, who she'll ne'er more see again.
They know not where he lies, or how he fell,
That's why I'm writing these few lines, the simple truth to tell.

Their graves are on Gallipoli, up on the very heights,
Above the first great landing place, scene of the first great fights.
Shrapnel Gully is on their right, Courtney's Post is to their head,
The wide Mediterranean at their feet, and the blue sky overhead.
Their burial march was the big guns roar, their greatcoat their
     winding sheet,
Their head is to the firing line and the ocean to their feet.

Officers and privates who fell, in that first great rush of fame,
They lie there side by side, their rank is now the same.
The city boy who left the pen, the country boy the plough,
They trained together in Egypt, they sleep together now.

Sleep on, fallen comrades, you'll ne'er be forgotten by
The boys who fought with you, and the boys who saw you die.
Your graves may neglected be, but fond memory will remain,
The story of your gallant charge will ease the grief and pain,
That we know your Kin are feeling, over there across the foam,
And we'll tell the story of your fall, should we e'er reach Home
     Sweet Home.

SIG. T. SKEYHILL
8TH BATT. A.I.F.

# Forward, the Light Brigade!

ONE DAY TOWARDS THE END of July, after a briefing by Major McLaurin to his officers, Charles returned to his trench in a very disturbed frame of mind.

McLaurin was very pessimistic about the course of the campaign and, like many of his superiors, thought that the armies should cut their losses and withdraw. Lord Kitchener, the British Secretary for War, decreed otherwise. Irked by the three-month stalemate on Gallipoli, during which time no gains had been achieved, Kitchener ordered General Sir Ian Hamilton to take urgent steps to end the deadlock—at any cost. Never having set foot on the peninsula, Kitchener had scant knowledge of the terrain, the strategic obstacles, the lack of vital resources and the health and morale problems which had decimated the Allied armies, although he had been well briefed from time to time. He was determined a decisive push must be made without delay, to make an end to what had been an ill-fated, poorly planned and disastrously executed campaign. This would make available tens of thousands of Allied troops who could then be deployed advantageously on the Western Front.

Hamilton consulted with General Birdwood and other high-ranking commanders and decided on one desperate throw of the dice. In theory his plan was feasible, but its ultimate success was dependent on the faultless execution and precise timing of each step of the offensive. In view of the bungling inefficiency that had characterised previous forays, McLaurin had very little confidence in the outcome.

Late in the afternoon of 6 August, the British were to make a feint at Cape Helles while the Anzacs launched an attack at Lone Pine, also with the intention of diverting enemy attention away from the main assault. This would take place during the night when the British IX Corps landed at Suvla Bay, north of Anzac Cove, after which they would reinforce the Anzac troops. Following this the New Zealanders would try to take Chunuk Bair as Australian troops lunged at Hill 971 to the north. The 8th and 10th Light Horse, under intense covering fire from their own artillery and the British navy, would charge the Turkish stronghold known as Baby 700. If all went well, and the vital high points of Chunuk Bair, Baby 700 and Hill 971 were secured, the way would then be clear to push the Turks back from the peninsula.

When McLaurin bluntly told his officers that they and their troops would be ordered to charge the enemy trenches and scale the impregnable heights of Baby 700 in shirtsleeves, armed only with fixed bayonets, grenades and unloaded rifles, he was greeted with total, incredulous silence. Their own trenches were perhaps 30 yards (27 metres) from those of the enemy, but they would face not just one row of heavily fortified trenches but up to seven tiers, each protected by a massive barrier of timber and sandbags and ranked one above the other on a hillside rising almost 120 feet (37 metres). Through these barriers could be seen the sinister snouts of the murderous German maxim machine guns, each of which could fire without endangering their trenches below.

It was a prospect to daunt even the bravest of men, a nightmare concept given credence only in the minds of the high-ranking officers who would be observing the carnage from a safe distance. It was obvious that any assault by the light horse would result in total annihilation. Was this the way it was to end for them and their troops, in a useless, hopeless charge?

McLaurin had argued that it was sheer murder, and Brazier of the 10th Light Horse had agreed with him. But Generals Birdwood and Hughes, and Colonel Antill, insisted that it was necessary, and that with the artillery covering the troops casualties would be light. However, it was apparent to anyone of the meanest intelligence that this was nonsense. The enemy would know they would be quite safe because the artillery could not lob shells so close to their own trenches, and as soon as the bombardment stopped the Turks would be ready to man their machine guns.

During the next few days, Charles and his brother officers cherished the hope that General Hughes would perceive the utter folly of the exercise. They were filled with impotent rage that the Allied Generals could even contemplate the criminal sacrifice of such a magnificent body of men. There was not the slightest chance that such an attack would succeed—it was a foregone conclusion.

Charles loved his men—their gallantry, their laconic humour, their generosity and unswerving loyalty to him and to each other—even though most of his original troop had been killed or wounded. He knew intimately their hopes and fears, their worries about their folks, their pride in their children, their love for their wives and sweethearts—his agony was not for himself but for these men and their families who were most unlikely ever to see their loved ones again.

Charles found it difficult to meet the men's eyes when they questioned him about the coming offensive. But bad news travelled fast, in spite of the strict secrecy surrounding the planned offensive, and the troopers soon understood the futility of the coming attack. Choosing his words carefully, Charles explained that it was considered essential to engage the Turks at the Nek, in order to allow Allied troops to land and to take the key points so vital to the success of the campaign. He expressed his hope that the charge would not be necessary.

As the days passed, however, it became apparent that there was to be no change of plan. Charles spent even more time with his men, talking to them, joking with them and listening to their news from home—a place never far from his thoughts, or theirs, as epitomised by the songs they sang accompanied by a mouth organ: 'Home Sweet Home', 'A Little Grey Home in the West', 'Keep the Home Fires Burning' and 'Gundagai'.

At night, when not standing to arms listening to the haunting melodies punctuated by sporadic gunfire, Charles's mind was free to retreat into the past, into the blissful security of his childhood in the valley—that Happy Valley.

SEA VIEW, GALLIPOLI
AUGUST 4TH 1915

DEAR NELL AND ALL AT HOME,

Your very welcome letters of 7th and 12th June to hand and am pleased to hear Mother and you are all well. By jove I can see Mother sitting on a stool in the kitchen reading those letters.

Lieut. Baker went away sick on Sunday and is going to look Fred up.

Well Nell I am writing this letter at six in the morning sitting in my dugout on the side of the Cliff overlooking the sea — its just lovely now. I went on duty last night at twelve and came off at Daylight then went down and had a swim and washed my pants and shirt, so I am putting in time waiting for breakfast — I am darned hungry too.

I thought by going down early I would miss the Snipers, but no fear. The beggars were sniping right along the beach soon after I got there. I managed to finish my swim and washing before they got anyways close to me but I had to run for it in the finish. They nearly got two other chaps who were a little further up the Beach from me. I saw them striking for the shore as hard as they could go with bullets lobing just behind them but they got safely in behind an old barge.

The damn Turk has no idea of sport shooting at a man when hes enjoying a swim.

But to give him his due he's a fair fighter so far as we know — not like those other Hogs [Germans].

We heard some awful reports of what they would do when we came here first if we fell into his hands, but I dont think there is one thing that can be proved against him.

I think I told you we were back in the trenches again. We have a better position this time — am pleased we had not to go back to where we were last time. The old Turks are still there and hum a bit still. We gained a couple of trenches Monday night on our right flank.

Well Nell you seem to be having a busy time of it with my stock. How did my cattle get on that were in Myrtleford — suppose old Frank starved them out. What horse do you do your boundary riding *on. If you can get old Nigger in condition you can sell him and keep the proceeds. How are the rest of my horses and old Bally and her foal — those fillies seem to be a darn nuisance — do you think they will make a* [carriage] *pair.*

*Jack has left his crop pretty late. It ought to be well up in June to do any good. Is he doing anything to his block at all. Fancy that damned old Hoban putting his cattle in that paddock — he ought to be shot.* [A neighbour had been pasturing his cattle on Carthew land, taking advantage of Charles's absence.]

*I never thought he would do that when a man is away on a job like this at any rate, the miserable dog. And speaking of dogs what is Black up to now — mooning around the creek I suppose.*

*I got a letter from Jean and one from Ethel, and the Stock Journal. Ethel has a job like yours, Boss of Craigie. She is giving the foxes nothing — poisoned two in one hit — they were killing the young lambs. Jean said Melbourne is likely to be in the first four for finals in the League F. ball.*

*I did not see where young Willouby was killed, only that he was wounded — he must of died of his wounds. Although we are only one and a half miles from the other chaps I very seldom hear or see anything of them. Every Unit has its own job and therefore one does not get much chance of seeing anyone, and a man wants all the rest he can get at this job.*

*Although I myself am tip top there is still an awful lot of sickness — the chief cause in my opinion is want of proper rest and regular hours which is impossible to get, also the flies. You dont know what flies are at home, they are rotten.*

*Well old Girl I can just about catch the mail so no more.*

*Love to all at home. Charlie.*

The days crawled by. White armbands and patches were distributed to all ranks to be sewn onto shirts (to make it easier to identify friend from foe in the aftermath of battle), and extra rations of potatoes, bread, tinned meat, jam and even eggs were issued. Charles was cynically reminded of animals being fattened for the slaughter, but he kept his thoughts to himself.

In spite of seventy reinforcements in late July, the regiment was still seriously undermanned. Morale was at an all-time low and the general health of the troops was immeasurably weakened by their poor diet, exhaustion from lack of sleep and the ever present dysentery. The water shortage was now critical and water was restricted to use for consumption and cooling of machine guns only. The transport of large stocks of ammunition was the first priority.

And so the men waited.

---

THE TRENCHES
AUGUST 5TH 1915

DEAR JEAN,

*Just a line in answer to your welcome letter. As you see we are in the trenches again — have been here a week but dont expect to be here long.*

*You can guess what that means. There is a lot a fellow would like to write about but carnt. I wrote to Mother and Ethel yesterday. You need not mention your surmise of the above either.*

*You are right I dont know what I would do without Nell at home. Fancy her lecturing old Hoban the miserable old dog. I'd like to have caught him.*

*Mother seems to be in good health which is great. I got a letter from one of my Boys yesterday — he got hit in the mouth and had his jaw broken. I never seen a gamer fellow — he is leaving for Australia but hopes to come back again if the war is still on when he gets right — his name Arthur Gay.*

*I have had no news of Fred atall [sic]. I have got two or three looking him up, but I havent the slightest doubt he is all right. I have been very fortunate since I have been here — no occasion to see the Dr.*

*Poor Minnie Green is having a bad time — I hope she gets cured all right. Kindly remember me to Minnie, also Mr. and Mrs. Mummery and Sir Dickie. Well old Girl its time I was getting my Bully Beef and biscuits for lunch so I ring off. Goodbye for the present.*

*Love from your old Bro, Charlie.*

In the late afternoon of Friday, 6 August, distant gunfire in the south of the peninsula heralded the anticipated attack on Cape Helles by the British. Simultaneously, close at hand, came the sounds of a desperate battle raging for the plateau of Lone Pine, where the Australian 1st Division made a concerted feint at the enemy.

Now began a period of intense anticipation for the 8th and 10th Light Horse at the Nek. Rations were issued and consumed, messages flew back and forth to HQ, were recinded, countermanded and cancelled, and the troopers made use of their time writing to wives, sweethearts and families. Moving with difficulty, the chaplains circulated among the densely packed trenches, hearing confessions, giving absolution, listening, counselling and leading prayers. It mattered not if they were priest, minister, rabbi or Salvation Army chaplain. When face to face with death, denomination means less than nothing. There is only one God, after all, the God of love, mercy and compassion, the Saviour of Souls.

By evening came the news that the Australians had taken Lone Pine, but at heavy cost. The Turks had fought back savagely during a bloodbath which resulted in the loss of eighty Australian officers and 2197 men. It was no consolation that the Turks had suffered three times the number of casualties.

More bad news was to follow. The landing at Suvla Bay of 20 000 untried and green British forces, who were to have marched inland to reinforce the Australians at Anzac and the New Zealanders at Chunuk Bair, had been a disaster. Their commander, Lieutenant General Sir Frederick Stoppford, had remained on his ship *Jonquil* well out to sea during the landing, indecisive and incompetent. Lacking cohesive leadership, the inexperienced officers and confused troops had milled around the beaches, easily routed and massacred by the far smaller but well disciplined Turkish forces from the heights above. The situation would have been laughable were it not so utterly tragic; a further episode in the sad litany of errors of judgment and the criminal wastage of human life that marked every facet of the Gallipoli campaign. (Stoppford had, in fact, never seen or heard a shot fired in warfare, his total qualification for his high office being an acceptable pedigree, sufficient money to buy and maintain a commission as a gentleman and an automatic rise in the military hierarchy. He had previously served as Commander of the Tower of London, and in fact it was even rumoured that he was senile. This incredible state of affairs was by no means peculiar to the British; history is punctuated by similar instances of such foolish appointments.)

Finally General Hamilton intervened, but by this time it was too late and the disorganised British troops were decimated by the Turks. The New Zealanders were subsequently driven back from the heights of Chunuk Bair, with massive loss of life on both sides, and the Australian attack on Hill 971 to the north met the same fate, with shocking casualties.

Back at the Nek, Charles and his fellow officers talked in low voices. There was still time for a reprieve, and each time a message was relayed from HQ their hopes rose, only to be dashed. There was nothing whatsoever he and his friends could do, and Charles knew they shared his frustration and impotent fury. (The officers could, of course, refuse to lead their men into action, but they would certainly be summarily court-martialled and perhaps shot for cowardice and insubordination.)

Majors McLaurin, Scott and Todd, and even Colonel White and Lieutenant Colonel Brazier, had bluntly voiced their doubts about the exercise, but to no effect. They could do no more. Both Hughes and Antill were Boer War veterans and felt entitled to claim superior knowledge and experience of military tactics, despite the fact that the South African conflict was mainly confined to guerilla fighting, which bore no resemblance to trench warfare.

Still the light-horsemen waited. They were told to snatch what rest they could in the crowded trenches, but few slept, in spite of—or perhaps because of—exhaustion and lack of sleep. Hopes were high that the offensive would be called off. However, in spite of the collapse of every phase of the campaign to date, which made the light horse charge irrelevant and pointless, the Generals decided to carry on as planned, using the attack on the Nek as a feint to assist the New Zealanders at Chunuk Bair.

Had there been the slightest chance of overrunning the Turkish trenches to gain the heights of Baby 700, Charles might have reckoned it worth the risk, but they all knew with absolute certainty that the attempt would fail. The odds were totally impossible, and he was filled with bitterness and grief that General Hughes and his Brigade Major Colonel Antill, safe in their dugout at HQ, were implacably resolved to sacrifice 600 of the finest men Australia had ever bred. To Charles, the welfare of his troops was paramount. He was endlessly proud of them, and the sure knowledge that tomorrow most, or all, of them would be maggot-ridden carcasses must have brought a bitter gall to his throat.

There were to be four waves of attack, each comprising 150 men, and four officers from the 8th and 10th Light Horse were invited to draw lots to determine the sequence of the assault. When the straws were drawn, to the 8th went the 'honour' of leading the charge. Watching the little ceremony, Charles must have known for certain that he would never return home to the land he loved; never hold his sweetheart in his arms again, nor raise their children in that Happy Valley of his childhood.

Charles had jokingly dubbed the ravine to the left of the Nek 'Happy Valley' after his birthplace. A place of death, where many hundreds of bodies, the bodies of friend and foe, lay rotting and unburied. A mecca for vultures, ravens, rats and other creatures which fed on carrion; a repository for the discarded detritus of war. The name had stuck—so totally, ludicrously inept was the title—and was adopted officially. 'Death Valley' would have been a far more appropriate name. Was this now to be his graveyard, and that of the 600 brave men of the light horse?

Did it, perhaps, occur to Charles that history was repeating itself with grim irony? That, sixty years before at Balaclava, 600 heroic British light-horsemen, allies of the Turks, had charged the Russians against quite impossible odds, and now, as allies of Russia, 600 Australian light-horsemen were to charge to almost certain death against the Turks? Did he, perhaps, think of Tennyson's great poem, written in homage to the Charge of the Light Brigade?

> Half a league, half a league,
> Half a league onward,
> All in the valley of Death
> Rode the six hundred.

'Forward, the Light Brigade!
Charge for the guns!' he said:
Into the valley of Death
Rode the six hundred.

This charge of the Light Brigade would be even bloodier and more senseless than its predecessor and the carnage far greater. Charles knew that the Turkish machine guns could each fire more than 600 rounds per minute, with a range of more than 1 mile (1.6 kilometres). From a distance of 30 yards (27 metres), every bullet would find its mark. Not even a blind man could miss.

There was no time, though, for idle regrets. Charles moved once more among his men in the crowded trenches—a joke here, a smile and a word there, a touch on the arm—seeking in his quiet way to justify the faith he knew they had in him, and to let them know of his regard, his pride and his confidence in their loyalty. A few were playing cards, cheating outrageously and wagering thousands of pounds on a single card, knowing that on the morrow all debts would be cancelled. Charles felt the tears come to his eyes as they laughed carelessly, but in the dim lamplight it did not matter. He took comfort in the sure knowledge that, come the dawn, these brave men would follow him wherever he led—trustfully, unhesitatingly and without question.

'Forward the Light Brigade!'
Was there a man dismayed?
Not though the soldier knew
Some one had blundered:
Theirs not to make reply,
Theirs not to reason why,
Theirs but to do and die:
Into the valley of Death
Rode the six hundred.

It would be both the longest and the shortest night of Charles's life. He reread all of his letters, lingering over the photographs in his wallet of Ethel and his mother and sisters. Margaret had sent him a time exposure of the parlour and he studied it minutely, as if seeing it for the first time, sick with longing for its shabby warmth and the security he had so taken for granted. There, in the corner, was the ancient burr-walnut piano with its yellowed keys and ornate brass candlabra, where Add would play hymns on Sundays and, on other days, the old familiar songs such as Gilbert and Sullivan's lively tunes, or 'Come into the garden Maude' and 'Home Sweet Home', while the rest of the family and friends gathered round singing lustily, with Black joyously adding his contribution.

Under the soft, mellow glow of the hanging lamp was the big, round table, covered with the shabby, ink-stained cloth of red serge edged with bobble fringe, where he had once wrestled with his homework. He could see his mother there now, darning one of his socks, her black curls escaping untidily from the careless bun at the nape of her neck, listening as Em or Babs read aloud from Charles Dickens or *Pilgrim's Progress* while the other girls crocheted or embroidered.

There were portraits in profusion—of his late father, framed in sable velvet, and other long-dead relatives. There was one of Uncle Albert Woolley, looking very brave and martial in his Boer War uniform, posing before an improbable canvas backdrop of military tents. By the time Albert had reached the Cape the war was well and truly over, but he still regarded himself as a veteran and had given Charles a great deal of soldierly advice. He smiled at the thought.

He took one last, lingering look at Ethel's portrait and pressed it to his lips before replacing it in his wallet, next to his heart. He had scribbled a short note to her, which he had given to the chaplain, assuring her of his eternal love, but asking her to find happiness with another should he go under. He knew, however, beyond a shadow of doubt, that in spite of what he had written Ethel would never marry. For her, as for him, there had never been, and would never be, anyone else. Theirs was a love so complete, and their committal to each other so total, that there would be no room for second best. His heart ached for her in all the long, lonely years ahead.

Charles's one consolation was that his young brother Fred, now recuperating in Egypt, was not among his comrades of the 10th Light Horse who would, in an hour or so, face the Turkish guns. He was thankful that his mother would not need to mourn the loss of two sons—at least in the immediate future. He did not want to dwell on her grief at his own death. That would be too much for him to bear, too aware as he was of her inevitable agony.

The endless night dragged on. Paradoxically, most men were shivering uncontrollably from apprehension, even as they sweated in the packed trenches. Thick slabs of bread and jam and mugs of sweet tea were circulated and, towards dawn, a generous tot of rum was issued to each man.

Charles watched the dark outline of the enemy trenches rising rank on rank to the summit of Baby 700. Deceptively still, deceptively quiet, yet he knew that the labyrinth of saps swarmed with vigilant men, waiting to unleash murderous fire from the deadly machine guns nestled among the wall of timber and sandbags they would have to scale. How could any mortal survive such a hail of death, he wondered bleakly?

Looking up at the unfamiliar stars, Charles sensed, rather than saw, an imperceptible paling of the eastern sky. It will be daylight in Constantinople, he thought, irrelevantly. He and his men had never doubted for a moment that they'd get there, and now they never would. The ill-conceived and disastrously orchestrated campaign had been doomed from the start, waged against an army of brave men who had been welded by their brilliant leader, Colonel Mustapha Kemal, into an efficient and grossly underestimated fighting machine.

The orders were brief and concise. The Australian artillery and the British naval guns would open fire on the Turkish stonghold of the Nek at precisely 4am, hopefully blasting and destroying the enemy machine-gun emplacements. On the stroke of 4.30am, the shelling would cease and the initial wave of light-horsemen would, at a signal, lead the assault on Baby 700, followed by the second, third and fourth waves at designated intervals.

As the appointed hour approached, the tension in the trenches became almost unbearable, the men's nerves being stretched to breaking point, and when 'all ranks to arms' was signalled there was an audible sigh of relief. They busied themselves rechecking their rifles, razor-sharp bayonets and the grenades they would use to clear out the enemy trenches—if they got that far.

Shockingly, at seven minutes before 4am, a deafening explosion was heard, heralding the bombardment by the British navy, followed by the Australian artillery. The waiting was over.

Charles threaded his way among his massed troopers for a last reassuring word and a smile, and each man reached out to grasp his hand for a silent and emotional farewell, or perhaps a benediction. Back at the parapet he shook hands with Colonel White (who was not required to lead his men in the charge but felt it his duty to do so), Major McLaurin, Captain Hore, Lieutenant Grant and Lieutenant Howard, exchanging a few words and wishing them luck and godspeed as the shells screamed overhead.

The naval guns appeared to be wildly inaccurate and seemed to be wreaking more havoc on the Australian lines than on those of the Turks, and the artillery, in trying to avoid hitting their own troops, overshot the target by a large margin, leaving the enemy machine gun emplacements relatively unscathed. Charles and his troop, numbering about forty men, were situated on the extreme right of the line, where there was no more than 30 yards (27 metres) separating their trench from the enemy. They were to mount the second wave of the charge.

Abruptly, at exactly 4.23am, the barrage of fire ceased, followed by an eerie silence. The seconds ticked away as they waited for the shelling to resume, but it was soon apparent that the ceasefire was premature and final. It was now twenty-six minutes past the hour.

The Turks, who had prudently retired to their saps during the bombardment, now emerged to man their maxims again, in anticipation of the expected assault. It was precisely twenty-eight minutes past four.

On the stroke of the half-hour, as a whistle blew, the first wave of the 8th Light Horse swarmed over the parapet. As Charles watched, appalled, he saw Colonel White immediately stagger and fall, but the officers and men who followed him never faltered as they raced towards the enemy trenches. In the melee, the dust and the smoke screened the terrible sight of wholesale murder, and Charles was unable to distinguish one man from another as one by one they fell like ninepins. He was never to know that within the space of two short minutes the entire complement of officers, including Colonel White, Major Redford and Lieutenants Anderson, Talbot-Woods, Wilson,

Borthwick, Dale, Marsh and Henty, had been killed and that most of their men lay mortally wounded in an area of less than half an acre.

There was no time to dwell on their probable demise as Major Deeble raised his whistle to his lips to signal the second charge. Poised on the fire step, Charles leapt onto the parapet, his figure outlined for an instant against the lightening sky, holding aloft his rifle, and his men rushed to follow him, proudly, unhesitatingly, to do or to die. And die they did—all but one—in a hail of blistering machine-gun fire. Those following their leaders trampled and fell on their mates in wild confusion, choking in the dust and cordite fumes as countless bullets tore up the earth of no-man's-land.

Charles had gone less than ten paces when he was hit by a stunning blow. His legs buckled beneath him and, as he fell, he was dimly aware that a herd of wild horses was trampling him. Then he knew nothing more.

> Cannon to the right of them,
> Cannon to the left of them,
> Cannon in front of them
> Volleyed and thundered;
> Stormed at with shot and shell,
> Boldly they rode and well,
> Into the jaws of Death,
> Into the mouth of Hell
> Rode the six hundred.

Sickened by the slaughter, Colonel Brazier sent an urgent message to the Brigade Major, Colonel Antill, requesting that the attack be halted. Brazier was told to 'press on'. When the second wave of the 8th Light Horse went over the top and was instantly massacred, joining the mounds of dead and dying on the Nek, Brazier, with Majors Scott and Todd, again petitioned Antill. Antill had heard that an Australian flag had been planted in an enemy trench by the second wave of troopers and, erroneously believing that the first line of trenches had been taken, maintained that the assault must continue as planned. In despair, Brazier went over the Colonel's head to General Hughes, who advised him to 'try another angle'. Brazier was thus forced to watch in anguish as his own 10th Light Horse went over the parapet and was decimated.

Meanwhile, Major Love cautiously reconnoitred the left flank, where the dead and wounded lay three deep, and reported to HQ that it was impossible for a man to advance even one yard and live. Filled with rage and grief at the loss of his beloved troops, Brazier confronted the General shouting that it was 'nothing but murder, bloody murder' and at last, reluctantly, he was given the order to retreat. Brazier was, however, heartbroken to discover that due to faulty communications half of the fourth wave had already charged to their deaths. (It was afterwards alleged that some of these men escaped death only because the Turks believed that no commanding officer would be stupid or foolhardy enough to squander any further men on such a hopeless attack.) The enemy themselves suffered almost no casualties.

When the tragic toll was counted, of the Western Australian 10th Light Horse, eighty were killed and fifty-six wounded. The Victorian 8th Light Horse fared much worse, with the death of 156 officers and men, and eighty injured, many of whom later died of their wounds. In less than half an hour, on less than half an acre, almost 400 men, the flower of Australian manhood, lay slaughtered and maimed on the bloody slopes of Gallipoli, their seed tragically lost forever. There was scarcely a family in Western Australia or Victoria that did not lose a son, a brother, a husband or a friend on that fatal Saturday of 7 August 1915.

When can their glory fade?
O the wild charge they made!
All the world wondered.
Honour the charge they made!
Honour the Light Brigade,
Noble six hundred!

# ⇥ The Aftermath ⇤

*B*ACK AT THE FARM in Happy Valley on that fateful day, Black disappeared shortly after lunch, failing to bring the cattle in as he invariably did. After a search of all his usual haunts he was discovered by Emily, crouched under Charles's bed. He lay quite still, his head on his paws, his ears and tail slack and motionless. Only his sorrowful eyes followed the women as they tried to coax him out with a plate of titbits and a succulent bone.

For three days and nights Black remained there, neither eating nor drinking, nor even voiding as far as they knew. In the late afternoon of 10 August he emerged, gaunt and unkempt, his tail limp and his eyes dull and lustreless, to empty his bladder and to drink a little water. It was to be some days before they understood.

Later that week, when Margaret heard Jack's car chugging up the road and saw his grave face, she knew at once that he was the bearer of bad news. He handed her the *Herald* after a brief greeting, and when she saw the glaring headlines her heart gave a sickening jolt and her legs turned to jelly.

SHEER HEROISM. AUSTRALIAN LIGHT
HORSE ATTEMPT THE IMPOSSIBLE.

———

Tornado of Fire Defends Eight Fold Turkish
Trenches. Soldiers Fight Over Bodies Three
Deep. An account by C.E.W. Bean, War
Correspondent of Gallipoli. August 15th '15.

The attack on Lonesome Pine had already
forced the Turks to rush Brigades of reinforce-

ments South, and it was now necessary to prevent them from moving troops to the centre. For this purpose, the 8th and 10th Light Horse Brigades were ordered to charge, from an angle of our line, the immensely strong positions held by the Turks opposite them.

The Turkish lines consist of trench after trench, sometimes eight deep, across a gradually rising background.

(Our men were ordered to wear only shirt-sleeves and carry only bayonets and grenades, and charge an amphitheatre of tiered Turkish trenches which gave clear fire from up to seven tiers, onto the defenceless men. It was clearly suicidal to the lowest mentality.)

The main attack was made at dawn (Aug. 7th). After half an hour's bombardment by our Artillery, which because of the proximity of our trenches to the enemies', as close as thirty yards, killed probably as many of our men as theirs, and others tried to avoid this and missed the enemy.

The bombardment ceased at 4.30 a.m., and some minutes later (owing to a discrepancy of synchronisation) the order was given to charge. At the same instant there broke out such a rattle of rifle and machine gun fire as was never heard before.

Into this fusillade our men went. The 3rd Light Horse (comprising the 8th and 10th Light Horse) was attacking a narrow ridge only a hundred yards broad (the Nek) across which the trenches faced each other at a distance of fifty to thirty yards on the right.

The attacking party was divided into four lines of 150 men in each.

The first line, on a signal given by officers, watch in hand, jumped over the parapets. Many fell back wounded, but the rest rushed on, into the dust caused by the bullets and the shrapnel from the Turkish 75 Mill. guns, and poured across the whole Nek. Into the thick haze, the figures of hurrying and falling men could be dimly seen.

Two minutes later, the second line followed. This line reached the R. hand corner of a Turkish trench. A small flag which they carried with them in order to mark the captured trench appeared for a couple of minutes only.

The third line was immediately sent forward, of the 10th Light Horse, and the men leaped from the parapet without having the least hesitation, but when the flag disappeared, the attack was ordered to cease in time to check a few on the left (of the fourth line) who had not reached the fire zone.

## SHEER HEROISM

The Victorian 8th Light Horse led the charge. (They had drawn lots as to order.) No trenches were gained in this fight, but for sheer self sacrifice and heroism, this charge of the Australian Light Horse is unsurpassed in history.

A Cable message received yesterday stated that the 8th and 10th (Western Australian) Light Horse were practically wiped out in the fighting on August 7th.

The casualty lists grew longer every day as more and more deaths were confirmed, bringing heartbreak and grief to hundreds of homes. Those whose sons were not mentioned today read of friends and relatives who had lost loved ones, and they lived in dread of what tomorrow might bring. The war was no longer an exciting event that was happening thousands of miles away in someone else's country, but a ravening monster that stretched its tentacles into every corner of the land, voraciously demanding more and more human sacrifice to feed its insatiable maw.

Many of the names and faces in the printed photographs were familiar to the Carthew women. There was the Reverend Morrison's son, George, a member of Charles's troop, young Ilsley and Sid O'Neill, Lieutenants Henty and Dale, Alf Healy, Reg Bruce, Colonel White and the two Cole brothers. There were significantly less wounded. The Turks had repeatedly raked the mounds of fallen soldiers with machine-gun fire, leaving only a handful of survivors, and it was soon apparent that few, if any, had been taken prisoner. 'Practically wiped out'—the terrible words returned again and again during those agonising days to those who waited. (At this stage, due to the length of time if took for letters to reach Australia, the Carthews had no knowledge of Fred's illness and subsequent convalescence in Egypt. They only knew that both the 8th and 10th Light Horse had, with incredible heroism, taken the leading role in the most disastrous charge of the Gallipoli campaign and had paid the ultimate price in blood.)

Four days after delivering the newspaper account, Jack again drove up in his motor car bearing a telegram from the War Office.

---

11.40pm 18th Aug. 1915
T.H. Carthew Esq
Ovens Vale Via Myrtleford

*Regret to inform you it is officially reported your brother Lieut*
*C. Carthew was missing seventh inst. any further particulars*
*received will be at once communicated to you.*
    *Colonel Hawker*
    *Victoria Barracks Melbourne*

---

Friday

My Dear Babs,
    *We have just received a wire from the defence department*
*stating that Charl is missing, and has been from the 7th inst. —*

*its just about the worst we could hear, Mother is greatly cut up
about it. I hope to God he is alright — its awful not to know how
or where he is — goodness only knows what happens to them
when taken prisoners, we can only hope for the best, which seems
but cold comfort.*

*I wonder if Ethel got a wire, I daresay she did poor girl — she
will feel it.*

*Well Babs you know as much as we do now, I do hope we get
good news later.*

*Goodbye, from Nell.*

FITZROY

DEAR SISTER,

*Saturday's Herald brought the unfortunate tidings of Nephew
Charles' mishap. 'Missing' which has broad meaning either wounded
or taken prisoner. If taken prisoner I learned that he will be well
treated as all officers are. At any rate, keep up your spirits, knowing
that he has done his duty to his country, his kindred and his family.
I can say no more, time is fleeting and must be gone.*

*Goodnight Sister Maggie and give a strong lead to your family
by not showing the 'White Feather'.*

*'Come forth in the armour of the Spartan mothers, who gave of
their sons freely to their Country ...'*

*Brother John*

In the days that followed, Nell and Adelaide repeated staunchly that no
news was good news, and Margaret prayed constantly to her merciful
God to spare her beloved sons, but deep down she knew that Charlie
would not be coming home to them. She said nothing of this to her
daughters, letting them cherish their hopes for a time at least, but she
was convinced that the strange, mystic bond between Charles and
Black had endured—even though they were many thousands of miles
apart—and that the dog had known, inexplicably but surely, that something terrible had happened to his beloved master. Indeed, it was later
confirmed that 4.30am at Gallipoli, the time of the charge, corresponded with 1pm in Melbourne, the time Black had disappeared.

Like the family, Ethel Seymour was almost demented with worry and fear, and Margaret's heart ached for the poor girl who made no secret of her adoration for her Charlie.

The days crawled by. Eventually, Jack received a cable, not from official sources but from his younger brother, Fred, in Egypt.

---

23RD AUG 1915
HELIOPOLIS, EGYPT
J. CARTHEW
MYRTLEFORD

*Charlie has been killed in action on seventh. Fred.*

In haste, Jack drove over to Happy Valley with the Anglican minister, the Reverend Morrison. Margaret read the yellow slip of paper exhibiting an almost unnatural calm, as though she had known all along—as indeed she had. She quietly thanked Reverend Morrison for his support, expressing her sorrow for the loss of his son, George, and enquired after Mrs Morrison's health.

In one way, the cable brought the good news that her youngest son was safe in Egypt, for the time being at least. She had much to be thankful for that the good Lord had spared him, and she tried not to wonder why He had seen fit to take her Charl, surely the finest son a mother could have.

A few days later, the *Myrtleford Mail* reported Charles's death to the district.

### KILLED IN ACTION—LIEUT. CHARLES CARTHEW.

---

Widespread regret was felt throughout Myrtleford District when it was learned that a cable was received Thursday stating that Lieut. Charles Carthew was missing. Although this news was bad enough, hopes were entertained that he might turn up alright, but these were dispelled on Monday when a notification was received that Lieut. Carthew was dead.

The Rev. Morrison and Mr Jack Carthew drove at once to Happy Valley and broke the sad news to the deceased officer's mother and sisters, who, needless to say, were prostrated by the heavy stroke. They will have the heartfelt sympathy of everyone throughout the district in their time of trouble.

The late Lieut. Carthew was the second son of the late Thos. Henry and Mrs. Carthew of Happy Valley where he had always resided, having as quite a young lad, taken his late father's place in managing for his mother — a duty which he well carried out up to his departure for the front.

On the formation of the L. Horse at Myrtleford, he was one of the first to join, always taking the keenest interest in everything concerning it and was afterwards placed in charge as 2nd Lieut.

On the outbreak of war he lost no time enlisting and left for Broadmeadows Camp in September of last year. Whilst there he had the reputation of being a 'good alround man' noted for his dash and daring, keen judgment, a fearless horseman, and he was most popular with both brother officers and men, who placed in him their greatest confidence.

On leaving Broadmeadows he was promoted to 1st Lieut., and later was marked for further promotion.

Possessed of a splendid physique and a most fearless nature, he never had a fear for himself, but constantly expressed a wish that his young brother, who is also at the front, would come through safely. In a recent letter to his mother he entreated her not to worry over them, for 'if wounded we will be well looked after, but if we should go under, remember that we did our duty and were not afraid to die for our country, and did not stay at home like some who could, but would not go'. A good son and a good brother, his loss to his family is a severe one, and for his fine qualities he was held in the highest esteem by all.

No truer words can be said of him: 'He was a soldier and a man'.

From the length and breadth of the country, telegrams, mourning cards and black-bordered letters poured in from near and distant relatives, friends, brother officers, convalescent former members of Charles's troop and their parents. The latter all begged for photographs of Charles, and Margaret and the girls were kept busy replying and sending copies of his portrait.

There were also visits from neighbours and mere acquaintances, garbed in deepest mourning, who descended on the bereaved ladies to offer their condolences, mopping their eyes ostentatiously with black-bordered handkerchiefs all the while as they partook of tea and fruitcake baked daily by Adelaide.

---

To THOS. HENRY CARTHEW

MY DEAR SIR,

*Words cannot convey to you my feelings of sympathy with you in your deep sorry.*

*Your brother was a splendid young fellow in every way and gained the esteem and admiration of all.*

*I have no doubt you have already received full particulars of how bravely he died in a heroic effort to take the Turks trenches.*

*Yours very faithfully,*

*F. Hughes*

*Brdr. Genl. Commanding 3rd Light Horse Brigade.*

MY DEAR MRS. CARTHEW,

Have just heard of your great trouble in losing your splendid soldier son Charlie. Please accept my deepest sympathy. I am so very sorry for you and your girls and boys in your sad trouble.

With love from Yours Sincerely, Albert Woolley.

'SALFORD', CASEY ST. C'WOOD

DEAR MRS CARTHEW,

It was with deep sorrow that I heard of the great loss of your noble, loyal soldier son. Try to feel that it is for the best and trust in God — He will never leave thee nor forsake thee. We all know that your brother is happy now and free from pain. If you could only see some of the poor boys who have come back without some of their limbs, you would feel that your loved one is better off.

Your sincere friend, Linda Johnston.

THE CHERRY TREE, MURROON
SEPT. 11TH 1915

DEAR MRS. CARTHEW,

I just received a letter today from my husband. He and your son were great chums and shared the dugout together. He had the greatest admiration and respect for your son and he told me to a man everyone in his Troop just adored him.

Just as my husband was leaving for Egypt where he had been sent owing to having his knee cap displaced through a fall from the parapet of the trenches, Mr. Carthew was the last to say Goodbye and said if he was sent home to call and tell his sister that he was quite alright.

Your boy often sent kind messages to me as I was very anxious and I met him at Broadmeadows. I feel so for you, but how very proud of such a son you must be.

I can see his grand, strong face now, and he just had to have a hero's death. My husband's one regret was that he was not by his side helping him. They were so fond of each other. So I just wanted you to know that though I am overjoyed at knowing I will have my husband back again, still I can weep with you in your loss, for I wanted to see them come home together, and I shared your anxiety when I saw he was missing and sorrowed when I saw that he had fallen.

You must be a grand woman to have a son that men loved and could be led by, and your pride in him will temper your grief, for he was a hero.

Believe me, Dear Mrs. Carthew,

Yours very sincerely, Viva Mulder.

---

DALESFORD

15.9.'15

DEAR MADAM,

Allow me to convey my deepest sympathy to you for the loss of your son, who was my officer in Egypt and the Dardanelles.

I was with him all the time from when he joined us at Broadmeadows until I was wounded on June 1st, and I can say there was no officer there more respected and honoured than Lt. Carthew, right from the first he became a favourite with the men, indeed to us he was more like a mate than an officer, and his loss must be deeply regretted by everyone. Hoping that knowing that he died in a good cause will help to ease the pain of grief.

I am sincerely yours,

Tpr. A. Gay, B Troop, 'C' Squadron, 8th. A.L.H.

There was even a letter from Margaret's nephew Frank Carthew. She hadn't cared for him greatly as a youth, when he had trapped little Fred under a washing tub, sitting on it until the child was hysterical and almost asphyxiated, and as far as she could tell by his letter he hadn't greatly improved.

---

BOWEN, N. Q

20TH SEPT. '15

DEAR AUNTIE AND COUSINS,

I visited you with my Dear Mother 12 or 14 years ago. I read of poor Charlie's death in the paper and was indeed grieved at reading same. Poor chap, he died the bravest of all deaths fighting for his King, Country, and all of us at home, and it is no doubt hard losing him, but for the sake of us, who through some tie or other must stay behind.

Heaven only knows if I were single I would have been at the front long ago. However, I am doing my little bit at home financially and rearing my family. God forbid that any of them will ever turn out such specimens as these 'Huns' the atrocities they have committed are beyond relization [sic] when you consider they are supposed to be a civilized nation and Kultured at that.

All has happened for the best you may depend. It was his turn and the Almighty took him.

Our boy is nearly 17 months, we had him dressed up as a soldier on Patriotic Day, and he collected seven pounds, four shillings which was very good Eh.

Well dear Auntie I must conclude.

Your aff. nephew Frank Carthew.

P.S. I received word today of a rise of ten pounds per annum.

---

No. 699, Cpl. M.H. Griggs
8th L.H. Reg., 3rd Brig., A.I.F.
Heliopolis, Egypt. Oct. 2nd 1915

Dear Mrs. Carthew,

I am writing these few lines to let you know that I am sending by the same mail, a notebook belonging to Mr. Carthew. I thought perhaps that you would like to have it, you will please excuse the delay in sending it, but it was in my kitbag and I was in hospital for 2 months after the charge, where we lost such a lot of fine men. It would have been very hard to find such a good lot of Officers as those of the 8th. L.H.

I had the good fortune to get into Mr. Carthew's Troop. Dear Mrs. Carthew, we all sympathize with you very sincerely in your sorrow, he was loved by us all, as a man first, and a gentleman. I can say no more than that, for there is nothing else to say. We would have followed him wherever he went, and he died like the brave man that he was, for country and honour.

This is all that I had of his given to me, and although I would have liked to keep it, thought that you had the most right to anything that *he had used, so please accept it from me.* [Margaret later returned the notebook to Corporal Griggs.] *I was one of the few that got through that Charge by God's help, for he surely must have been near me to protect me.*

*Again, I apologise for the delay in sending it to you. Believe me to be —*

*Yours in sorrow, M.H. Griggs.*

POST OFFICE, OVENS VALE
OCT 9TH '15

DEAR BABS,

*Received your letter last night, and also got one from Ethel, sorry to hear they have not been well — they must be a very delicate family.*

*I had a letter from poor old Charl, dated 4th. Aug., probably the last — he was then in the best of health, what a blessing he had little or no suffering. I was afraid he might have been wounded and lingered for a time.*

*We had a letter from a Mr. Daniels, his son was a Sergeant in Charl's Troop, but was sent to Lemnos in July, thus his life was saved, for a time anyway — the old fellow met Charl at B'Meadows several times. His boy said Colonel White and Charl were seldom out of the danger zone, always doing something for the men instead of resting themselves, and they had the name of being the two bravest men in Galopoli* [sic] *— and the men thought the world of Charl. Its nice to get these letters, but its like getting it all over again.*

*About those photoes Babs I think you had better get half dozen to see what they will be like, this Mr. Daniels wants one too.*

*My bridle came up Friday night — I did not get it yesterday as I had parcels enough on the saddle. I got a black dress made by Miss McFadygen, she made it alright I think, 11/- she charged, a bit stiff for no lining. She is the only one in Myrtleford now.*

*We are putting the place up by auction about the end of next month I think so if it sells we will all be on holiday.*

*Well I'll close now, with love from Nell.*

RAGLAN ST., DALESFORD
17.10.'15

DEAR MISS CARTHEW,

In reply to your welcome letter I will just write a few lines to let you know how I was hurt, and how I am getting on.

On the morning of June 1st. the day I was shot our troop were relieved in the firing line after 48 hours work to take our turn in the rest trenches just behind the firing line, for 48 hours — that is the way we used to work, 2 days in and 2 days out, the ones who are out doing the fatigue work for the others — well in the afternoon after we had finished work I thought that I would take the rifle and go into the first trench to see if I could get a sniper who had been troubling us a bit so I took up a position at a new loophole where I could enfilade a small section of trench running up the hill from the place where the snipers used to work from — I watched there from 12 o'clock until about 4 p.m. when I saw the top of a man's hat start to move towards this piece I was watching and as soon as his head appeared I got in one shot which missed I think for he ran but stopped him with a second. It was getting late then and the sun getting behind us was throwing my shadow across the loophole. I saw the danger of it but thought I would just take one more look. (I knew they had located me as you only had to pass your hat over the loophole to draw their fire.)

Well I just moved sideways over the loophole until I could see out with one eye only, but that was enough — for then two or 3 bullets came throw the hole and got me in the top lip just under the nose and the bullet striking the top teeth broke up and travelled along the jaw and down the throat after shattering the lower jaw and cutting two arteries in my throat so you can see what a narrow escape I hud.

Captain Campbell our Medical Officer saved my life and was killed a few days later himself poor fellow — he was very popular amongst the men.

Poor Charlie helped to carry me out on a blanket and when I felt myself going from loss of blood and the morphia that they injected into my arm I thought was dying — I shook hands with him and poor old man he nearly broke down — I think it hurt him more than it hurt me — he couldn't stand to see anyone suffering — even the Turks — he said to me on the day of the Armastice when they were burying their dead 'Isn't it a shame to see all those game men lying there' and he felt that badly it was days before he got his old spirits back.

There is a lot I could tell you about him but it would take a week to write. Anyhow he will always rest in my memory as the straightest and best man I ever met.

I will enclose a letter I rec'd from him only the other day written about a day or so before he was killed. You will see by that what a hopeless task the 8th had before them. I would like it back and if you could spare a photo of him I would be very thankful for it.

Hoping this finds you well I will close with kind regards from Yours Sincerely, Arthur Gay.

I don't know any of our troop that are in Egypt now. There are some of them invalided home and I think the rest have gone back to the fight as far as I know. (You will see Charlie's signature across the censor stamp he used to censor all our letters.)

---

ANZAC, GALLIPOLI
30.10.'15

DEAR MR. CARTHEW,

I expect you will be wondering why I had not replied to your letter re your brother's death, but shortly after I returned after being wounded, (slightly, I am glad to say) I had the bad luck to sprain my ankle and only returned here recently, during my absence all my letters were sent after me, and they are only now coming back, hence the delay.

After the Charge on the 'NEK' on the morning of August 7th, Charlie, amongst a lot of others, was reported as missing, as there was a probability of some being taken prisoners, but later on, taking the evidence of some of the very few men who were on the Right of the line, the Board decided they were all killed and reported accordingly.

I was in the charge and have not the slightest doubt that this is correct. We have not the faintest idea how it could have appeared in the papers that he had died from unknown causes.

You have my deepest sympathy in your sad bereavement, and I can assure you that I feel Charlie's death very much.

He was the best troop leader I had and one of the best in the Regiment, and was one of my dearest friends, besides which he and I were in the same Regiment in Victoria and I knew him well and appreciated his many sterling qualities, he was a 'Soldier and a man', and was beloved not only by his men (who all died with him) but by the whole Regiment, to which he is a distinct loss.

Your one consolation is, that he died fighting for his country, with his face to the foe, the best death a soldier can die.

Will you please convey my deepest sympathy to all the rest of his family.

With kind regards,
Yours faithfully,
A.W.G. McLaurin.

Many months later, a postcard arrived which gave Margaret much pleasure. It was a picture of Charles's favourite horse, Silver, sent from Palestine. The reverse carried the following letter, addressed to her son Jack as all military communications were.

---

PALESTINE
15. 4. '17

DEAR SIR,

You will probably be surprised at receiving this photo, but I am taking the liberty of sending it to you, for this horse was your late brother Chas' favorite horse. He was very much attached to 'Silver' and Silver is a horse that responds to kindness — therefore the attachment was mutual. I have had Silver for nearly 18 months and he is the favorite and pet of this Regt. Although I was not in the same Sqdrn as your brother I knew him well, and several brother officers have asked me to send this. It does not really do him justice but it is only an amateurs work.

Kind regards from,
M.W. Cowell Lt. 'C' Sqdrn. 8th Light Horse.

One hot day, wearing her old, shady hat and carrying a large basket, Margaret set off for the creek where, early in their marriage, Thomas had planted almost every variety of fruit tree for the benefit of his growing family. For once, Black was nowhere to be seen, but she assumed that he was with Nell who was grooming the horses in the stables.

The apricot trees were groaning with heavy branches laden with luscious, ripe apricots, and, intent on reaching for a cluster, Margaret failed to see the coiled tiger snake in the long, dry grass until she had almost stepped on it. At the same instant, Black appeared from nowhere and sprang, sinking his jaws in a death grip on the back of the reptile's neck, but not before the snake had struck viciously, biting the dog on his front paw.

With tears streaming down her cheeks and dripping onto his coat, Margaret sat with Black's head on her lap, stroking him gently. His faithful eyes never left her face until gradually they glazed over and Black was dead. In dying, he had fulfilled his beloved master's last request.

Margaret remained by the dead reptile, holding Black until Nell came in search of the two. Together, weeping, they buried the faithful dog by the creek, where he and Charles had spent so many happy hours.

→ PART TWO ←

# *Fred*

# → Behind the Lines ←

AFTER SPENDING CHRISTMAS 1914 at home with his family and his mate Jack Regan, young Fred Carthew made his way to Broadmeadows Camp near Melbourne. As a member of the Signalling Corps of the 10th Light Horse, Fred had already completed a few weeks training in Swanbourne, Western Australia, which he was to continue at Broadmeadows.

St. Paul's Soldiers' Tent
Broadmeadows
5.1.1915

DEAR MOTHER,

*Having a gay time here, they are doing the Tango and its causing a dust. This is the city tent and its very nicely fitted up, they are in opposition to Young and Jackson's on the opp. corner. Tell Babs and Nell their very much appreciated tin of pudding and Add's cake arrived Saturday after a prolonged joyride around the state, the ham was very much mildued the pudding likewise on the outside but we cut that off and it went O.K. the cake was very nice tell Add. I suppose your foot is about right again by this time Mother so dont go chasing pigs and sprain it again. Our school is closing Friday and we may leave on the Katoomba on Wednesday. Why not take a run down with Add to see us off. I may get leave in the West so will take a trip up to see Harry and James Holman. I'd like to go home with Jack but don't think I will have time.*

*Your Affectionate Son Fred.*

To Margaret's disappointment, the wharf was out of bounds to the general public for security reasons, and she and the girls were unable to farewell Fred when he and his unit boarded the *Katoomba* on 13 January 1915.

On arriving at Fremantle several days later, Fred and his mate Jack Regan were granted a week's pre-embarkation leave and Fred was able to spend a few days with his brothers Harry and James. In early February, the men of the 10th Light Horse, together with their horses, set sail on the troopship *Mashobra*, bound for Egypt.

---

'MASHOBRA' TROOPSHIP A 47D

DEAR MOTHER,

*Just a line to let you know that we are still on our way to 'where ever we are going'. I havent missed a meal since I left Fremantle. The weather is perfect and we are sailing along at the rate of 260 miles a day. We had half a day off at our first port which we are not allowed to name, but had a good time having rickshaw races. The natives are the greatest lot of rooks on the face of the earth — they ask 15/- for a 1/- article and gradually come down but we Australians usually come off second best. I was disappointed that the 8th Light Horse was not with us as I expected to have a chat with Charl per medium of the signallers. There are three boats with us, namely the 'Clan MacGillvary', 'Chilka' and the old German prize 'Hassan'. When we crossed the line Father Neptune came aboard and everyone got a severe ducking, some tried to escape by climbing the rigging but were seized and ducked when they came down. At C.— [Colombo, now Sri Lanka] we anchored in an artificial harbour of about fifty acres created by a stone breakwater and we went ashore in small boats. The Governor of C— did his best to prevent us going ashore at all, because the second contingent misbehaved and nearly pulled the place down — about 300 swum ashore and went uptown in bathing costumes and caused such a stir the whole white population drew up a petition to the effect that no Aus. troops were to be allowed ashore again. Apparently when they left the native hospital was overcrowded which speaks for itself. Anyway Colonel Antill had such a good opinion of us he guaranteed five pounds a head for everyone of his men who misbehaved and insisted on sending us ashore, and I can safely say that he had no cause to regret it. Must draw to a close now with love to all From Your Affectionate Son, Fred.*

When not on watch, Fred occupied his time by writing a diary, although there was little to write about until they left the vast Indian Ocean and entered the Red Sea, near the Arabian coast, which was swarming with ships and fishing boats.

---

MAR. 1ST

*Was innoculated yesterday. The barber will shave for twopence and a haircut is threepence and the Indian crew will do your washing for fourpence an article. We signallers dont have to do any stabling work and spend all our time on the bridge watching for signals. We also sleep on the top deck and as it is 70 ft above water we get plenty of fresh air. Expect to see land soon. Horses are getting very tired, been standing for 3 weeks and are starting to go down.*

---

MAR. 3RD

*The Arabian coast in view today — very mountainous. One man was sentenced to 28 days in barricks, and his own portion (not his wife's) of his pay stopped, and is to be put ashore to serve his time then put back in reinforcements, for having in his possession several articles that did not belong to him. Hope to reach Aden this evening. Arrived Aden but only stayed a few minutes while a motor boat came out for the mail. An officer came aboard probably with orders and two signal stations flashed an enquiry as to what ship we were. The poor horses have been standing for nearly a month with no room to lie.*

---

MAR. 4TH

*We are now in the Red Sea. We see quite a lot of ships now as this sea is only 90 miles wide. We lost our fourth horse today. He had injured himself and had to be shot, it was hauled out of the hold by the neck and suspended over the side for a long while as they have to turn the*

*stern of the boat so as the horse wouldn't get mixed in the propellors.*
*The land is very rocky, barren and hilly rather like Albany Harbour.*
*Had a rifle drill today and instruction of the prismatic compass. We*
*have had a bad case of pneumonia.*

---

MAR. 6TH

*Post day — we'll reach Sues tomorrow. We received news of the*
*Dardenelles victory — came through by wireless, we were all paraded*
*to hear the great news.* [Fred is probably referring to the British naval
attack on a Turkish fort guarding the Dardanelles, which had been
successfully destroyed on 5 March.]

---

MAR. 7TH

*Arrived in Suez today. The town is ancient looking, the houses square*
*stone with ugly corners. The harbour is guarded by an English war ship*
*and a French one and we played the French National Anthem as we*
*passed up the Canal. The Arabs are as crooked dealers as the Hindus*
*and refused to leave the ship's side so we put the hose on them. The*
*Canal is only about 150 yards across and the banks are all entrenched*
*and guarded on both sides by Indian and English troops and we passed*
*the place where the skirmish with the Turks had taken place. Leaving*
*Port Said after a few hours when the ship took on coal carried in baskets*
*by the natives, we arrived in Alexandria next morning. The harbour was*
*full of sailing ships making a forest of masts. We disembarked and*
*boarded a train passing through what I would call the richest country in*
*the world, the Valley of the Nile, just one continual stretch of green all the*
*way. The villages are a heap of hovels with winding streets the width of*
*a gutter. Most of the ploughing is done by cows dragging a long pole with*
*a stake attached. Camels work the home made water wheels for irriga-*
*tion. Lucerne grows about three feet high and the natives load the camels*
*to bring it into camp so all you can see is the camel's neck projecting from*
*the mass of green. The natives wear clothes like you see in the Bible but*
*the higher classes are very well dressed in European clothes but the men*
*always wear the little round red caps. We arrived in Cairo about 10 p.m.*
*but most of us had to lead our horses about 10 miles to Mena Camp as*
*they cannot be ridden yet for some time. Arrived at Mena about one a.m.*

and had to put down horse lines and feed the horses so it was almost day-light before everything was in order. The largest and oldest of the pyramids 'Cheops' is only a few minutes walk from camp and there are two others and the Sphinx together in a group. There is a beautiful road and train line bordered with trees running through the Nile Valley. This road was supposed to be built by Napoleian for the special purpose of bringing his wife out to see the Sphinx etc.

MENA CAMP, THE PIRIMIDS, EGYPT
18.3.'15

DEAR MOTHER,

We landed in this land of sand and sorrow last Tuesday, and have been working hard getting the camp in order. The horses were in very good condition, considering that they were a month on their legs, we will not be able to ride them for a week or two but have to exercise them every day.

The camp is situated on the edge of the fertile valley of the Nile and it makes a strong contrast, the rich green of the clover, lucerne etc and the bare sandy hills. We are just under the Pyrimids but have been too busy to see much of them, although three of us pinched off the other day and explored one, but we were caught and had to do night 'picket' for it — they are wonderful old things, there are nine of them altogether, but seven of them are ten miles from here. The largest pirimid is over 400 ft. high and they were originally covered with marble but only one of them has any left on it, the rest being taken off years ago to build some place in Cairo. The one we went into, the toumb was about 200 ft. below the surface, you climb down a long shoot with your back bent as its only 3 or 4 ft. high, then turn and go down some more shoots in different directions until you finally come to a pink granite chamber, and on a big flat slab at one end is where the King was laid. I'm not going to attempt to pronounce his name. He also had a hole in the rock to hold his money etc. The marvellous part of it is how they got the rocks into position, as some of them weigh a thousand tons, and no modern machinery could have handled it.

*Above: The Myrtleford Light Horse Militia, c.1910–1914. Lieutenant Charles Carthew (centre, middle row) was the troop's commanding officer.*

*Below: The officers of the 8th Light Horse. Charles is standing in the back row, second right, and Captain (later Colonel) McLaurin is seated in the centre.*

*Left: Margaret Carthew (née Macaulay), mother of Charles, Fred and James, arrived in Myrtleford as a young bride in 1872.*

*Right: Adelaide Carthew, elder sister of Charles, Fred and James.*

*Right: Nell and Jane ('Babs') Carthew, sisters of Charles, Fred and James.*

*Left: Lieutenant Charles Carthew, before his departure for Gallipoli in February 1915.*

*Above: The 8th Light Horse on board the* Star of Victoria. *In his letter of 17 March, Charles describes being 'shaved' with a bucket of paint and a wooden razor.*

*Below: Charles holding Captain McLaurin's horse while mounted on his own horse Silver, whom he brought with him from Happy Valley to Mena Camp, Egypt.*

*Above: Mena Camp, in the shadow of the pyramids near Cairo, was the base camp for Australian and New Zealand troops arriving in North Africa.*

Left: As they mentioned in their letters, Charles and Fred found time to do some sight-seeing during their stay in Egypt.

*Above: The parlour of the Carthew's home at Happy Valley. Margaret sent this photograph to Charles to remind him of home.*

*Below: Charles's map of Monash Gully, indicating the proximity of the Turkish trenches to those of the 8th Light Horse. He enclosed this map in a letter to Nell.*

Above: Members of the 8th Light Horse at Gallipoli, moving out of a ravine close to the beach. The rugged, steep terrain provided many obstacles for the troopers.

*We had our first leave yesterday and had a look at Cairo, its about 10 miles from here and we got there in a train. The country is marvellously rich, seems to grow anything. We had one windy day and the sand storm was awful, the sand is like beach sand and the water washed stones show that it was the sea bottom once.*

*We have between 30 and 40 thousand men here now, they stream over the hills in an endless chain like ants when they go on parade.*

*Cairo is about the dirtiest place on earth I think, nearly all slums and a disgrace to civilization. Our officers are very proud of our conduct and congratulated us on our behaviour in Cairo.*

*Must go to the stables now, love to all.*

*From your affectionate son, Fred.*

---

MENA CAMP
21.3.1915

DEAR MOTHER,

*Hope you can read this pencil, ink is hard to get. Was disappointed when the mail came, most of the other chaps got mail but I drew a blank. Charl has not arrived here yet but we expect his regiment in a few days time.*

*We have to exercise the horses every day but they are too stiff to ride so we have to lead them around the desert and its hard work walking on the sand. We get a fair amount of leave here but havent been paid for quite a long time, so its not much use taking leave when there is no money to spend. The money is rather confusing here, they deal cheifly in a coin called a piastre so they cut things very fine. Most things are fairly cheap if you have the time to beat the Arabs down. I will send you a few curios when I can raise a few shillings together, but as they only pay two shillings a day here we will not have much to burn, and I left three shillings to be paid into my account in the Commonwealth Bank, dont know whether they are doing it or not. Its getting near lights out Mother so will close with love to all.*

*From yours Fred.*

MENA CAMP, EGYPT
25.3.'15

DEAR MOTHER,

*I am sending off a small box of trifles home by next post, not as much as I'd like to send. When we were here a fortnight they paraded us for pay and gave us seven shillings and sixpence and that doesnt go too far.*

*I climbed to the top of the largest pyramid yesterday, it is 470 ft high and covers 13 acres, and is about 4,500 years old. You get a lovely view from the top of the camp and Nile Valley with its straight tram line bordered all the way to Cairo by an avenue of trees. When you get to the top, there is an old Egyptian there, old and withered who offers you a cup of coffee about the size of an egg cup for a penny farthing. He has his spirit lamp there for the purpose of keeping it hot, he told us that he was a doctor and that he had walked up the pyramid every day for forty years and that he was sixtyeight now, but judging from his looks I should say he was about a hundred and sixty eight.*

*Its marvellous how quick these Egyptians are picking up the Aussie slang. I think some of the swank ladies who come out here touring will get a few shocks as they say things that are not in the dictionary and dont know what the meanings are.*

*Well Mother I will have to close now hoping that you are all O.K. as this leaves me.*

*From your Affectionate Son Fred.*

On the afternoon of Good Friday, 2 April, Fred and his mate Jack Regan caught the tram into Cairo, along with hundreds of other light-horsemen and infantry, as half the camp had been granted leave and all were raring to go.

The streets were soon full of Australian and New Zealand troops, sauntering along in high spirits, bargaining with the natives, laughing uproariously and studiously failing to see the British officers they were supposed to salute—to those officers' fury. The Australian and New Zealand enlisted men were not well regarded by the British, who regarded them as undisciplined, boorish and insubordinate, while the

Anzacs believed that Johnnie was as good as his master. Most hated of all were the British Military Police, or the Red Caps, who lost no opportunity to victimise the boys from Down Under.

Some of the units were rumoured to be off to the Dardanelles shortly, and the men were determined to have a final fling before going into action to give the Turks a good trouncing. After an hour or so, a good percentage of the troops were very drunk on the vile liquor sold by the Egyptian and Greek vendors and were looking for mischief. Several New Zealanders had been infected with venereal disease by the local prostitutes, and they and their friends decided to get their revenge. They descended upon the brothels responsible, which were situated in a slum area known as the 'Wozza', and began to take the places apart, smashing down the doors and dragging out all the furniture and bedding into the street before setting fire to it. Soon, hundreds of onlookers had gathered, mostly soldiers who enthusiastically cheered the miscreants on.

It was not long before about thirty Red Caps arrived, brandishing pistols, to be greeted by a hail of stones. In retaliation, they fired into the crowd of innocent bystanders, wounding one Maori and four Australians and killing one soldier. The rest of the crowd was so incensed by this that they all joined in the melee and the rioting went on for several hours. A company of British Tommies, who were brought in to quell the riot, advanced with fixed bayonets but were merely hooted at by the crowd, and it was not until a squadron of Mounted Dragoons arrived and backed their horses into the rioters that the streets were partially cleared.

A number of men were arrested and subsequently disciplined, though all claimed to be innocent bystanders, but the Australian top brass were determined to make an example of the rioters. Fred noted in his diary: 'It is a great pity it happened as they have behaved splendidly up to date; they are going away tonight and this will leave a blemish on the name of the whole Aus. troops. It was only a mixed few of the roughs who caused the trouble. The New Zealanders took a very prominent part, in fact they started most of the trouble, but it is the poor old Aussie that has to take all the blame, and it seems to be their fate to get more blame than they deserve.'

Mena Camp
3.4.'15

Dear Mother,

Still no letter from home after nearly three months and am getting anxious to know how you are all getting along. I expected Charl here before this but he has not put in an appearance. The Infantry contingent are moving out of camp at the moment, I can hear their band playing as they march out, poor devils they are glad to get away from here as they have been working hard in this sand digging trenches, and marching across the sandy desert at all hours of the day and night. I think they are going to the Dardenelles. I believe more than 200 men discharged themselves from the hospital in order to try to embark with their units.

Yesterday we went to see the Citadalle which is one of the most beautiful buildings in the world, and really is magnificent to say the least — it is beyond me to describe it. The whole building is built of beautiful alabaster which is suppose to come of the Pyramids but you get so many different tales from the Arab guides that one doesnt know who to believe. The Mosck (Arab church) roof consists of 5 large domes and 4 semi domes and the insides are carved and inlaid with most brilliant colours with chandeliers of cut glass, the biggest centre one a present from the last King of France and also the clock on the outside.

In one corner surrounded by a massave iron barracade is the toumb of the Sultan who build the Citadalle, the grandfather of the present Sultan. This tumb is a magnificent affair all inlaid with pure gold and silver costing 14,000 pounds and brought from Mecca. It used to have a large double door at the entrance, but Napolian snared one half of it and the other half is in the London Museum.

At the rear of the Citadalle is Joseph's Well but it is now nearly built over by the Arabs. The hospital for the Indian soldiers is nearby, there are nearly a hundred Indians there wounded in the fight with the Turks on the Suez Canal and a few hundred sick ones.

We went to the Cairo Zoo Sunday, it throws the Melbourne one well into the shade but of course labour is very cheap here. They have two of the 'punts' that the Turks attempted to cross the Canal in, they are about twenty five feet long and are made of zink or something of that sort, they must be light, but it must have been a contract bringing them across the desert. They are fairly riddled with bullet holes and a few shells went through them leaving great holes in them, I wouldnt have been in them when they were fired on for a trifle. I am sending a view of the camp, of course it is only a small portion and the Pyramids.

Jack Regan wishes to be remembered to you all, he is just as hard a case as ever, always has the tent in roars with his irish wit.

Well Mother this is all my news so will close with love to all.

Your affectionate Son Fred.

---

DEAR JACK,

Charl turned up today, I thought I would drop you a line and let you know. He is looking very fit but has been going hard since 5 a.m. yesterday and is just about 'beat', so havnt had a good talk to him yet. Well John, its getting near 'lights out' so must close.

Remaining Yours, Fred.

Cant get stamps so you will have to pay.

---

MENA CAMP
18.4.'15

DEAR MOTHER,

Just a line to let you know that I am still in the land of the living but as I have had no word from your quarter I am beginning to think that you are not. We are shifting to Heliopolis Camp as this is considered unhealthy. Charl came around and wanted me to go for a walk around the Sphinx with him but as I have to do stables we are going this afternoon. I had a trip up there with Jack and a couple of others on camels and one on a donkey and had our photo taken so will send you one. We also had a look at the inside of the largest Pyramid of King Cheops which besides being the biggest is the oldest. You have to take your boots off as the rock is as smooth as glass and you have to asend *up the inside to a hight of 250 ft to the king's chamber where he was buried, the empty granite coffin is still there but of course the old man himself is in the london mueseum. I had a look through the Cairo Meuseum Sunday, it is very interesting and of course Melbourne cant compare with it especially for ancient statues, the real originals some very much battered, the mummies are marvelliously preserved you see them almost the same as they were buried and they have been there for thousands of years. Some of the pyramid builders are there, Rameses the Pharo and dozens of others who were heads in there time.*

*There are a few hundred wounded Australians landing at Alexandria from the Dardenelles but as for getting any definite information as to what they have been doing and how many have been killed, it cant be done, the newspapers here are as bad as the Myrtleford mail for news.*

*I seen Haden Hewitt yesterday, I didn't know he was here and he told me about quite a lot of the Myrtlefordites who were here until recently.*

*The flies here are getting awful — there seems no end to them, they are as thick as a swarm of bees in the tent now, I think they are the cause of a lot of the sickness.*

*Ive heard nothing more of the Turks who were supposed to be advancing on the Canal, must have been a false alarm.*

*Well Mother will close with love to all and remember me to all the Happy Valley people if there are any left now.*

*From Your Affectionate Son Fred.*

---

HELIOPOLIS CAMP
2.5.'15

DEAR MOTHER,

*We are still in Egypt but this camp is a slight improvement on Mena. I got a letter from the land lady of the cafe we used to patronise in Perth and one from Poll* [the wife of the Carthew's cousin 'Old Fred'] *but none from you.*

*The wounded from the Dardinelles are rolling into the hospitals by the hundreds — they are making a great name for*

*themselves and Aust. but are paying the price in blood. We dont
see much of the chaps in hospitals as they are not allowed out
and we are not allowed in without some very good reason, and
of course the seriously wounded are put into the Alexandria
Hospital which has something like 1800 rooms — it was
originally built for a gambling casino to rival Monte Carlo, but
the Egyptian Government wouldn't grant a licence so they turned
it into a hospital.*

*We are all anxious to get away and give the Turks a stir but they
say there is no work for Light Horse at present, but we hope its just
a matter of weeks for us.*

*Three thousand odd reinforcements left here on May 1st.—
they were in great glee too. I would have given anything to have
been going with them. I was talking to night* [sic] *to a chap who
has been sent back with a bullet wound through the leg and he
says that some of the regiments are practically wiped out, but I
suppose before you get this you will have had a full account of it
all in the papers. Anyway its enough for us to know that our
chaps have proved themselves as good if not better than anything
in the world.*

*Charl was telling me tonight that Capt. Sergeant who was
attached to his old Regt. had been wounded and captured by the
Turks and he was afterwards found terribly cut and slashed about
by the devils.* [This rumour is probably untrue.]

*Some of out Aust. Officers gave the men the tip before landing to
always keep a cartridge for himself so as to take his own life rather
than be taken prisoner.*

*I am sending along some photoes of Charl and myself on
camels at the Sphinx, I have registered them so you should get
them.*

*Well Mother must go and feed my horse. Hoping this finds you
all fit and well.*

*I remain your Affectionate Son, Fred.*

HELIOPOLIS CAMP, EGYPT
8.5.'15

DEAR NELL,

Your very welcome letter to hand, had almost given up hope of ever hearing from you. So Jack and his Troop [light horse militia] have been camping at Broadmeadows, I hope he enjoyed the dust, it was the mud we had to contend with.

We are having rather a good time here and are now on Garrison hours — get up at 5 a.m., stables, 6.30 breakfast, on parade at 7.30, come back 11.30 , stables till 12.30 then finish, except for one hour of stables in the afternoon — this is on account of the heat but I dont feel it very hot.

We hope to go away and try our luck with the Turks on Friday, but we are loosing [sic] our horses and are going as dismounted Light Horse, as the country is not suitable or feed and water is not available or something, but we hope to get them later on as its a bit too far to walk to Constantanople, and something must happen when the 10th A.L.H. arrive on the scene.

There are a few thousand wounded here in Egypt now, but a great many only slightly wounded as they are very much afraid of blood poisoning.

Remember me kindly to all the Happy Valley and Running Creek people.

From your Affectionate Brother Fred.

F. CARTHEW
10TH. AUS. L.H. 3RD BRIGADE, A.I.F.
14.5.'15

Dear Mother and All at Home,

We are leaving tomorrow night and most of the chaps are in Cairo tonight having their last night out. Would have liked to be with them but had to stay and write letters. We were out on parade with our full marching gear on, puttees and packs — we looked like a climatised Santa Clause — its getting very hot here now.

*I saw Haden Hewitt and he told me that Jack's dog had bitten a Myrtleford girl and that the result was disasterous. Well Mother I must close now hoping this finds you in good health, and whatever you do dont worry about Charl and I as we will be quite alright tho we will not be able to write as offen. Affect Son Fred.*

# → The Real Thing ←

ON HIS ARRIVAL AT GALLIPOLI, Fred took up residence in his communication billet, a dugout burrowed into the hillside above Anzac Cove in the area known as Monash Valley—a quarter of a mile or so south of the Nek where his brother Charles was garrisoned.

---

ON ACTIVE SERVICE
24.5.'15

MY DEAR MOTHER,

*Just a few lines to let you know that all is well with us, we are seeing some of the real thing now, that is in the war line. We are living in holes in the ground 'like warmbats' quite out of harms way.*

*As the conditions are quite unsuitable for visual signalling here, we do our work with field telephones. The weather is all that could be desired, were it not for an occasional shower of rain, brought on by the heavy firing of the big guns.*

*Its rather a relief to see the green shrubs that grow on the hills here after the barren desert of Egypt, its really a very pretty place.*

*I have seen Charl two days ago but I think he has gone ahead with his Regt. Well Mother must close, hope this finds you as well as it leaves me.*

*I remain Your Affectionate Son Fred.*

*Love to All at home, hope to hear from you soon.*

*Thrown into our trenches by the Turks. This is word for word as written on the original. Fred.*

English soldiers taken by us state that they have been told that each soldier who has fallen into our hands will be killed. Dont believe that lie only told to persuade you to prefer being killed than surrender.

Be convinced that everybody of you who has been taken prisoner will be treated just as well as international law commands.

France, England and Russia have been beaten awfully and suffered tremendous losses — during the last few days more than 100,000 Russians have been taken prisoners by the Germans in Polonia. Liban, a Russian harbour in the Baultic Sea has been taken by the Germans. Dunkirk has been bombarded by the heaviest guns, Calias [sic] and Warschaw [sic] are in danger.

The very next days will bring new losses to the allied forces of the Entante.

There is no chance for you to get the narrows.

SIG. F. CARTHEW. ON ACTIVE SERVICE
28.5.'15

DEAR MOTHER,

*All is well with us here. We are doing a bit of 'Turkey shooting' here now and find it excellent sport. Our tents are a thing of the past, we are living in dugouts, that is holes in the hillside. We are quite at home and take no notice of the shells going overhead, in fact they keep firing so continually that we miss them when they stop for a while. Will write more next time,*

*With love to you all. From your Affectionate Son, Fred.*

SIG. F. CARTHEW. MONASH VALLEY, ON ACTIVE SERVICE
2.6.'15

MY DEAR MOTHER,

Just a line to let you know we are still going strong in this part of the world. Our boys are doing very well making quite a reputation for the 10th already. The weather here is perfect only we get an occasional shower which makes things rather unpleasant in this dugout world of ours. I havnt had any mail since arriving here but there must be some at Egypt and it will be sent on in due course. I havnt seen anything of Charl since the day after our arrival here — he is about a quarter of a mile from here. I cant say very much otherwise I could give you rather interesting reading. We are all enjoying ourselves here and are now quite used to seeing the horrible sights that modern war presents.

The first contingent that landed here certainly did a marvellous piece of work, when one sees the rugged wild country, you would think it would be a matter of impossibility for a party to land at all, especially when we know that they had been waiting for our arrival for months.

We are being fed well and get a good issue of tobacco every week, so we are not doing to bad are we. You should see Yours truly with a large 'cherrywood' in his mouth sending clouds of smoke out of his dugout ducking his head under the protecting bank when a shraphnell shell bursts in the vicinity.

Well Mother I must close now with love to all. Give my regards to all the people known in that quarter.

Your Affectionate Son Fred.

SIGNALLER FRED CARTHEW
ON SERVICE
6.6.'15

DEAR MOTHER,

Just a few lines to let you know that I am still in the land of the living. I am on night shift on the field telephone, and as there isn't much work doing I am putting in the time writing a few notes. We are now in rest camp — the Regt. having done rather good work and are having a day or two spell. We get very little news of the outside *world. I seen in orders last night that Charl has been promoted to 1st. Lieut. so he is alright evidently. Have only received one letter in four months but expect to any day. I cant say much but we are keeping our end up and I think with credit. From where we are now camped one can get a full view of the sea, and its a very novel scene to see the sides of the hills all burrowed into with blankets etc for shelters.*

<hr>

*9.6.'15*

*Its three days since I started this so I suppose its time I finished it. Charl came along to my camp last night, he has just come out of the trenches and is now resting as we are.*

*I met old Mart Gavin* [an acquaintance of Margaret's from Myrtleford] *on the transport ship from Alexandria — he gave me all the family history and informed me that he was a married man — there ought to be a chance for me after that.*

*Well Mother must close now with love*

*From your Affectionate Son Fred.*

*What do you think of our home made envelopes F.*

Around the middle of June, Fred fell victim to influenza. The close daily contact among the troops, and the lack of proper hygiene, made influenza and other infectious diseases, such as measles and scarlet fever, endemic. Where possible, troops suffering from illness were removed from the peninsula to Lemnos Island. From there they were either sent back to the trenches or to Egypt for further convalescence.

<hr>

SIGNALLER F. CARTHEW
FROM LUNA PARK HOSPITAL EGYPT. 10TH REG. H.Q.
29.6.'15

DEAR MOTHER AND ALL AT HOME,

*Just a few lines to let you know that I am back in Heliopolis again. The last time I wrote you I was in the stationary hospital on Lemnos Is. I was there about a week with influenza, but it seems to have settled on my lungs as a result of inattention due to an overtaxed hospital.*

*I arrived on Sunday and I think the sea trip and change has done me more good than anything else, am getting pretty fit again, but still have a cough. Im afraid Ive neglected writing since Ive been off colour — we received our first mail on the Peninsula just before I left. I see the drought has broken at last — things were beginning to look very blue werent they. Charles was quite alright when I left, I was glad to hear that you were looking so well. I had a letter from Jim last mail. The L.H. turned him down, but the Infantry might take him if it wasnt for his Girl. Its just as well someone stopped him as its no place for anyone with lung trouble, living in a hole in the ground isnt all beer and skittles especially when it rains, but personally I wouldn't miss the experience for anything and wont be sorry when I get back with the boys.*

*Its now dinnertime so will close. Love to all,*
*From your Affectionate Son, Fred.*

---

TROOPER F. CARTHEW. HELIOPPOLIS, EGYPT. 10TH. BATT.
17.7.'15

DEAR MOTHER,

*Hope you got the photoes. Am going to Hellewan Hospital tomorrow, convalescent. And whatever you do dont start worrying if I dont write regularly. I havn't felt like writing somehow, just laziness on my part. I am quite recovered and going convalescent to get my strength back as it pulled me down a bit — its over a month since I came here. They are keeping all the sick and wounded here in Egypt with the horses when they recover, but I am going to do my best to get back with the boys when I get fit. I received Nell's letter this morning but most of my mails have gone to Gaba Tepe and I suppose I shall never see them.*

*It's funny that you knew nothing of us leaving Egypt but it does take a long time for mail to go through. I havn't heard anything of Charl but he is alright or I should have heard.*

*They are very slow getting the Casualty list through — they only have hundreds where there are thousands. There are two thousand men here now who are to go back to Aus. and N.Z. as unfit for further service, of course some will come back when properly cured.*

*Well Mother I shall have to close now with love to all.*
*From your Affectionate Son, Fred.*

TROOPER F. CARTHEW. HOTEL AL HAYET. EGYPT
19.7.'15

DEAR MOTHER,

You see I am now in my new residence and its really something classey. I am quite satisfied with my surroundings, its one of the largest hotels here and a great watering place for tourists, natural sulphur barthes for rheumatism pts. Helowan where I am now looks like a nice little place. I dont expect to be here long as I only want to pick up a bit and the food is very good so Ill soon be my old self again. There are about 1,000 men here, I struck one of the Forbes boys, was badly wounded in the leg. I cant see my way to get back to Gaba Tepe as all the sick and wounded are sent to the horse lines to look after the horses in Egypt, but you never know your luck. Well Mother, dinnertime so I will close with love to all.

From your Affectionate Son, Fred.

---

TROOPER F. CARTHEW. HOTEL EL HAYET, EGYPT
24.7.'15

DEAR NELL,

I am being discharged from here today. I can assure you it is some class, heaters in every room etc. It looks odd to see about 800 men in the grand dining room, of course the furniture has been replaced by deal tables and stools but they still have the natives to serve the food and I couldnt wish for better tucker.

Helowan is built in the desert on the edge of the Nile Valley and the date palms are beginning to bear, the Valley is smothered in the trees with dates hanging in large green clusters.

I havent heard anything from the front in six weeks since I have been here. There are about 150 men leaving Helowan for Aus. as unfit for service — its surprising the number of cripples the few weeks fighting has made — of course there are a few cold footers working their way back, but very few.

Its marvellous how soon ones gets used to gorey sights — men get their heads blown off etc. The Japanese bombs we use do the most damage, they are a very powerful explosive, I've seen them draging [sic] the Turks out of our trenches after they had an unsuccessful charge on us — when our bombs had been to work — with their heads smashed to pulp, legs blown off, in fact they are like a piece of raw meat in human shape, but our chaps have become so hardened to all this that they take no notice, just take them by the heels and drag them down the hill at top speed.

I suppose the worst of the Winter is over in Aus. now. We have had two summers on end now. [End of letter missing.]

---

TROOPER FRED CARTHEW
CHAUBUCA HOSTITAL
8.8.'15

DEAR MOTHER,

Just a few lines to say that I am getting on O.K. with my measles, in fact I havn't felt better in my life, but suppose I will have to see my three weeks out. It's worse than being confined to barricks. Nothing of importance comes to us from the front. I heard that one of the Crouchers from Dederang had been killed, he was in the eighth L.H. Its been as high as 125 degrees in the shade here, we've had two years of heat and never any rain.

This is the natives month for fast — they neither eat nor drink nor smoke during daylight, a gun is fired at seven o'clock and then they are at liberty to carry on. They have a sacred carpet here in one of the mosques — and every year it is carried with much pomp and ceremony to Mecca where it is blessed, but as things are a bit too warm around Mecca this year, the carpet has to miss its usual blessing.

Egypt is still full of troops, as fast as they are drafted away to Gallipoli they are poured in from Aust. The last of our original Regt. went back Sunday.

If I hadn't had the bad luck to catch these dashed measles I should have been with them and in my dugout by this time. I havn't heard a word from Charl since leaving but Ive been shifting around so much in the last eight weeks.

The Nile will soon be rising now, and all the channels will be full of water, but the people wall it up so it does no damage to the crops. It always seems to be Springtime on the Nile — they get three crops a year. I wouldnt mind about 300 acres — they say its worth 200 *pounds an acre, mostly owned by rich Egyptians, in lots of an acre up. Lord Kitchener has a big interest here they say. Even the most ignorant people know of Kitchener.*

*There are about 60 measles patients here, most just arrived having cultivated measles on the troop ship. The strain of hanging on at Gaba Tepe seems to be telling on the men, there are Red Cross trains coming in every day, full of sick men etc.*

*Well Mother hoping this finds you O.K. I will close with love to all. From your affectionate son, Fred.*

It was to be some days before Fred read in the casualty lists that Charles had been missing since the fatal charge on the Nek on 7 August. The hospitals in Egypt were overflowing with the wounded from the peninsula, and Fred was given permission to interview the few survivors of the 8th Light Horse. Two weeks after the battle, Corporal M.H. Griggs, the sole survivor of Charles's troop, informed Fred that his brother was dead.

TROOPER FRED CARTHEW
HELIOPOLIS CAMP, EGYPT
21.8.'15

*Dear Add,*

*I received two letters from you yesterday, it is evident that your previous correspondence has been going astray so you will have to forgive me for not answering them, however I am glad to hear from you. I also had a letter from Em, also her first, and she speaks of having previously written, really it is scandalous how the mail goes astray, Nell's letters come fairly regularly now.*

*I have been unable to get any more information about poor Charl, except that he has been officially reported missing, probably the authorities will wire you to that effect; but I think poor Charl has gone from us forever.*

*I was speaking to one of his troop who was with him in that terrible charge — and he told me that when he fell wounded near Charl he was laying quite still evidently being shot dead. Other than this I can get no information as to what happened in the last few terrible minutes.*

*I am writing to Mother today, hope she is keeping well when you last wrote.*

*I have just been out of hospital a week now and am getting strong again, suppose I will soon be going back to the front again.*

*Some of the Canadians are coming here, I seen some of the advance party last night — they are fine big fellows.*

*I think this Dardanelles question is going to be rather a tough one. The rumour here has it that, the two days casualties when the advance was made at Gaba Tepe (where I was) were 2,200.*

*Well Add there is really nothing to write about just now so will have to close with love to all. From your affectionate Brother Fred.*

HELIOPOLIS CAMP, EGYPT
22.8.'15

MY DEAR MOTHER,

*You will have to forgive me for not writing to you last mail, but you will know what to expect in my letters and the shock of receiving the terrible news will be spared you.*

*I know Mother, the shock when you received the news of poor Charl, must have almost broken your heart, but you must bear up and accept God's will. He will soften the blow you have received.*

*I got a friend in Alexandria to inquire at the enquiry office at the base, and he informed me that Charlie has been officially reported missing, and I know the anxiety would be killing you — thinking that perhaps something terrible had happened to him.*

*Well Mother I have found one of Charl's troop who was with him in that last terrible charge — and he tells me that he fell wounded near to where Charl lay, and from what he told me, I am afraid we have lost poor Charl forever.*

*It was a terrible affair Mother, that charge — the men had to charge the Turk's trenches under a most terrible machine gun fire — they knew that they were probably going to their doom, but they went out like the heros that they were, and very few came back alive — the Eighth Regiment led this charge, and only one officer came out without a wound.*

Lieut. Robinson had his hand badly shattered and will probably be sent back to Aust. as he will be some considerable time before he will be well again, he is a fine fellow and one of Charl's best friends, and would like to see you and have a talk with you, when he goes out to Aust., so I would suggest that you ask him up home for a while. You have met him of course. Poor chap he was in a very bad state when I first seen him in the hospital; he has an awful looking wound — when he was telling me about poor Charl he nearly broke down, he said Charl was the best friend he ever had and they were always together.

Well Mother, you must not fret too much, for although you have suffered a terrible loss, you have given a son to the nation, and he died like the hero that he was, and you can well afford to be proud of him. His men thought a great deal of him, and I know he was one of the most popular men in the Regiment.

But you know its all for a good cause and it remains for those of us who are left behind to carry on the good work those brave chaps have done.

I am having rather an easy time of it here — this is our days work.

Signal practice before breakfast for about an hour — after breakfast we Signallers go out onto the Nile for station work with the heliograph, and I can assure you that it is a pleasant ride, the roads are all shady avenues, with beautiful crops of maize over ten feet high — cotton fields one mass of white woolley balls, it is now being picked by the natives and it is a pretty sight — to see them working among the cotton.

The children are always half naked and live in filth from the time they are born, they are often blind in one eye, and I dont wonder, the women carry the little kiddies across their shoulders, their faces black with flies — One is always seeing strange and novel sights here. Its funny to see the natives crossing irrigation channels as big as rivers — they take off their few clothes and tie them in a bundle on their heads, then swim across and dress on the other side.

We passed a native funeral yesterday — the chief mourners walk in front chanting for all they are worth, and the coffin follows on the shoulders of 4 men, the coffin is a gay affair draped in gaudy cloth,

with the dead man's fizz (cap) on a peg on the end — the corpes is
not buried in this coffin, dont know how they do them up, but I
know the same old box is always used, as you see it coming back after
the ceremony. In Cairo you see dozens of funerals every day — they
seem to die like flies.

With the better classes it is quite different. They live in grand
houses, have fine gardens and apparently live on the fat of the land
— they are always well and tastefully dressed in European style, but
always keep the red 'fizz' — its funny to see them in a theatre all
wearing these little red caps.

The hotels in Cairo are of the oriental style — with little tables
right out across the pavement — where men and women alike sit
and drink iced drinks — and all the time I've been here I havent
seen one of these Egyptians drunk — that is of the higher classes.

The Grand Continental Hotel and Sheppards Hotel are among
the best in the world they say, but one would need to be a millionaire
to stay there — haven't seen the inside of either one of them yet —
two shillings a day will not allow it.

Well Mother I will close now, with love to you all.

From your Affectionate Son Fred.

---

HELIOPOLIS RACECOURSE, EGYPT
SUN. 29.8.'15

DEAR MOTHER,

We are still with the horses, there is nothing definite as to where we
are going. The Nile is now in flood but they do not waste the water —
they have large dams built up the river which irrigate the valley when
the river is low — Lord Kitchener was the originator of it.

Out of our 10th L.H. Regiment there were over 100 men killed, I
dont know how many wounded but I'm afraid there will be some
broken hearts. I suppose before this reaches you the papers will be
giving some of the casualties of our brigade.

I was in Cairo seeing about Charl's things, his sword and saddle
and officers uniforms etc. which he left at Cooks with instructions to
be sent home if anything happened, but they cannot send them until
they receive instructions from the Military Authorities.

There are a lot of sick men coming back from the front now, its getting very unhealthy there, a great many dysentery cases, this is the result of camping so long in the same place, the flies are very troublesome.

Polly was telling me they made six thousand pounds for the sick and wounded soldiers in Perth at a sale on Australia's Day.

Eighteen of our old hands of the 10th are going back to the front tomorrow, but they wont take signallers as they say we will be wanted for the mounted regiment.

Our poor old 3rd. Brigade has been again badly cut up since the fateful 7th. Aug. — in this last advance over eighty more of our 10th. L.H. were killed, and Ted Croucher was telling me last night that there was only one officer and twenty men left in the Eighth L.H. Regiment.

This is terrible considering that all those regiments of the 3rd Brigade have been reinforced five times, and there are as many men in five lots of reinforcements as there are in a regiment.

Nell seems to have her hands full with all those sick and dying cattle — things must have been very bad; what bad luck losing that young draught too, but we never seem to have much luck on that farm.

There are very few Aust. soldiers left in Egypt — the 28th. Battalion have gone away and they were the last to arrive here, all that now remain are reinforcements.

There are of course dozens of rumours as to where we are going with our horses, but no one knows really, but it is certain these horses are eating their heads off here in Egypt.

Poor Australia has suffered a great deal heavier than the home people think, as the authorities do not let all the names go through, only a few at a time, I dont think its right myself. The people of Aust. should know exactly how matters are.

I hope you are not worrying too much Mother as its useless and injurious to yourself. Remember that you have given one son to the Nation, and I hope to be able to conduct myself with as much credit as did poor Charl, if I ever get back to the front. My work here is not so dangerous, as we are with the Headquarters Staff, and they do not often charge, only when the whole regiment advances, but the work is important as all orders from Brigade Headquarters comes through us, and a small mistake may mean a great deal.

*Well Mother I hope this finds you quite well.*

*I remain your Affectionate Son Fred.*

LATER. *Have been busy today getting equipped for the Mounted Regiment — we are being inspected in the morning by General Spence who is in charge of all the L.H. in Egypt. Captain Shannon has been transferred from the 8th. Reg. and is now in charge of the 10th. — he is shaking things up a bit to — we were getting very slack.*

*I have been made Acting Cpl. from today, and I think I have a good chance of keeping the stripes — though I'm the youngest of the Signallers — it will mean 10 shillings a day, so that is not too bad eh?*

*I am writing this in the YMCA and there is a sermon going on at the other end.*

HELIOPOLIS RACE COURSE. EGYPT
28TH. SEPT. '15

DEAR ADD,

*Your letter arrived today dated 15th. Aug. — was glad to here from you. Things must be very bad in Aust. but hope they are improving — fancy fat cattle being such a price — something unheard of before.*

*Nell was telling me in her letter how McGrath was causing trouble with those roads — what a beautiful specimen of humanity he is — stays at home and takes advantage of a man who lays down his life for the country he lives in. There is as much principle about McGrath as there is in a dingo.* [McGrath was a neighbouring farmer who continually tried to cause trouble for the Carthews. Furthermore, not one of his five sons enlisted.]

*I am in charge of the signallers as I am the only N.C.O. Sig. in the Brigade. Capt. Shannon was temporally* [sic] *in charge of our Regiment but he has gone away to the front with reinforcements for the 8th. L.H. I often wondered if he remembered the time he used to trap rabbits for a living.*

*I hope Mother is keeping well and has got rid of that cold — you must try and keep her from worrying as it can do no good you know. Things are much as usual here. I dont know how the natives would manage without the donkeys and camels — we meet them every morning carrying enormous loads of maize, lucerne and cotton.*

There is always a shying match with our horses when we meet a camel loaded up with lucerne so that you can only see his head and legs — the horses never seem to get used to them.

These agricultural classes are about the most ignorant of all the Egyptians — they live in dirty hovels, built out of mud bricks, they are low, shapless and flat roofed, and all the rubbish is thrown onto the roof — the animals live in these hovels with them, but they seldom have cats or dogs as they can't afford to keep them.

Jack Regan is back in hospital somewhere with ear trouble — I havn't heard from him for some time.

The Army is doing good work in France, according to this mornings paper, and Russia is also doing big things.

Well Add I must go and do some 'buzzer' work now, field telegraphy is used largely at the front.

Hoping this finds you all well as it leaves me, Love to all, From your Affectionate Brother Fred.

---

HELOPOLIS
OCT. 8TH. '15

DEAR MOTHER,

Just a few lines before we go away — We expect to be away in the morning so we are all busy sewing on buttons and getting our kit ready.

Nell was asking if it was Jack Regan who was reported killed, but I am glad to say it was only a namesake of Jacks. I had a letter from him and he is now back at the front. He would have written to you but he is a funny chap and cannot write to anyone he is not familiar with — he has often asked me to write to a stranger for him.

I was sorry to hear that poor Minnie Green has been so ill, but hope that its nothing really serious.

Its a pity for the Bright district loosing Dr. Kidd, but good doctors and surgeons are badly needed here, as there are such a lot of so called doctors in the Military who are only here for the experience it gives them and the poor chaps who come back sick and wounded have to suffer for it.

Things are very quiet at the Dardenelles just now, they say they are diging themselves in for the Winter, but I hope we havn't to spend all the Winter there as it will be very severe.

*One of my pals has lost a brother at the front. He is coming with us. I received twenty letters from the front but they were of course very old.*

*Mrs. Forbes, the lady I used to board with in the West has had her son-in-law killed — one of her sons wounded badly and sent back to W.A. and the other son wounded for the second time. All of them were in the first landing party so you see she has had a lot of worry. Poor old lady I feel very sorry for her and write her regularly.*

*There is a mail from Aust. in today so I am looking forward to some from home — you cant imagine how we look forward to mail day — even more than pay day and that is saying a lot.*

*By the way Mother if you have any of your own photoes just send one along — I would like to have one. With love to all at home.*

*From your Affectionate Son Fred.*

# → An End and a Beginning ←

*D*URING LATE AUGUST and September, continued assaults by the Allies on the Turkish strongholds at Gallipoli caused further massive casualties, and as a result recruitment in Australia dropped sharply. To make good these losses, convalescent troops in Egypt were recruited instead, and to Fred's satisfaction he was among those selected to return to the peninsula.

As soon as he was off duty, Fred made a pilgrimage to the Nek to see the place where his brother Charles had charged to his death. As he stood on the fire step, surveying the rugged terrain, he must surely have tried to recognise his brother's body among the pathetic mounds of the dead.

GALLIPOLI
28.10.'15

DEAR MOTHER,

*Just a few lines to let you know that I am back at the front again. Arrived here on the 24th. We had a splendid trip across, on the Frankonia, were well treated, and had no rough weather.*

*Things have altered a great deal since I was here last, a vast improvement all round, so you see those terrible sacrifices were not made for nothing. Of course there is still plenty of work to do; but dont mind that so long as I keep my present fit condition.*

*The weather here is not so cold as I expected to find it — I think the really cold weather is in January, but its just cold enough to keep the flies from being to much of a nuisance, and with the flies will go a deal of sickness.*

*I am back in my old job on the field telephone, but have lost my stripes as expected as there is no vacancy here at present. By the way Mother, Sergeant Carr is in charge of the signal station, the same gent who used to work for you — he asks me to send his regards to you all — its rather a mystery to me how he became Sgt as he seems to be a bit of a dead head.*

*Babs says in her letter that Jack has enlisted, but hope he hasnt as someone ought to stay and look after the farm. Polly says Jim got knocked back again. Jack Regan is writing to you he told me.*

*Our 10th. L.H. Regiment has been making quite a name for itself — we now have one V.C.* [Second Lieutenant Hugo Throssell] *and three with D.C.M.s — we are of course very proud of the fact. Well Mother I suppose it will be Xmas when this reaches you. Wishing you all a merry Xmas and Happy New Year, with love from your Affectionate Son, Fred.*

---

Trooper Fred Carthew
Gallipoli
9.11.'15

My Dear Mother,

*Just a line to say that I am fit and well. Am sorry to hear that you were not keeping so well and trust that you will soon be your own self again.*

*There was a mail in today but only recieved letters from W.A. I was a bit disappointed, should like to have heard from you, especially as it is my twentyfirst birthday.*

*Old Fred tells me that Jim has again enlisted and finally been accepted and was to go into camp a month ago — they didn't say which battallion he is in — suppose he will soon be leaving for Egypt — I havn't had a letter from him since last June, cant understand why he doesnt write.*

*We have just heard that all our Xmas mails have gone to the bottom of the sea, so if you do not recieve a Xmas letter you will take the greetings for granted. I sent a card to each of you.*

*We had it very wet and stormy a few nights ago, and the sea was very rough for them to land supplies washing away one of the jetties.*

*Its not altogether pleasant in the trenches when its wet — one gets all covered with mud and there is very little shelter.*

*I am writing this from my phone box and have the receiver strapped to my ear for our call.*

*Just fancy its 13 months today since I joined the Regt. Well Mother I hope this finds you quite well again.*

*With love to all on the occasion of my 21st. birthday. Fred.*

*P.S. I seen Lord Kitchener the other day — he was here for a few hours. He doesn't seem to be any the worse for the work he has to do. There is practically no signalling done now, so we have to go with the troops doing trench work, so I will not be able to write much Mother, but do not worry as I will be alright as things are quiet just now.*

During mid November, violent storms sank many of the lighters which ferried stores and ammunition from the big ships that stood out to sea beyond the range of the Turkish guns. The shortage of ammunition was now critical, particularly artillery shells. Lord Kitchener, who visited the peninsula briefly on 13 November, and General Monro of the Allied Forces, agreed that there was no point continuing to hold Suvla Bay and Anzac Cove. Evacuation, beginning with the artillery, was to take place as soon and as secretly as possible.

GALLIPOLI
22.11.'15

*Dear Emm,*

*Just a few lines to let you know I am still in the land of the living and not doing too badly. We are getting it pretty cold now, one has to go around with his greatcoat on all day — we expect it to snow any day now. The trenches get into a terrible mess when it rains. I suppose Jim will be over here soon. I think our family are doing 'their Bit' at least, to hold our end of the stick up.*

*Babs was saying Geordy Matthews was going to enlist — well its just about time one of them found out that they were needed. What think you?*

*I recieved Babs birthday present, jolly acceptable too — just fancy how old we are — the 'kid' is now a man.*

*Lord Kitchener came here on the 13th. I was lucky enough to see him — happened to be on the beach when he came ashore from a destroyer. The men all cheered him and he said 'The King asks me to tell you how splendidly he thinks you have done.' He is a very tall man with a florid face and walked along the trenches for a couple of hours before going back on board.*

*Fancy old Ned coming to light like the bad penny he is.* [Uncle Ned Carthew was the family skeleton in the cupboard. Believing he had killed a policeman in a fight, he prudently absconded to New Caledonia until things blew over.]

*Well Emm must close now. Ever your affectionate brother, Fred.*

As Christmas approached, things were anything but festive at Gallipoli. By the end of November the peninsula was blanketed in deep snow and there was extreme hardship in the trenches. Due to the cold, and having to stand in a foot or more of melting snow for days and weeks on end, the men suffered greatly from frostbite and trench foot. Mortality was high because the men had no feeling in their frozen limbs, and boots and other clothing were sometimes not removed for weeks at a time. When at last they took off their sodden boots and socks, often the entire rotten skin and flesh came off as well, and sometimes even the toes. Many had one or both feet amputated hastily to prevent gangrene spreading up the legs. Frequently, by the time gangrene was discovered, it was too late even to amputate.

One method of warming frozen hands was to fire one's rifle four or five times in quick succession. This heated the barrel and the men would clasp it, although the pain experienced by the returning circulation to the fingers was almost worse than the numbness. Although this practice was officially frowned upon, most officers turned a blind eye to it.

The shortage of water was critical. Although there was snow in plenty, and water in the pools and gullies, these were polluted and poisoned by the thousands of decaying corpses of men and animals, and there was no wood to boil it. The men tried futilely to boil snow over a candle and made tiny, ineffectual fires in holes in the side of the trenches with slivers of wood from biscuit boxes, trying to keep out the wind and snow flurries with only a small waterproof sheet.

Almost worse were the fleas and lice that tormented them night and day. While the weather was warm, the Aussies had kept far cleaner than the Tommies by swimming and washing their clothes in the sea, but now they were all filthy and louse-infested as well as thirsty.

The Turks had no such problems, having good lines of transport, but they were well aware of their enemy's predicament and redoubled their shelling. One of their biggest guns, christened 'Beachy Bill' by the boys, was making life even more intolerable by sending shells at the rate of one per minute, both day and night.

---

GABA TEPE
2.12.'15

DEAR MOTHER AND ALL AT HOME,

*Just a few lines to let you know that I am still pegging along in the same old spot. We have been a little bit frozen over this last week, had a heavy fall of snow, about 3 inches I think, and its still lying about. I can assure you we were none too warm, especially those of us who have been in Egypt of late. The trenches were a great old mess, and the hills were too slippery for the mules to come up with the supplies, so we were on iron rations for a few days. This is quite a novel (if severe) experience for most of the W.A. chaps, most of them have never seen snow before, and hope they never see it again. There were quite a lot of chaps frostbitten. I've seen dozens carried down to the beach with their feet wrapped up.*

*I told you our Xmas mail had gone down. Well, we have since heard that the incoming mail was also sunk — the boat was torpedoed, so I guess our luck is out. It will be disasterious if our Xmas 'billies' go down.*

*Bill Carr has been shifted — transferred to the 8th L.H. and I am taking his place here — with the elevated position of temporary corporal, but getting paid this time, and 10/- a day is very nice to, I think. I'm pretty sure to be made permanent if I dont get sick and I'm feeling very fit now. I'm in charge of the telephone with 2 men and a Cpl. eh what!!! But I say dont start putting Cpl. on my letters as anything may happen.*

*Well Mother its 3.30 a.m. so will close. Hoping this finds you fit and well as this leaves me, I remain your Affectionate Son, Fred.*

GABA TEPE
11.12.'15

DEAR MOTHER,

Well we are getting along first rate at present. Though we very seldom get a sunny day it is not nearly as cold as it was last week.

Of course there are heaps of things of interest to write about, but if one wants his letters to reach their destination you have to be very silent on the subject. Its a month since we heard from you, so I suppose it was your mail that went down.

Babs was saying George Matthews was coming home to enlist. Nearly time, I should say, that some of them made a move, as they havn't anything to keep them — except Evan, of course, with his wife and children.

I must tell you Mother, that I have had my promotion confirmed, and am now a full blown Corporal — my chest measurement increases visably. Jack Regan is still away at rest camp, he went a month ago.

We are getting plenty of tobacco and cigarettes here now, all gift stuff. I think I smoke more in a week now than I ever smoked in my life — the old pipe is my best friend, as its about the only thing there is to do — smoke.

The biggest trouble is keeping oneself clean — we cannot always get our full issue of water — which is a bottle full a day — and we spend more than three parts of our time in the trench, which is anything from 7 to 15 ft. deep, and just wide enough to let 2 men pass, and of course the wind's in and out a lot. My dug-out is also the trench, a very good one to, by the way it was built for Capt. Shannon, and when he went away sick I transferred my belongings into it. My phone dugout is right in the firing line, its 2.30 a.m. and there is a fairly constant crack of the rifles, with an occasional burst of machine gun — the Turks bullets often hit the parapet over our door, but cannot reach us, and the only damage they do is bring a shower of dirt down.

Well Mother I shall have to close now and hope this finds you all quite well. With love to all, From your Affectionate Son Fred.

During the first two weeks of December, clandestine preparations were made to facilitate the withdrawal of troops from the Dardanelles, the Australian sector being orchestrated by Brigadier Brudnell White. At first his plan was opposed by the British General Byng at Suvla, but Byng was overruled by General Birdwood. Nevertheless, Byng still planned to evacuate his troops from Suvla early, leaving the Anzacs unprotected. Luckily his treachery was discovered and Birdwood ordered him to adhere to White's plan.

Although the troops were kept in the dark as much as possible, it was patently obvious that moves were being made to vacate the area. Surplus stores were destroyed or consumed so as to leave nothing useful for the enemy, and rations of food and cigarettes were considerably more plentiful. None had any regrets about leaving the Peninsula, except for the sadness of deserting their dead mates. In the last few days, more durable, solid wooden crosses were lovingly carved from building materials and trench supports as the men made their last, poignant farewells.

Although there was almost a full moon on the night of 17 December, 200 men, their boots muffled with rags, slipped stealthily down the steep slopes and into the waiting boats to be rowed out to the ships offshore. The following night, the main forces from all over Gallipoli, including most of the artillery, were evacuated between the hours of dusk and dawn, thousands melting like wraiths down the cliffs to join the rendezvous off Imbros Island 17 miles (27 kilometres) away. Some left tins of food and messages for their enemies: 'Too roo Jacko, pleased to have met you' and 'So long Johnnie Turk, hope you enjoy the tucker'. One wag, forced to leave his beloved gramophone behind, had, with typical Australian humour, left a record of the Turkish national anthem on the turntable ready to play—an ironical concession to the Turks that they had finally won this battle, but no hard feelings.

The few remaining troops made themselves very visible, in order to give the impression that it was business as usual. They brazenly played cricket on Shell Green, ignoring the bombardment from Beachy Bill and the other enemy guns, noisily conducted races and boxing matches, and sauntered about smoking and playing two-up uproariously. All this activity caused the Turks a great deal of uneasiness and bewilderment, and they finally concluded that the mad Anzac devils were celebrating some sort of infidel holiday. They had not the vaguest suspicion that most of the enemy had been spirited away. (Although, as Charles Bean scathingly reported, British naval idiots shouted at the top of their English voices, doing their best to alert the Turks that there was Allied troop movement.)

At 3am on 20 December the last few men, including Corporal Fred Carthew, who had helped co-ordinate the withdrawal by field telephone, hurried down the paths and ravines to the deserted beach. Weaving through the tangled, rusty barbed wire and sunken wrecked boats, they waded out to the waiting ferries, at once jubilant and sad. Behind them they could hear the fusillade of shots from the damaged rifles the men had rigged using two bully beef cans, some water or sand and a piece of string. (One can, with a small hole in its base, was filled with water or sand, which trickled slowly into the other can. When the second can was heavy enough, it pulled the string attached to the trigger, and fired the gun.) Shortly afterwards, there was a deafening explosion as the fuses the sappers had laid under the Nek exploded.

At 7am, as the ships stood out to sea, the naval guns opened fire on all remaining artillery, ammunition, stores and mule carts, leaving little or nothing of value for the enemy. It was not until after 1pm that crowds of Turkish soldiers were seen excitedly running across to the deserted Allied trenches, realising that at last victory was theirs and the invaders were vanquished. Incredibly, casualties for the entire evacuation of 41 000 men amounted to just two wounded at Anzac and three at Suvla Bay.

The tragic total of Allied casualties on Gallipoli numbered 252 000, with 50 000 killed. Their gallant adversaries, the Turks, suffered over 300 000 casualties and lost more than 86 000 men.

In a letter to Winston Churchill, war correspondant Ellis Ashmead-Bartlett wrote: 'There was never an army worse looked after than the one in Gallipoli. The hospital arrangements were awful and thousands of wounded were left to die between the lines who might have been saved. When the true history of the events in the Dardanelles comes to be written, it will amaze the world that any staff should have piled blunder on blunder as they did and the manner in which thousands of lives were thrown away to absolutely no purpose at all.'

The ill-fated Gallipoli campaign had achieved precisely nothing, except undying glory for those men who paid the supreme sacrifice, and for the many thousands, maimed in body or mind, whose lives would never be the same again.

It was also to be the catalyst for the eventual severance of the umbilical cord that linked Australia to the mother country. The Australians had arrived as British colonials, but they left proudly as Anzac Diggers. The Australian nation had forged its own identity on the bloody slopes of Gallipoli, and had come of age.

# → In and Out of Battle ←

*F*OLLOWING THE EVACUATION of Gallipoli, most of the infantry was sent to France to join Kitchener's three million British volunteers, leaving the British cavalry and the Anzac mounted regiments to guard the vital Suez Canal and patrol the Sinai Desert against the incursion of the Turks from Palestine. British General Sir Archibald Murray held the Anzac Mounted Division in high regard as 'the only reliable mounted troops I have ... any work entrusted to these excellent troops is invariably well executed'.

Except for some reinforcements, the men of the 3rd Brigade (comprising the 8th, 9th and 10th Light Horse regiments) were all veterans of Gallipoli and already a legend. Only men of perfect physical condition were accepted. Most of them were bushmen, farmers' sons, stockmen or shearers, lithe and muscular, tanned, laconic and monosyllabic, with the inevitable fag drooping from their lips. Like their horses, they were able to survive the scorching heat and bitterly cold nights of the desert on little or no rations and, bush-trained as they were to note every facet of terrain as they rode, their sense of location was infallible. Magnificent in the saddle, and more at home on a horse than on foot, most of their leisure time was spent playing equestrian sports, often bareback: steeplechasing, peg sticking, racing, wrestling, tug o' war, polo and even musical chairs—games at which Fred excelled, having played similar ones with his brothers for most of his life.

They were feared by the Egyptians, and for good reason. The Australians, who regarded the Egyptians as filthy, cruel and dishonest, were not above giving them a good hiding when they felt they merited it. On one occasion, several Egyptians had tried to purloin two young wallabies, the beloved mascots of the infantry (who had smuggled them out of Australia), to supplement their meagre diet, and were beaten to within an inch of their lives by the incensed troopers.

---

HELIOPOLIS
26.12.'15

MY DEAR MOTHER,

*Just a few lines to let you know that we are all back in Egypt again, just in time for Xmas. I suppose you have heard of the evacuation of Gaba Tepe by this time, but we are forbidden to mention any particulars. We had a good Xmas, considering the circumstances, we were all paraded for our 'billies'* [the Red Cross organised gifts for the troops, packed in billy cans] *on Xmas morning and also recieved a pkt of smokes. It was great fun opening the billies, each one had a note in it, some of them very amusing. Mine came from a young lady in the Young Lady's Collage, East Melbourne, and it contained all sorts of useful little things. The Xmas mail came along after we recieved our billies and I got quite a dozen letters, also the 2 prs of socks. I got the note in your pair, so jolly good of you to make them, they would have been just the thing had we been over in the snow. My birthday present didn't arrive, but it may turn up if it didn't go down in the 'Orange Prince' that went down with some of our mail.*

*Love to all from your Affectionate son, Fred.*

---

2.1.'16

MY DEAR MOTHER,

*The New Year finds us here in Egypt, but I hope the next Year will find us back in good old Aus. Just fancy its nearly 12 months since we arrived in this land of sand and sorrow, a year full of change and new experiences.*

*Polly tells me that Harry is still talking of coming away but I think he should stay home with his wife and kiddie. We expect to be going away soon to have a go at the Arabs — they are starting to give a bit of trouble. So the old home was not sold, money must be scarce or else people must be afraid of the future.*

*Jack seems to be successful in all his deals. I must write and thank Mrs. Woodside for the parcel I recieved on Xmas Day and my 'billie' girl. We had a Cinematograph picture taken of our Brigade today. You may see it in Aus. I met Ted Croucher and he tells me Jack has bought a motor car. So they are talking of conscription in Aus. I thought it would never come at that and I hope it never does. Charl's baggage should have reached you by this.*

*With love from your Affec. Son Fred.*

---

JAN. 30TH. 1916

DEAR MOTHER,

*Recieved Em's letter written on Xmas Day. Jim's young lady must have been a surprise. How did you like her? Jack Regan has been made a Corporal. We went to Cairo the other day and seen the gayest funeral I ever seen. Some old Coptic Judge — we pushed through the gaily attired gyppos to the church which was lit up with hundreds of candles. The old priest was holding forth at the top of his voice just like a dingo in a trap, and the choir boys kicked up a great old row. Finally they carried the corpse down the isle dressed up but no boots. The hearse was a gay affair, all gold and cream with big black plumes and the horses were all decked with large plumes on their heads.*

*We have been in the saddel seven hours a day for a week desert training and feel a bit stiff — would have thought nothing of it once. It makes rather a fine sight when all the Brigade is out together. What a lot of beauties the romans are around Myrtleford — evidently they are taking the same stand they did in the S. African war — as you say it would be a good thing they brought in Conscription. I used to think it would be a disgrace on the Empire if we had to have it, but evidently its the only way to induce some of these people out of their chimney corners. Hoping this finds you in better health Mother.*

*With love from your Affec. Son Fred.*

The men felt a natural affection for their mounts—they were their partners, almost an extension of themselves. Often their very lives depended on the ability of their horses to survive the harsh, blistering conditions of the desert, and the animals' welfare was paramount. When not on patrol, most of the day was taken up with grooming, feeding, watering and exercising the horses. They were mostly Walers, a breed that originated in New South Wales and was noted for its extraordinary stamina and endurance. (One officer, Major Shanahan, and his Waler Bill—a big, bad-tempered chestnut of nearly seventeen hands, who would buck and unseat any but his master—rescued four of his men whose horses had been shot under them, and were in great danger, during the battle for Romani. Risking his life, Shanahan rode up to the group and told two men to jump up before him, and the other two to ride on his stirrups, pleading with Bill to behave as they mounted. Carrying the five men, Bill galloped back to safety.)

Each horse was expected to bear tremendous loads of stores and equipment as well as his rider, who carried a .303 rifle and 100 or more rounds of ammunition in his bandolier. Sometimes, when the patrols ranged far into the desert, it was necessary to carry sufficient rations and water for several days, plus blankets, greatcoat and ground cover, mess utensils, folding bucket, horseshoes and grain (for there was no forage to be had in the harsh, inhospitable desert, except for the wiry camel grass).

Bored by the endless desert training and camp routine, Fred tried to transfer to the cavalry in France. Anything, he decided, would be better than the torrid heat, plagues of flies, mosquitoes, midges, fleas and lice that tormented both men and horses, and the daily desert storms that blotted out everything with a wall of red, swirling, stinging sand, making it impossible to open one's perennially bloodshot and swollen eyes.

However, Fred was soon to get the action he craved as scouting parties and skirmishes with the Turks became frequent, a type of guerilla warfare that often involved no more than a single troop of about forty men. Among the deep wadis and stony hills of the Sinai Desert, a large outcrop of rock could hide fifty or 100 Turkish cavalry lying in wait for the light-horsemen. Because the light horse and the New Zealand mounted rifles were highly mobile it was their role to patrol the Sinai Desert, the tongue of land between the gulfs of Suez and Agaba, bounded in the east by the Egypt–Palestine border. It was the ultimate goal of the Turks, who had occupied Palestine for the past 400 years, to cross the desert and capture the Suez Canal, the 'jugular vein' of the British Empire. To prevent this happening, the troopers moved constantly along its banks, from Suez to Ismailia.

The Anzacs were somewhat of an enigma to the Moslem Turks, for whom war was a serious business—a Jihad, or holy war. The Australians and New Zealanders would charge joyously into the fray, laughing, coo-eeing, yelling encouragement and insults, clearly enjoying the deadly challenge. Moslem and infidel were fairly evenly matched: both were superb fighters adept at hand-to-hand combat, and they respected each other highly. Unlike their German masters, the Turks were fair fighters and never fired on soldiers carrying wounded men in the Sinai. The Germans, who often used the Turkish mosques to store ammunition, knowing that the Anzacs respected the Moslem shrines, simply regarded the light-horsemen as madmen.

---

Tel El Kebir
14.6.'16

My Dear Mother,

*Since coming here I have received about 20 letters, all old ones. Anyway they were very acceptable as it is three months since I recieved any. I have had whooping cough since I last wrote. It was bad luck missing Jim — we passed each other in the train the day he landed apparently. He wrote a note and gave it to one of my mates, but he lost it.*

*Jack Regan and I are now in a regiment formed out of the details of the Third Brigade. We are glad we are not in the old regt, for one thing there is too much favouritism shown to the reinforcements who took such a long time to find out that the war was on.*

*All flags are flying half mast here now and the officers are wearing black armbands on their arms, as a mark of respect for Kitchener, it was an awful blow to England to lose him at such a time as this, but I suppose there are as good fish in the sea as there are out of it eh? It is very hot here now and dust storms nearly every day, you cant open your eyes. I was very sorry to hear of poor Kitty Morrison's death, the poor girl was never very strong.*

*Well Mother its getting near dinner time — its only bread and jam and tea but one has to eat well to keep fit. Tell the girls I've taken a great dislike to writing so this will have to go round.*

*Ever your loving son, Fred.*

Early in June, Lord Kitchener and his entourage had embarked on the armoured cruiser HMS *Hampshire*, en route for Russia. As they approached the Orkney Islands the ship was sunk, presumably by a mine or a torpedo, with all hands. This was seen as a crushing blow to the Allied cause by most people, despite a wild rumour that the tragedy was no accident but a desperate move by the High Command to get rid of Kitchener, who was proving intransigent and a liability with his outmoded ideas which might have been relevant during the Boer conflict but were redundant in the present situation.

---

TEL EL KEBIR. NEAR SUEZ
21.6.'16

DEAR MOTHER,

*Just a few lines to let you know I am still well. Our 16th and 17th reinforcements have just arrived so there is quite a crowd here now. There used to be 59,000 before the Infantry went away to France. We are on the move again, destination unknown, but we are hoping it will be out of Egypt. There is a phonograph here grinding out ragtime so excuse mistakes.*

*It is very hot now so we have to do our parades at 4 a.m. till 7 a.m. and 9 a.m. till 10 a.m. and 5 p.m. till 7 p.m. I recieved letters from all the girls last week and a parcel from Nell with tobacco and malt, the latter was just what I wanted as I had a bit of a cough and it seems to be doing me good.*

*We are very anxious to get to France and I am quite satisfied that this is not a white man's country. Nothing but sand with not a tree or a shrub of any kind. We get into the Suez Canal every few days for a swim and that is about the only thing to look forward to.*

*Well Mother it is useless to mention anything about military affairs as it would only be crossed out. With love to all,*

*From your Affectionate Son Fred.*

In late June, Fred and his fellow light-horsemen moved towards Romani, 22 miles (35 kilometres) east of the Suez Canal, in order to prevent the enemy from invading Egypt and gaining access to the canal. Following several skirmishes in July, the Australians were attacked at midnight on 3 August by a far superior enemy force, outnumbering them ten to one, and by 7am the Turks had pushed the Australians back and taken possession of the strategic Wellington Ridge. Following more battles later that day, involving the British and New Zealanders, General Chauvel, Australian commanding officer of the light horse, devised a trap and after a fierce battle on 5 August the Turks were routed, with high casualties and many prisoners taken. The Allied casualties were little more than 1000, most of whom were Anzacs who had, with their horses, borne the brunt of the battle. The exhausted survivors, who had been more than thirty hours in the saddle, slept as they rode into Romani. The victory had quelled the threat of a Turkish invasion of Egypt and paved the way for the routing of the Turks from Palestine.

SUEZ CANAL
6.10.'16

DEAR OLD BABS,

*I have just returned from a weeks holiday in Alexandria. We had a splendid time and I feel a good deal better for the trip.*

*One of the chaps in my sqdrn was attacked by an aeroplane and he got shot. He was only a boy and a really good chap.*

*I suppose Harry will be joining up next month if he passes the Dr. but I dont think he will pass the test. I dont think he could stand the hardships unless his health has improved, and I hope the war will be over before he gets here. I had a letter from Jim the other day, he was buried in a dugout by a bursting shell but was not badly hurt, and should be back in the firing line by now. We voted on the Conscription question on the 19th. Oct. We expect to be leaving this camp shortly, destination unknown.*

*Im writing this in our little lookout box and was called up by some chaps about 8 miles away with a heliograph. You can picture me on a high sandhill in a home made box of matting, with phone and a* couple of helios outside mounted on a wooden platform to keep their legs from sinking into the sand, a telescope and binoculars, also an electric lamp for night work. Flags are out of the question as our nearest station is about 7 miles. The front view sand and still more sand, sandhills without number, tussocks of camel grass here and there as coarse as wire and it should be recommended for conspicuous bravery for trying to grow. Barbed wire entanglements without end. On the left about three miles away an oasis where dates can be had in unlimited quantities. Behind us we can see the Canal with the big boats passing to and fro. The outward bound shipping makes us think of the time when we will be aboard on our way home. The ones coming the other way makes us wonder if they have any mail aboard for us.

And so we live and keep our bodies and souls together with bully beef, stew, bread and marmalade.

Do you remember me telling you about the Forbes boy being killed, well Ive just had word that his brother is being returned blind — what rotten luck that family has had, brother and brother in law killed and the other blind — it will just about break the old lady's heart. I wonder if Add or Nell dropped her a note. I think she wrote Mother when we had our trouble. Well Babs old Girl I must close now and go to tea.

From your affectionate brother, Fred.

---

HQRS. 4TH AUST. CAMEL REGIMENT
8.11.'16

DEAR MOTHER AND ALL AT HOME,

Just a few lines to catch the Xmas mail. Your Xmas parcel arrived here last night, it was a jolly fine parcel and we enjoyed the contents thoroughly.

Well we are on the move and are being formed into a Camel regiment. We are going into camp near the city for a few weeks to be introduced to our camels so I guess there will be some fun when we board our lofty mounts.

I am writing at the YMCA and there is a crowd writing their Xmas mail. Jack is writing for his life at the other side of the table. He is very much taken up with those fortune telling cards you sent — he has been keeping all the boys amused telling their fortunes.

*I suppose you will have a quiet Xmas, well I hope to be with you for the next one. It is rumoured that Conscription went down — well I suppose the men back there can be spared — most of them would be more expence to the Govt than they are worth.*

*Enclosed is this poem written by a Lighthorseman.*

We're sick, we're weary, we're wounded,
With death up above and below,
But I'd rather be here with the heros,
Than back with the men who said "No".

*Well I think that is how a good many of the chaps feel about it especially the old hands.*

*We are camped on the Canal banks for a few days and are having a good old time — the chaps are like a lot of ducks after being in the desert for three months.*

*So you havn't heard from Jim for a few weeks, well dont let that worry you, as you have no idea how hard it is to write in the trenches and no news is good news you know.*

*Thanks so much for remembering me so hansomely — the boys reckoned my Xmas parcel was just IT.*

*I expect to be made a Sergeant shortly.*

*Wishing you all a merry Xmas and a Happy New Year.*

*Your Affectionate son Fred.*

*P.S. Thank Babs too for her bonzer parcel, it was greatly enjoyed by me and the boys.*

Britain had introduced conscription following the terrible loss of life on the Western Front during 1915, and Australian Labor Prime Minister Billy Hughes was anxious to follow suit. Public opinion on the issue was divided, but a referendum held in October 1916 rejected conscription. The majority of the Labor Party, along with the Roman Catholic Church, did not favour conscription. Many of the men at the Front also preferred to do without the 'cold footers'.

ABBASSIA
13.12.'16

MY DEAR MOTHER,

Well we are right among the camels now and are getting quite expert in the art of steering them, but some are as rough as a heavy sea. I think we will find it much better in the desert with the camels than with the horses, as they can go five to seven days without water comfortably, and we carry fifty pounds of grain (Dhura) which is the ration for the camel for five days. We also carry a five gallon tank of water for our own use, so you can see when we are loaded we have a fairly good load. One can make himself fairly comfortable on a camel saddle — its a bowl shaped arrangement — we sit up cross legged on our blankets. One can travel much further without getting tired than you can riding a horse, once you get used to the swing. Some camels are much rougher than others, and if you are unlucky enough to get a rough one its worse than a fast ride in a spring cart over the Running Creek road.

Jack Regan is still in hospital having a rather a bad time with his eyes. He had to undergo an operation as soon as he went in and the Dr. told him had he been a day later he would have been blind. He has a good chance of getting a trip back to Aus. Im going to see him this afternoon.

I got that third stripe — am Sig. Sergeant Carthew 4th. A.C. Reg.!!! some class eh? Recieved Add's and Nell's letters and one from Babs dated 2nd March. I hope the Xmas Cake and pudding dont take as long. (More than nine months.) I also rec. a parcel from Harry so am not doing bad eh.

We are camped by a big aerodrome with aeroplanes flying over us all day — in fact one of our officers was knocked off his camel by one the other day, and got a broken arm and a very bad shaking.

Well I believe Conscription was turned down. One would think there are as many Germans in Aus. as in America. [End of letter missing.]

In late December the Turks launched another assault on the Suez Canal. Had they succeeded in capturing the canal the result would have been catastrophic for the Allies. Fortunately, British and Anzac light horse units were able to repulse the attack and the Turks were forced to withdraw into southern Palestine where they established a strong defensive line running 50 kilometres from Gaza, on the coast, to Beersheba, inland.

Early in January 1917, the Australian light horse and the gallant New Zealand mounted rifles captured Rafa, the coastal town on the border of Palestine. The way was open to the 'Promised Land' of rolling, green, fertile country. The Anzacs moved rapidly from place to place—to Egypt, north by sea to Tripoli in Lebanon and back to Egypt again.

---

PALESTINE
4.1.'17

DEAR MOTHER,

*Just a line to let you know that I am O.K. and hope this finds you all as well as when I last heard from you. I gave you a description of the 'Stunt' at Suez in my previous letters but I don't know if they got past the censor.*

*I havn't heard from Jim for some time, the last I heard he was suffering from a slight attack of gas, but was carrying on in the trenches, so evidently it was nothing serious.*

*Our 4th Camel Reg. has been broken up, and we dont know what our next move will be.*

---

SIG. SERGEANT F. CARTHEW. EGYPT
1.2.'17

DEAR MOTHER,

*Just a few lines to catch tomorrow's mail. There never seems to be anything fresh to write about. I recieved a letter from Jim the other day — he is in hospital in Oxford England and has evidently had a pretty bad time with his wounds but seems to be on the mend now.*

*He didn't even tell me where he was hit, only just said it might have been worse. I am glad he is out of France anyway as one carries his life in his hands there, judging from all accounts. Jim reckons its the worst place he has ever been in, so suppose I ought to be thankful*

*I am in Egypt, but all the same I would like to get a shift out of it. Its only a week short of two years since I left Aust. and it seems like ten years. Well Mother, more next time.*

*Love to all from Your Affectionate son Fred.*

---

AUST. MOUNTED DIVISION. TRIPOLI
20.2.'17

DEAR MOTHER,

*You will be wondering what has become of me. My right hand went paralized and remained so for nearly a month — was getting electrical treatment and my hand in an iron splint so I couldn't write but am glad to say it is quite O.K. again. My two officers are away so I have to cope with the troop of 62 men so I've got plenty to do.*

*We are camped 5 miles from Tripoli, a seaport town the size of Bright — with white stone houses and red tiled roofs, it looks rather pretty from the sea, but like all these eastern towns distance lends enchantment. The snow-capped Libian mountains are a few miles inland, they are 10,000 ft. high, very rugged, reminding one of the Buffalo Mts. The civilian population (Syrians) are in a state of utter poverty — they had a terrible time while the Turks were here — more especially the christians. They tell us that as much as 60% of the population of some towns died of starvation, people died in their houses and there was no one to bury them, the result was the country was reeking with disease when our troops came through, and we lost an awful lot through sickness, Spanish influenza, Blackwater fever, Malaria, etc. Well no news that I can write about. Love to all at home, and Many Happy Returns Mother of 17th. March.*

*Your Affectionate son, Fred.*

---

ISMALIA
3.3.'17

DEAR MOTHER AND ALL AT HOME,

*We have been shifting about a bit since I last wrote. I think I told you that the Camel Regt. was broken up and we are now portion of a Camel Battallion so my address will be — Headquarters, 4th. Camel Batt. Egypt.*

*We are camped near Ismalia at present having trecked from Abbassia a few days trip throuh the desert. We expect to move off again shortly so you may not hear very often now.*

*I recieved two letters from Babs recently but only a paper from you.*

---

KUBRI
2.4.17

DEAR MOTHER AND GIRLS,

*We are stationed on the Canal only a few miles from Suez, it is a good camp but frightfully monotonous and the army rations leave much to be desired.*

*I was awfully sorry to hear that poor old George Matthews had been killed, it must have been an awful shock at home especially as he was the family favourite. I have just written a letter of sympathy to Mrs Matthews.*

*Jim was getting on O.K. when he last wrote to me, and I hope they keep him out of France till after the Spring, as I think it will be very hot there then.*

*Well it looks as though the war won't last long now, I think this year will see us on our way home and I can assure you we wont be sorry.*

*I met Bill Carr or rather Lt. Carr when we were trecking through from Abbassia — he has been home to England on leave and the ship he was on got torpedoed — of course Bill had a great tale to pitch about it. He sent his love to the girls.*

*Well must close now with best love.*

*Yours ever, Fred.*

In March 1917 the Anzac Mounted Division, led by Chauvel, and the Imperial Mounted Division, led by British officer Major General Hodgson, together with Fred's Camel Brigade and three British infantry divisions, assaulted the Turkish stronghold of Gaza. The enemy resistance was crumbling and the city was almost in Allied hands when General Sir Archibald Murray (who had orchestrated the battle from the safe haven of the Savoy Hotel in Cairo, hundreds of miles away) ordered Chauvel and Hodgson to withdraw, due to the lack of available water. Despite Chauvel's protests, his men were forced to surrender a victory they considered already won. The British Prime Minister, Lloyd George, was later to remark that this incredible blunder was typical of the stupidity of Generals on both sides of the war.

On 19 April, Murray ordered the troops to retake Gaza, this time using six tanks and a supply of gas. The Turks, however, had had time to rally and the Allies suffered a heavy defeat. It was to prove to be one of the greatest disasters of the war in the Middle East, with Allied casualties totalling over 6000.

Believing that Murray had sent them into a death trap, the Australians openly accused the General of murder. Eventually Murray was replaced by General Sir Edmund Allenby, a man different in every way from his predecessor. Allenby moved his headquarters into the Sinai Desert, close to the action, and reorganised the mounted divisions, which included the Camel Corps, the Australian light horse and the New Zealand and British cavalry, into a single 'Desert Mounted Corps'. He placed Chauvel in charge, promoting him to Lieutenant General, which caused much resentment among the British officers. (When one of Allenby's subordinates was heard to remark that it was absurd to award supreme command of the world's greatest ever cavalry force—a force of 40 000—to a colonial, and an Australian at that, Allenby retorted that Chauvel was the best man for the job and he cared not a jot whether he was black, white or kickapoo Indian.)

Allenby was feared by his own troops, but the Anzacs soon learned to trust and admire him for his fairness and plain-speaking ways. Allenby in turn appreciated the Anzacs' courage and initiative and the fact that they, like himself, called a spade a spade. He did not believe in leading an army from the safe distance of the Savoy Hotel in Cairo, as his predecessor had done and many of his senior officers had been wont to do, sipping wine as they pored over desert maps, and he lost no time making this abundantly clear to them.

British Red Cross, Order of St. John
Ferry's Post Ismalia
25.4.'17

Dear Mother,

*Just a line to let you know that I am O.K. I was sent to hospital with influenza and was on the point of returning to camp when a chap in our ward contracted scarlet fever, so I am shut up in an isolation camp for 10 days and I can assure you it is dull in every sense of the word.*

*I suppose there is great things doing in Aust. today, Anzac Day, well there are great things doing over on this side too, only of a different nature. The fighting at Gazza is going on again thick and heavy, and there are hundreds of wounded coming in daily — our chaps are up against one of the strongest positions the Turks have, so of course we must expect heavy casualties.*

*I had a letter from Polly recently and Old Fred has got into trouble with the [Railway] Dept. and was sent away up country as punishment, so to get away from it all he has enlisted ...*

*I hear rumours of Jack doing a matrimonial deal, tell him I wish him all sorts of luck and hope it turns out as successful as his other deals appear to have done.*

Southern Palestine
10.10.17

*Many thanks for the parcel of silk shirts Mother, they are just the thing for this place, so strong and light and cool. We see some rather good air fights here and they are very exciting, our chaps brought down 2 enemy planes last week so they are not doing to badly. Thanks to for the Myrtleford Mails — who was it forgot themselves so far as to put that piece about me in?*

*From your affectionate son, Fred.*

# ⇢ Charging to Victory ⇠

AFTER THE ALLIES again failed to take Gaza, due to General Murray's bungled orders, Allenby devised a daring plan for the capture of southern Palestine. Seven infantry divisions (each of 4000 men) and three mounted divisions would attempt to break through the left flank of the Turkish lines at Beersheba (reputedly the place where Abraham dug the 'well of the oath'). It was a risky plan because of the difficulty in supplying such a large force of men and horses with water. The Turks had destroyed all the known wells in the surrounding desert, and unless the town and its life-giving wells were captured on the first day, there could be dire consequences for both men and animals.

---

PALESTINE
29TH.OCT.'17

DEAR MOTHER,

*Was glad to hear from Add and Babs that you were all O.K., and that you enjoyed your trip to town. We were all glad to hear that the strike had come to a satisfactory termination, it certainly threatened to be very serious.* [A strike by the waterside workers, partly orchestrated by the Communist Party, had occurred.]

*We have just returned from a week's stunt, only a premelary* [sic] *to what is to come, we are going out tomorrow, so you see we havnt much time for letter writing.*

*Am pleased to be able to tell you that Jack has been promoted to Sgt — I often see him as we are camped close together.*

*Well Mother hoping this finds you all O.K.*

*Your Affectionate Son, Fred.*

Throughout the day and night of 30 October, the Desert Mounted Corps crossed the desert and, by dawn, had taken up positions in the Judaean Hills which surrounded the saucer-shaped valley in which the town of Beersheba was situated. The 1500 Turkish defenders had skillfully exploited the terrain, building an elaborate network of trenches in a horseshoe shape around the sides of the valley. They were supremely confident that their defences were impregnable and that the Allied forces would never be able to cross the waterless desert.

Early on 31 October, the Allied infantry divisions assaulted the town. The battle raged on throughout the day without making a dent in the Turkish resistance, and towards evening the plan of attack appeared to have failed, with the town still firmly in Turkish hands.

Chauvel believed that the precarious situation demanded bold, decisive action. He had been holding the 4th Light Horse Brigade (comprising the 4th and 12th light horse regiments) in reserve, but now he ordered them to ride out of the hills on the south side of the town, where there were no barbed-wire entanglements, and to break through the Turkish lines. This sector was heavily defended by artillery and machine guns, and they would be facing massive bombardment from the enemy trenches.

As the 500 light-horsemen rode up over a ridge and headed down into the long, open valley towards Beersheba, the Turks opened fire with their heavy guns. A hail of shrapnel was soon bursting around the ranks. To lessen the impact of the bombardment, the troopers fanned out across the valley, advancing at a headlong gallop, yelling and coo-eeing in the euphoria of the furious charge, as they always did, revelling in the deadly challenge and shouting insults at their opponents, who were shrieking, 'Allah, Allah Akbar' ('God is Great').

'We'll give you Allah, you bastards!' they bawled. The Turks in the trenches must have been dismayed at the sight of hundreds of horsemen thundering towards them in a full-blooded cavalry charge, for their artillery had difficulty in finding their range. Two green German Albatross aeroplanes swooped low, machine-gunning the horsemen, but with little effect. They failed to stem the swift momentum of the attack.

When the cavalry were within range, the defenders opened up a barrage of intense machine-gun and rifle fire, which proved not nearly as efficacious as planned, due both to the speed of the attack and to the fact that the machine guns had been carefully calibrated to cut down approaching infantry, not cavalry. Most of the bullets passed harmlessly through the horses' legs. As the Australians neared the trenches and closed ranks for the assault, the fire from the panic-stricken Turks became even wilder and less effective.

Ian Idriess, who witnessed the attack, wrote (quoted in *800 Horsemen*, C. Stringer, self-published, 1998): 'This charge was the grandest in history. A magnificent cheer went up from the watching British troops and even some of the Turks stood and applauded, such was the magnificence of the feat. Hopelessly outnumbered and outgunned, they thundered on, their [emu] plumes fluttering proudly, and the gateway to Jerusalem was opened that day.'

Troopers Healy and O'Leary were the first to reach the Turkish lines. O'Leary jumped the first trench and charged alone towards Beersheba, pulling up at last to capture a gun emplacement and its crew, who dazedly surrendered. He then brazenly ordered one of his prisoners to hold his horse while he seated himself on the gun and leisurely rolled himself a fag. Healy, meanwhile, leaped off his horse into the first trench to attack its occupants, and hard on his heels came the others, clearing the heads of the cowering Turks. Some continued on into the town and others dismounted, plunging into the trenches to attack the enemy with bayonet and rifle. Such was the fury of the assault that the Turkish resistance crumbled, and in the rear lines demoralised men surrendered by the score, sometimes to a single trooper.

The 12th Light Horse then galloped into Beersheba to secure the vital wells. These had been wired with explosives, but taken by surprise with the fury and suddenness of the attack, the officers responsible for their destruction had had no time to detonate the fuses before they fled.

At the end of the day, the Australian light horse brigades had captured 38 officers and 700 men, losing only 39 of their own men in the attack. Uncharacteristically, the Turks had fired on the Anzac ambulances, having been told by their German masters that they were carrying ammunition. One trooper, having captured a group of Turks who had surrendered, was shot dead by their German officer (who was later executed). Another German Major, who was taken prisoner, summed up the feelings of the defenders when he said of the Anzacs: 'They are not soldiers at all, they are madmen'.

As the troopers thankfully rode up to the wells, thirsty as they were having been without water for many hours in blistering 50°C heat, their first thought was for their beloved mounts, who were allowed to drink their fill before they themselves slaked their thirst. The troopers and their horses had delivered what is referred to as the world's last great cavalry charge, and their legend would go down in history.

The capture of Beersheba led to the speedy collapse of the whole Turkish defensive line. Gaza fell on 6 November, and Jerusalem followed on 9 December. After the capture of Beersheba, the push into the Judaean Hills brought incredible hardship for men and horses. Heavy rainfall soaked their greatcoats and below-zero temperatures caused frostbite and terrible pain when hands and feet thawed. Many men died from gangrene.

---

13.12.'17

DEAR MOTHER,

*Just a few lines to let you know that I am O.K. We are back in Palestine where we were before the 'Stunt' and are having a bit of a spell and clean up after seven weeks hard work on bully beef and biscuits. We had a fairly hard time and rather a heavy casualty list, but it was an interesting trip, tho' the experience was rather painful at times. It was rather disappointing to be withdrawn before we seen Jeraselum [sic], which was occupied soon after we left the front. We had a good deal of wet weather and it was very uncomfortable sleeping in wet blankets, but the greatest hardship we had to put up with was the camel itch which we have all contracted, it is exactly like the exma [sic] Jim used to get and we are awake all night scratching ourselves raw, but the camels are being taken away from us soon untill we get rid of the disease and there is also rumours of leave to Cairo, and I hope we get it. I havnt tasted fresh meat for 2 months; so I guess a few days leave in Cairo wouldnt hurt much Eh?*

*Well Palestine is certainly a beautiful country, I have never seen richer country — miles of beautiful red soil without a tree or stone, but it is practically waisted on the Bedouins and Jews who work the ground with the same old implements as were in use B.C.*

*Beyond Gaza the country is richer and more thickly populated, and sprinkled with red roofed villages, and the inhabitants are mostly Jews of various nationalities. They were overjoyed at the appearance of our troops as Jacko was not giving them a very pleasant time of it. Nevertheless, they remained true to their traditions, and asked about 3 times the value of everything they sold us. We could only get brown bread and oranges as they didn't have too much themselves.*

*Must close Mother with love to all,*
*Your Affect. Son Fred.*

Palestine had been occupied by the Turks for 400 years, during which time both Christians and Jews had been cruelly pesecuted. So great was their joy on their liberation, they literally kissed the dusty boots of the light-horsemen as they rode in.

The Arabs, who often fought side by side with the Anzacs, were regarded as superb horsemen and brave fighters. Unfortunately, they welcomed the Germans and Turks with equal impartiality, depending on which was the more expedient, which made them very unreliable allies.

---

PALESTINE
16.12.'17

DEAR EMM,

*We are now about 60 miles behind the lines. Well it was a pretty rough 'stunt'. We lost a good number of men — 39 casualties in 15 minutes, the night before we left so you see we got into some hot corners.*

*Jaffa is a fairly large place and I was in for a swim on the beach. I took some photos of Bersheba but dont know how they will turn out. Bersheba is not a very big place, but there are a few nice buildings there, a big Mosque, hospital, Railway station all stone with tiled roofs. The flour mill was blown up, but the wells were the main thing to us, and the Turks evidently didn't have time to destroy them, tho they had explosives packed around some of them.*

*We rode thru Bersheba early the morning it fell, there was a cinametograph man there taking our picture so you may see the Camel Corps on the films. Thanks for the tin of tobacco Emm, it arrived when we were in the trenches and was worth its weight in gold — we were over a month without a cigarette issue. 'Nuf sed'.*

*Goodbye Yours as B.4.*

By this time, the Turkish army and the native inhabitants of the Holy Land had been severely decimated by the pneumonic influenza, and soon many of the Anzacs contracted the dreaded disease. The victims' lungs quickly filled with fluid, severely restricting respiration, so that the body became starved of oxygen. This manifested the ominous, characteristic blue-black patches of dead tissue over the body and usually resulted in death. (During the following two years, the disease spread like wildfire, becoming pandemic and causing more than sixteen million deaths worldwide—more, in fact, than the entire previous four years of conflict had claimed. Some estimates of the death toll were as high as thirty to forty million.)

---

PALESTINE
20.1.'18

*Dear Mother,*

*We are having splendid weather, I think the winter is just about over. I havn't heard from Jim for a good while, suppose he is having a rough time of it. It is very evident that some of my letters ended up at the bottom of the sea, the boats seem to be always being sunk so if you dont hear from me regularly dont worry. Suppose you recieved the cable I sent along at Xmas, thought you would be wondering how things were when you seen the reports of the big advance.*

*Well the troops are very much disgusted about the defeat of Conscription, we were quite sure Aust. would put it through under those conditions, but it looks as if she is turning her soldiers down.*

[Conscription was again defeated in a second referendum held in December 1917.]

*Well I think that is how a good many of the chaps feel about it, especially the old hands. Well Mother I hope this finds you as well as it leaves me. Love to all From your Affectionate Son Fred.*

---

22.2.'18
PALESTINE

*We are having very rough weather here, just now, blowing a gale off the sea. Suppose you are having it hot and dry in your part of the world. I would very much like to be back in the old orchard under the apple trees.*

*A chap from Myrtleford came over the other day, it turned out to be Tom McKeoh, its a long time since I have met anyone from the old spot and it does one good to have a yarn to someone from home. I havn't heard from Jim for sometime suppose he is like myself very often not in a writing humour and its really hard to find anything to write about.*

*Must close now Mother hoping this finds you well at home.*

*I remain your affectionate son Fred.*

---

ABBASSIA
31.3.'18

*Just a line to let you know I am O.K. and doing well, am at present down at the base awaiting for the flying school to commence. I think I told you in my last that I was going to try myself as a flying man, well that school is not starting till next month so am taking the 'rest cure' back here. Have had no news from home since Jan. 1st and as you always write regularly I came to the conclusion that something has gone wrong with the mail bags.*

*I had a note from Polly saying that Old Fred had been called up in the railway unit, and of course she was in a state about it, but she must remember that she is not the only one who has to make sacrifices, besides Fred is leaving her Two pounds nine shillings a week and young Charlie is earning his own living. Its too dark to write so must close with love to all from yr Affec. son Fred.*

During the next few months, the Desert Mounted Corps moved rapidly from place to place in Palestine, clearing up pockets of resistance. From Gaza in the south they went as far north as Tripoli in Lebanon, via Jaffa on the coast, and inland to Jerusalem, Jericho, the Dead Sea and the Jordan Valley.

---

EGYPT
7.8.'18

MY DEAR MOTHER,

*Just a line to say that I am still carrying on with the soldiering but am a non combatant for the time being. There doesnt seem to be much chance of me getting into the flying Corp now, as Ive heard nothing about it for some time.*

*Poor old Jim seems to be having a bad time according to a letter I had from Babs, but I think he will get a trip home now, and I dont think the gas has a lasting effect. Ive just returned from seven days leave in Alexandria, enjoyed the spell away from the military, its the longest leave Ive had since I joined in 1914, but one cannot really have a good time, as a soldier in Egypt is regarded by the civil population as something to be avoided, and then of course there is very little English spoken.*

*I had a very pathetic letter from Mrs. Forbes, my W.A. landlady — one of her sons has returned from the war so mutilated and smashed he is practically a maniac, and has turned their refined little home into a bedlam and has made one of his sisters so ill that they had to send her away to the East to save her from becoming a permanent invalid — they have been a very unlucky family in this war, one of the girls lost her husband, one of the sons was killed in France, and the other one comes home sightless, without teeth or jaw and partly insane. So you see we have something to be thankful for.*

*Ted Croucher was here for a few days, he was in hospital with fever but was quite O.K. again. The Jordan Valley is a very unhealthy place and I suppose I should be thankful to be out of it. We get up at four o'clock and work till 11.30 as its too hot in the afternoon. Have the Woodsides sold their place. If they do it should be a good opportunity to sell our place, I think the sooner we get out of it the better, as the St. John's Wort is becoming a menace in the district, and people will be afraid to buy property in the effected parts.*

*Well Mother must close now with love to yourself and all at home.*

*I remain, your Affect. Son Fred.*

The campaign in North Africa finally culminated in the triumphant entry of the 10th Light Horse, led by Lieutenant Colonel Olden, into Damascus on 1 October 1918. This brought about the complete collapse of the Turkish and German forces in Palestine, and spearheaded the liberation of the Holy Land. In two and a half years of compaigning in the desert, only 73 light-horsemen were captured, while they themselves had captured 40 000 of the enemy.

Paying tribute to the Anzacs in later years, General Allenby wrote (quoted in *800 Horsemen*, C. Stringer, self-published, 1998): 'The liberation of the Holy Land is one of the greatest epics of modern history ever to take place, achieved by the greatest body of cavalry in the history of the war. The Australian light horse has earned the gratitude of the Empire and the admiration of the world ... I doubt that the modern nation of Israel would exist today were it not for the magnificent courage of the Australian light horse.'

According to one Australian trooper, 'It was our horses that did it—those bloody marvellous horses'. The Walers were often on campaign for up to sixty hours in blistering heat without food or water, and although dehydrated they carried their heavy burdens proudly and unfailingly, easily outdistancing the Arab horses. The troopers often broke down in tears if one of their mounts was killed or injured, and always shared their precious water with them. One trooper, who lost his stripes after punching an officer, protested that 'He whacked my horse, and nobody belts Nipper—he's my mate and he's often saved my life'.

After the end of the war in November 1918, the troopers of the Australian light horse and New Zealand cavalry learnt, to their fury, that the powers that be had no intention of repatriating their beloved mounts, now that they were no longer necessary to the war effort, stating that the cost would be too high. Devastated at the thought of abandoning their faithful companions—who had shared with them the dangers and vicissitudes of war for so many years—to the tender mercies of the Egyptians, the men decided to shoot them all. Eventually, the most fit were sold to the Indian army and the remainder, after a final race meeting, were humanely put down by their riders. (Only one horse, a Waler named Sandy, was returned to Australia. He had been the personal mount of Major General Sir William Throsby Bridges, commanding officer of the Australian army. Bridges was fatally wounded at Gallipoli in May 1915, and in 1917 the Minister for Defence gave orders for the General's beloved horse to be shipped back to Australia. Sandy ended his days peacefully in the lush paddocks of Duntroon Military College.)

Fred Carthew remained in Egypt with other members of the light horse as a peace-keeping force during the Arab uprising of 1919. Tragically, many who had survived Gallipoli and the Sinai campaigns were killed during this period.

---

MOASCAR
4.4.'19

DEAR MOTHER,

*Just a line to let you know that we are still here with the Gipos and are likely to be for some considerable time. I think the last time I wrote was from Tripoli Syria — well as you see by the above we are back in Egypt again, and when we arrived here we found that the Egyptians were in revolt — wanted their own government etc, and started in to wreck the railway lines and make themselves a general nuisance, the result being the light horse having to be fitted out with horses and all the gear they had handed in, and sally forth again to guard the railway lines and the European population. All demobalising has been suspended much to the disgust of the mob.*

*I think I told you I had applied for the furlough to England, well its been granted so expect to get away shortly — that is if the Egyptian situation allows.*

*Jack Regan's regiment (15th) is moving out of camp on garrison* duty this morning. He has just come out of hospital and is looking very much worn out.

My address in England will be A.I.F. Headquarters, London so please address the next letters there. I have no programme mapped out as to what Im going to do when I get there but hope to have a good time. I havn't recieved a letter from anyone for ages, so am going to give up waiting.

Must close now with love to all at home,

From Your Affect. Son Fred.

---

JULY 4TH 1919

MY DEAR ADD, NELL AND EMM,

It seems ages since I have written to anyone except an occasional note to Mother; so will now endeavour to give you an idea of what I have been doing since I left the land of sand, sin, sorrow and sore eyes. Leaving in Port Said on board the very much overcrowded 'Caledonia', we arrived at Marsailles after a rather uneventful trip — except that my two mates and I had to burst open a fruit locker up on deck before we could get a place to lay our head — on May 6th were marched into a rest camp there and remained two days, this gave us time to have a look at the place, and I was rather surprised at the size of the Burg. It is purely a commercial town, and its immorality is typical of the French.

We were fortunate enough to get a converted hospital train to travel across France in, instead of the customary cattle trucks, and so had a great deal more convenience and room than we expected. Springtime is France at her best, and I can assure you that here best is very hard to beat.

The whole place is like a beautifully laid out park, with its green fields, orchards and vineyards; Hedges, and beautiful old slate roofed houses that age seems to have given a charm and softness unknown to our too new, and too modern homes of Australia. The railway tunnels are a very striking feature of the French railway between Marailles and Le Harve, we must have gone through at least 60 tunnels during the fifty two hours trip.

Arriving at Harve, we were marched into a big infantry camp, and *at once realised how much better the infantry had been catered for when they were out of the line, than the L.H. of Egypt — Big oval roofed galvanised iron huts with board floor and a stove — hot water baths, huge recreation and Y.M.C.A. Huts Canteens etc, all of which were foreign to our rest camps in Palestine, where a rest camp usually meant knocking of work to carry bricks. We were surprised to see the pink and white complexions of the infantry chaps — have never seen Aussies with such complexions before, and think I prefer to see the good old tan, what do you say?*

*Stayed in Harve three days, and had a look at the town which is a very dead place with nothing of interest to see. Left France on 13th for Southampton, arriving there about 11pm, and stayed on board the boat (Lydia) all morning — It was supposed to be early summer; but we had no blankets, and I don't remember feeling so cold for ages, had to walk the deck all night to keep warm.*

*Went ashore on morning of 14th and entered London about midday, then carried our kits from Waterloo Stn to Horsferry Rd where A.I.F. Hqrs are. Met Old Fred on the way just outside Westminister Abbey, and of course, Carthew-like he took command, bussled about and found lodgings etc for about eight of us, then proceeded to show us the sights of London.*

*If I had half of Fred's brazen impudence, and cheek, I may have been a captain today; but I glad Im not* [this remark may have been prompted because Old Fred, who enlisted in March 1918, had already been promoted to Sergeant, after only a few months' active service]. *After seeing everything of any great interest, Tower of London, Tower Bridge, Houses of Parliament (I hung my hat on the peg in the House of Lords that Kitchener used to hang his on) Westminister Abbey Grenwich observatory, The Blackwell Tunnel under the Themes* [sic], *we walked through and went through China town at the other end, and seen there the house where Billie Carlton used to have her opium etc. shavoos.*

*Well after seeing most things that the londoners havn't seen, I have come to the conclusion that there is only two things in london that I really admire, and that is the Tubes and the London police. The former is the most business like, and bussle breeding arrangement you can imagine, and the latter is a real live fountain of information with a helmet on.*

*Well we only stayed in london about a week and then 'catched up our hats and rund away' to Scotland. Leaving London at midnight the express dropped us in Glasgow about seven thirty next morning with only two stops on the way. But enough for one day will tell you about my experiences in Scotland another day.*

*Love from your Affectionate Brother, Fred.*

---

A.I.F. Hall, Australia House
Strand
London, W.C.
July 4th 1919

Dear Mother,

*Just a line to let you know that we are still carrying on with the good work. My mate and I are juggling ledgers and figures about at Clarks Business College Chancery Lane, right in the heart of the City and I find my rotten education my worst enemy. We don't expect to learn a great deal in three months, but will get a good knowledge of the principals of book keeping.*

*I have still had no mail from Aust. Cannot understand where it all is, but suppose it will turn up in a body one of these days. You know I don't even know whether the home is sold, or not yet.*

*I met a chap who has just arrived from Egypt, and who left Aus. with me; so have been showing him around a bit. You see we are beginning to know this Burg, went out to St. Paul's yesterday.*

*Well Mother as it is nearly an impossibility to write with this pen, so Ill have to close. Hoping this finds you in the best of health, I remain, Your Affect. Son, Fred.*

*P.S. Am staying at Tulse Hill now, but its too far away from the city, so am going to shift, so please address mail to C/o CLARKS BUSINESS COLLEGE. Living is dreadfully dear here, you cannot get a decent meal under 5/-.*

*Am writing to the girls today.*

ST. JOHN'S HOUSE
LONGSTOWE
CAMBRIDGE
4TH AUGUST, '19

MY DEAR MOTHER,

You see I am back at my adopted home again; the colledge has closed down for a fortnights vacation, so we packed up and came home again.

We brought Bert Ulrich — one of my old pals that left Aussie with me — along with us; there are three other Aussie chaps staying here too, making a total of six guests.

We were punting on the Camm river in Cambridge on Saturday and also went to a service in St Johns Colledge chapel — the choir was splendid, and it's a most beautiful chapel.

We all went along to see the 'Hounds' yesterday — the master of the hounds has about three hundred of the brutes there, and they are worth from two to three hundred guineas each; (a guinea is one pound & one shilling) but personally I'd rather have Laddie and Spider than the whole lot of them; their upkeep is a matter of two thousand (pounds) a year. If I had them I'd send them to Hudsons Bay, put them in a sledge, and make them earn their living.

Am going to Longstowe Hall to play tennis tomorrow — 'When the Squire's away the mice play'.

Affectionately Yours, Fred.

14TH AUG. 1919

MY DEAR MOTHER,

Just a few lines to let you know that I am still at my country residence, but think we shall have to return to the big smoke this afternoon. Mrs Gray wants us to stay on for the weekend, but unfortunately we made other arrangements, so will have to face hot and smokey London again worst luck.

I have been here fourteen days, and have had a glorious time, used to play tennis at the Hall etc; but my mate made a bit of a hash of things by poaching pheasants on the Squires estates on Sunday afternoon!!! Of course being a Church warden, and a J.P. was not at *all pleased, being an offence against Church and state as he said.*

*I said it must have been in the family as his father was sent out [as a convict] for the same thing. Mrs. Grey is an absolute brick and fixed the thing up satisfactorily. She is coming out for a trip to Aust. probably next year, and I do hope we will be in a position to entertain her for a few weeks. She is an aristocrat to her fingertips, but absolutely unconventional.*

*We go back to Clarks on Monday next, and its going to be hard.*

*Well Mother I do hope this will find you quite well,*

*Love to all from Your Affectionate Son, Fred.*

---

Y.M.C.A. WITH THE AUSTRALIAN IMPERIAL FORCE
7TH SEPT. '19.

MY DEAR MOTHER,

*Carrying on in the big smoke, nothing to report — haven't heard from Aussie since I wrote to you last.*

*Have just been down to Hyde park to see the swells give an exibition of their inability to ride a horse as it should be ridden, also seen the guard change at the palace, but it is really nothing showy now as they are only ordinary tommies in ordinary tommie uniforms.*

*Our time is drawing near, now, and expect to be on our way home by the end of the month — There is a lot of boats available now and they expect to get eighteen thousand away by the end of the month, leaving only six thousand to go. I wonder if you have disposed of the place yet? Give my kind regards to all the people in that part of the world; Hope to see you all personally in a month or so. Love to all, From Your Affect. Son, Fred.*

---

Y.M.C.A. SUTTON VENEY CAMP
WARMINISTER, ENG.
25TH. SEPT. 1919

MY DEAR MOTHER,

*You see by the address that I am no longer a civilian. We arrived back in camp yesterday, and find it very hard sleeping musty blankets on the floor; but hope it will not be for very long, its very uncertain, but expect to get a boat in a week or so. Its getting very bleak and cold here now, so will not be sorry to get back where the sun shines daily.*

*I went down to Cambridge to say goodbye to Mrs. Gray and got a bit of a cold and had to stay on for a week after my leave was up, but she got the doctor to give me a certificate to the effect that I was unable to travel — have never been laid up under such pleasant conditions in my life — She is the most charming hostess — came back to london with me when I came — went to a theatre, and seen me off at the stn yesterday. She may come out to Aussie on a trip next year, and I do hope I'll be in a position to entertain her for a time.*

*I'm thinking of going to Queensland when I go back to see what opportunities there are in the land line — I hear the Q government give the returned men every chance to make a start. Hoping this finds you all quite well, I will close with love to all, From Your Affectionate Son, Fred.*

---

AUSTRALIAN IMPERIAL FORCE
BASE RECORDS OFFICE, DEPT OF DEFENCE, MELB.
27TH OCTOBER, 1919

*Dear Madam,*

*I am in receipt of advice to the effect that No. 12, Sergeant G.F. Carthew, 2nd. Light Horse Signal Troop, is returning to Australia per transport 'Pakeha' which left England on 6/10/19 and will probably arrive in Melbourne about the 19/11/19. Further information as to the exact date of arrival and time of disembarkation will be published in the press when available.*

*It should be noted, however, that owing to possible mutilations in the cabled advice, and other causes, this notification may not be correct pending verification from the roll after the arrival of the troopship.*

*Any further inquiries should be made to the Staff Officer Returned Soldiers, Military Headquarters, Perth W.A.*

*Yours faithfully,*

*J. McLean, Major.*

*Officer in Charge, Base Records.*

*Above: The heroic charge of the 8th and 10th Light Horse Brigades at the Nek on 7 August 1915 was described by Charles Bean as 'unsurpassed in history'.*

*Left: Fred Carthew enlisted in the 10th (Western Australian) Light Horse in October 1914.*

*Above: Fred Carthew (second from left) and his fellow signallers of the 10th Light Horse, c.1915. As Babs noted, Fred is sporting the largest emu plume.*

*Below: Fred (far right) and some of his fellow troopers in North Africa, on a break from the front line.*

*Australian War Memorial B01627*

*Above: An official photo-graph of the Australian Camel Corps, of which Fred was a member, in Palestine, January 1918.*

*Right: Sergeant Fred Carthew, prior to his return to Australia in October 1919.*

*Left: James Holman Carthew, Margaret's second youngest son, in 1914.*

*Right: Nellie Browne, to whom James became engaged at the end of 1914, prior to his departure for the Western Front.*

*Above: James (second from right) poses with friends for a photograph at the pyramids, at the same place where his brothers Charles and Fred had their photograph taken a year earlier.*

*Above: A reserve trench at Gueudecourt in the Somme Valley, in November 1916. The quagmire of mud and the dugout (left of picture) give some idea of the appalling conditions James endured.*

*Above: Gassed Australian soldiers awaiting medical aid at an overcrowded first aid post, following the battle of Villers-Bretonneux where James was gassed.*

*Below: The Crescent War Hospital, England, where James (centre, beneath clock) was sent to recover from the effects of being gassed and temporarily blinded.*

*Above: James (fourth from left) in the kitchens of the Crescent War Hospital. He wrote on the back of this photograph: 'I find it a wise plan to keep in with the cooks. I could not look up owing to the light in my eyes.'*

*Left: Gunner James Carthew in 1918, partially recovered, prior to returning home to Australia. He is wearing his Military Medal ribbon.*

# → PART THREE ←

# *James*

# → Love and War ←

DEEPLY DISAPPOINTED at being rejected by the Western Australian 10th Light Horse because of his asthma, James Carthew decided to seek consolation from his sweetheart, Miss Nellie Browne, who lived in Kalgoorlie but was currently staying at the YWCA in Adelaide Terrace, Perth.

Nellie, who was secretly delighted that her Jim had not been accepted into the army, was so sweetly sympathetic that James was emboldened to press his suit, which he had been trying to get up enough courage to do for more than a year. He had little faith that such a wonderful, beautiful girl as Nellie, with her honey-gold hair and green eyes—a schoolteacher and superior in every way—would look favourably upon his proposal, but he knew his future happiness depended on her answer. Sinking to his knees on the linoleum floor of the hostel sitting room, surrounded by aspidistras, he began: 'Nell, sweetheart, would you do me the honour, the very great honour, of becoming my wife? I know I'm not worthy of you but I love you very much ...'

He was unable to go on. He waited, his heart in his eyes, for the answer that was to give him the courage and inspiration to endure three terrible, endless years of horror and heartbreak on the Western Front.

Nellie looked down into the dark eyes of this quiet, unassuming man she had loved for nearly two years, and smiled. 'I would feel happy and honoured to be your wife, Jim,' she said softly.

To Mrs. F. Fordham Browne
58 George Street, Kalgoorlie, W.A.
28.12.1914

My Dear Mrs. Browne,

*Having obtained Nell's consent to our engagement, I thought it my duty to write and ask you for your consent also, before making any further arrangements. I am not going to talk of anything more serious, until I am in a position to give her as comfortable a home as what she has now, which in my opinion she is justly worthy of, and which time I hope is not far distant. In granting me your consent, which I feel sure you will, I hope you never have any cause to regret having done so.*

*Well I will close now and anxiously await your reply.*

*Yours Most Sincerely,*

*J.H. Carthew.*

By October 1915 the war had been going for a year. People had ceased to predict optimistically that it would be over by Christmas, and following the reports of the dreadful massacres on Gallipoli, recruitment had fallen off dramatically. Women garbed and veiled in deepest mourning, men wearing black armbands and wounded men in hospital blue were a common sight on the streets of Melbourne and elsewhere, and the military promoted their recruitment drives with less and less effect. No longer were they able to portray the AIF as a career fit for heroes—a glamorous, exciting adventure—when the newspapers and the casualty lists told another story. *The Age*, on 1 October 1915, reported a marked decrease in enrolment in Victoria, with only 74 volunteers applying the day before, and concluded with the news that 'another organised effort to stimulate volunteers to fill the gaps at the Front will be made directly'.

The situation was no different in Western Australia, and men who had previously been rejected by the army were now accepted to fill the vacant places. At the end of October, Margaret Carthew received the letter she had been dreading.

GUNNER JAMES HOLMAN CARTHEW
BLACKBOY HILL CAMP, MT. HELENA. W.A.
23.10.1915.

MY DEAR MOTHER,

*I suppose you have been worrying why I have not written before. Well, dear Mother I have been waiting until I got into camp here and got a little settled. I came here about a week ago, so consequently do not know much about it.*

*Mother, I do hope you are keeping well in health and not worrying, since the receipt of our terrible news.*

*I felt that it was my duty to go and try to take his place, although everyone was against me. Polly would not hear of it, also the Girl [Nellie], who is very broken up, and I find it very hard to have to leave her, she is such a splendid girl. My landlady thinks there is nobody like her, we had arranged to be married next Easter, which makes me feel it more.*

*I don't know how the asthma is going to treat me here. I have had slight attacks of it already. Would like very much to get a trip over there before I go, to have a look at you all, but I suppose there is no such luck.*

*I hope Jack is not thinking any more of going, as I think that three of us is quite sufficient out of one family and besides you want a man to look after you to keep you away from the cow yard etc. Its ages since I have had any news from home but I only have myself to blame for not writing. Hope the girls are in good health.*

*This is a very different place to Merredin, the place is full of fun and amusements, the YMCA have a splendid building here and they hold concerts every night. It is very hard to take sleeping on the hard boards after being used to a soft bed but it is wonderful how quick one gets used to it. I suppose you have no more particulars re Charl's death, Fred says that he is still being reported missing, if that is the case there might be a chance.*

*Well dear Mother will have to go now so will close. With love and good wishes.*

*From your Affec. son, Jim.*

To Miss Browne
Kalgoorlie
Nov. 17th 1915

*Leaving tonight express return same day. J.H. Carthew. Perth.*
[An 800-mile (1288-kilometre) round trip for a few hours with his 'Girl'.]

To Miss Nellie Browne
58 George Street, Kalgoorlie

Dear Sweetheart,

*Just a few lines on the eve of my departure from the State, it pains me very much Darling at having to leave practically without saying goodbye to the only girl I ever loved. My short stay in Kalgoorlie did not allow me to say what I might otherwise have said, had we had a few nights together.*

*Tonight darling you are the one and only thing that my thoughts are on. My one hope is that you will be the same girl as you are now when I return, and you know to be that you must be good and not to fret because I am away. I forgot to tell Mum to look after you but I know she always does. You are very fortunate to have the parents you have, there are lots that are not nearly so lucky.*

*Well dear, we leave here at 9 a.m. and shall be up at 5 a.m. to catch the Indarra which is the boat we are to go by.*

*We had lots along the journey to say goodbye to last night. I did not know that I knew so many people before. Of coarse we could not get to bed till after Merredin, where there was a mob to see us off.*

*I recieved nine letters today including the bill of damage that I did not do. I am going to get a blank cheque and forward it on to save further trouble. I showed it to some of the boys and of coarse recieved some extensive enquiries as to my conduct when on the Fields.*

*There is some talk of going to Seymour in Victoria to do our trayning.*

*Well my darling I am afraid I must close this last letter from W.A. until I return. Now darling be good and remember that I am always thinking of my one and only little girl, and will look forward to the day of my return, because I know you will be waiting for me.*

*Well Sweetheart this place is closing up so will close with love and kisses from Your loving and effec. boy Jim.*

---

GUNNER JAMES CARTHEW
MELB. COFFEE PALACE. 216 BOURKE ST
5.12.1915

DEAR MOTHER,

*Just a line to say we have arrived safely. We were out at Broadmeadows at first but they shifted us to the Maribyrnong Barracks which is better and a little more handy to town. There are 1400 of Artillery here.*

*Babs met me on the arrival of the boat. She is still the same old hard case as she was, actually tried to drag me to Church last Sunday, but I declined to go. We do not get very much leave in this camp but I expect to get up for a few days at Xmas and am looking forward to seeing you all again. I am bringing a friend up with me, a mate of mine on the other side, so be sure and have roast sucking pig for Xmas dinner. Tell Add and Nell that a cake or two occasionally would be very much appreciated by the inmates of our tent.*

*Well Mother will close with love from your Affec son Jim.*

---

MILITARY CAMP, MARIBYRNONG
20.12.'15

DEAR MOTHER,

*Just a few hurried lines to say I expect to be up on Friday night if nothing unexpected turns up. In all probability I will have the Girl with me, as I got a wire from her last Saturday to say she was leaving Fremantle then, and she is due here Friday next. We get 4 days leave for Xmas but I am trying to get a week if I can manage it.*

*Tell Add I received the tin of cakes safely, which were commented on very favourable, it was quite a birthday party that followed their arrival.*

*Mother you will be able to find room for us all I suppose in the old home, there will be quite a houseful. The Girl does not start school until February, so she will have plenty of time with you.*

*Well Mum it is getting late so I will close with love till I arrive home. From your effect. Jim.*

The Christmas celebrations at Happy Valley were more subdued than on the previous year when Charles had been present. Two days earlier, Fred's letter had arrived telling Margaret that he was back on Gallipoli. It was two months old, and she lived in hourly suffocating fear of receiving another dreadful telegram from the authorities. The papers continued to print their tragic litany of casualties, bringing heartbreak and the death of hope to thousands of wives, mothers and sweethearts, and the hospitals were filled with crippled, blinded and shell-shocked young men. There was little to celebrate that Christmas of 1915.

In spite of this, Margaret and her daughters tried to put aside their grief to welcome home James Holman and his fiancée, Nellie, who had arrived by ship to make the acquaintance of her future in-laws and to spend Christmas with her sweetheart. Margaret wanted very much to like the girl her son had chosen, for he was possibly dearer to her than any of her other children. He had been a delicate child, suffering acute asthma and eczema almost from birth, which necessitated spending long periods of time in the Melbourne Children's Hospital. Often, as an outpatient, he had stayed at a nearby hotel, and the proprietor was so taken with the engaging child he repeatedly tried to adopt him.

Being rather shy and reserved, Nellie was very anxious to make a good impression on her future in-laws, but she need not have worried. Margaret was quite won over by the girl's quiet, unassuming charm, James's sisters also approved wholeheartedly, and soon Nellie felt very much at home. James clearly worshipped her, and it was obvious that she was deeply in love with him. Margaret thankfully felt sure that her son would be in safe hands.

On Christmas Day, twelve people sat down at the long kitchen table for dinner. Apart from Margaret and the girls there was Jack and his fiancée, the cowman Dave, Nellie and James, and James's friend from Western Australia, jovial Billy Lewis. When Jack stood at the head of the table to say grace, it must have seemed to Margaret that the past terrible months had all been a bad dream and that her beloved son Charl was speaking the familiar words, as he had on Christmas Day just one year before.

James's seven-day leave passed all too soon and it was time to leave Happy Valley for a four-week intensive training course at the artillery school, prior to embarkation for France.

METHODIST SOLDIERS' INSTITUTE, MARIBYRNONG
25.1.1916

DEAR ADD

*Just a hurried line to say that we are going on board on Thursday morning acting as advance guard so will probably see you down there. Goodbye for the present. Yours Etc. Jim.*

DEAR ADD,

*Am sorry there is no possible chance of getting up to see you as none of us are allowed off the ship. I have just been refused permission to go up. You will probably be allowed to come down to the ship's side tomorrow before we go. Am greatly disappointed at not seeing you So will say goodbye and good luck.*

*Yours Jim.*

DEAR ADD,

*I have no chance of getting off tonight. I have been onto the officer ever since but can get no satisfaction.*

*Thanks very much for fruit and cakes. It would not be much use you coming in tomorrow as I would hardly be able to see you. Well goodbye Add for the last time till I return, when I hope to see you all again.*

*Goodbye. Jim.*

James Carthew's passage to Egypt on the transport ship *Themistocles* was far less comfortable than the voyages of his brothers Charles and Fred. Packed like sardines in the stuffy cabins and saloons, he and his mates spent most of their daylight hours on deck, and at night all lights were extinguished. Enemy raiders and submarines were becoming far more active in the Indian Ocean as Germany tightened its blockade, desperate to prevent troops and vital supplies of armaments, fuel and foodstuffs from reaching Britain, France and Egypt. During the latter part of 1915, a number of vessels had been sunk and the *Themistocles* travelled in a convoy for safety, which slowed the journey considerably.

James's shipmates were a motley crew, from every walk of life. Some, like himself, had previously been rejected for health problems, and others were returning to Egypt having been wounded but now certified as fit for cannon fodder once more.

To James's acute disappointment there was only a brief stay in Fremantle to take on fresh stores, and no leave was granted. On previous occasions there had been a few desertions by men who had had second thoughts, while others, happily drunk, had arrived at the wharf in time to see their transport nearing Rottnest Island. This time the authorities were taking no chances and James was forced to kick his heels on deck, watching the lumpers load coal and stores, knowing that a scant 12 miles away his beloved was staying at the YWCA.

---

MEDITERRANEAN EXPEDITIONARY FORCE
No. 12277 COY. 14TH REINFORCEMENT F. ARTILLERY
EGYPT
3RD MARCH, 1916

DEAR MOTHER,

*Just a line to say I arrived here safely. We are camped a mile from Heliopolis about 7 miles from Cairo. I have saw nothing from Fred yet, the day we landed here the L.H. left for the Canal zone where a tremendous number of troops are camped. My friend's brother is second in Command of the 10th. L.H., a Capt. Kidd. We left the ship at Sewz and came by rail to Cairo. It is a wonderful sight along the Canal which the rail follows all the way, the journey took 12 hrs and there is almost one continual line of camps the whole way, they are expecting an attack by the Turks very soon and are making every preparation.*

*The Egyptian Government allow us equal to eightpence halfpenny in piastas each day to buy extra rashions, and I can tell you it is very exceptible, we live like kings compared with Aust. Dicipline is very severe, over here compared with the free and easy life we had over there, no staying an extra two days, and if one is absent from a parade it is 21 days C.B. [confined to barracks]. I was in Cairo once it is a wonderful place, purely a soldier's capital but the Egyptians run all the business and seem to be very shrewd, and will take you*

*down at every opportunity. They have an unlimited supply of oranges
which are the best I have ever tasted, they sell 4 for one piasta which
equals two pence ha'penny. Well Mother I will close with love and
kind regards to you all.*

*From your Affec. son Jim.*

21.3.'16

DEAR EMM,

*Just a line to say I am well. We have been in Egypt 3 weeks and
are leaving tonight for an unknown destination. Thornie has been
left behind and he is a very sore man, all our friends have been
separated.* [The British Generals pursued a policy of separating
friends and discouraging mateship, which they maintained was
bad for discipline.] *This place is just one big camp and everyone
seems to be doing their bit, the Indians and all, they are the finest
sample of men I have ever saw. I have saw nothing of Fred since our
arrival and will not see him at all now. Will write later.*

*Goodbye and love, Jim.*

# → Learning to Survive ←

*I*N EUROPE, MATTERS had reached a stalemate as early as the end of 1914, resulting in little activity on the Western Front for much of 1915. On Christmas Day 1914, the two armies in France had actually agreed to an armistice and, for an hour or two, friend and foe mingled freely in no-man's-land, cordially shaking hands and laughing as they tried to communicate, exchanging small gifts from their Christmas billies—packets of cigarettes, chocolate, bully beef, religious medallions and even uniform buttons—and exhibiting family photographs with mutual pride. Carols were sung with great gusto and bonhomie, along with 'Tipperary', 'Deutschland Über Alles' and, finally, 'Auld Lang Syne', before the whistles were blown and British and Germans returned reluctantly to their respective trenches. Then, on the stroke of midnight, the great guns opened fire with redoubled ferocity as if the strange interlude had never occurred.

A year later, following twelve months of unprecedentedly savage fighting, the gloves were off; all pretence of chivalry had vanished and camaraderie was dead. In June, British nurse Edith Cavell had been arrested by the Germans and accused of aiding British prisoners of war to escape. Found guilty, the courageous woman was brutally executed by a firing squad. And then, on Christmas Day 1915, a British private tied a white cloth to his rifle and climbed confidently from his trench. Shockingly, as he stood on the parapet joyously waving his flag, two shots rang out simultaneously and the soldier fell back into the trench—with both a German and a British bullet in his heart.

It was into this atmosphere of tension and all-out warfare that James Carthew was plunged, at the end of March 1916. The Anzac troops had been reorganised into two corps: I Anzac Corps, comprising the 1st and 2nd Australian divisions and the New Zealand divisions under the command of General Birdwood, and II Anzac Corps, comprising the 4th and 5th Australian divisions under the command of General Godley. I Anzac Corps (which included James's 2nd Field Artillery Battery, a sub-unit of the 1st Division) joined Kitchener's New Army in France, under General Sir Douglas Haig, and was deployed near Armentières in the northern sector of the Western Front, which stretched from the English Channel to Switzerland.

---

FRANCE
28.3.'16

DEAR ADD,

*Just a line to say I am well. We have not entered the firing line up to date, but expect to at any time as we are billeted only a short distance away from the guns. I think this is the finest country I have ever seen, even better than our native land, everything is lovely and green. There are plenty of aeroplanes to be seen, one can look up almost any time and see them patrolling over our lines keeping the enemy planes off as far as possible, but they get over sometimes by flying very high, then our aircraft guns open fire on it, and we can see the shells bursting around it. All the troops over here take possession of the farm sheds for billeting, and they are much more convenient than being camped in tents, and one never feels lonely owing to most of the barns being stocked with vermin.*

*I have only recieved one letter since I left home, I don't know where they have gone. We were inspected by General Haig a week or two ago and tomorrow we are to be inspected by General Birdwood, who is in command of Australian forces.*

*The front looks like a fireworks at night when there is a bombardment on, they shoot up star shells, and when they burst they light up the place like electric light.*

*Well Add, I will close now with love,*

*Yours etc. Jim.*

24.5.'16

DEAR ADD,

*Well our battery is in action at last. I am about half a mile from the German trenches in a dugout in the front line doing guard duty on the ammunition wagons for the night. All the farm houses around here are almost blown to pieces with shells, nearly every farmhouse is used for billeting troops and if the German aeroplanes see troops around a place it is certain to be shelled. The one we were camped in was shelled and the troops had to go for their life.*

*The civilians go about their work as if there was no war on at all, the women, children and old men are living on their farms right up to the first line of trenches, and they take no more notice of a shell bursting than if it was a penny cracker.*

*France is a lovely country but they are very much behind Australia as far as up to date farming goes, but the farms are so small it would not pay them to go in for expensive machinery like we do. There is one thing very funny, and that is a wooden wheel about eight feet in diameter and is fitted by a bar attached to the churn inside the house. When they want to make butter they put a dog on the inside of the wheel and start it going around — the old dog has to run for his life to keep on the bottom of the wheel, and thereby keeps the wheel going round — every farm has its dog wheel.*

*Our guns brought down a german taube yesterday, he flew right over our camp about five a.m. and we were all woke up by the guns firing at him, he was brought down some distance away.*

*Well Add, hoping to hear from you soon, I will close with love to all. I hope Mother is well.*

*From your effec. brother Jim.*

For the next few weeks, James's Field Artillery Battery was engaged in routine shelling of the enemy lines as a diversionary ploy while rumours of a coming 'Big Push' circulated. Haig had planned a concerted attack on the Germans in the Somme Valley, with the French playing the leading part, but a strong enemy offensive diverted the French forces to Verdun, a vital point in the Front only 130 miles (209 kilometres) from Paris. Forced to find another solution, the General decided to use the British Expeditionary Force instead.

The 'Big Push' began at the end of June with a seven-day bombardment of the enemy lines. This was standard practice and was designed to pulverise the enemy fortifications, barbed-wire barricades and trenches. (Unfortunately it also gave the enemy fair warning, enabling them to prudently vacate their forward lines for the duration of the attack, and because the German trenches were very deep and well fortified, casualties were light.) So intense was the shelling, with the guns roaring continuously along the 16-mile (26-kilometre) Front, that the ominous thunder was heard as far away as London. In the Somme Valley, the ground shuddered and shook incessantly, making it impossible to keep one's feet at times, and the gunners wore wax earplugs to prevent their eardrums from bursting.

As soon as the barrage ceased, at 7.30 am on 1 July, the Germans returned to their forward positions and retaliated, shelling the tens of thousands of British Expeditionary Force volunteers who massed in the trenches as they prepared to go 'over the top'. As usual, prior to a major action, there had been a church service, and the men were given a good breakfast and a tot of rum, no doubt to furnish a little Dutch courage.

Haig had issued a directive, assuring the 60 000 British infantry that they would be well covered by artillery fire, ordering them to walk in an orderly line and at 'a steady pace' across the 150 to 250 yards (137 to 229 metres) of no-man's-land to the enemy barricades.

In fact, it would have been quite impossible for them to go any faster than at 'a steady pace', burdened as they were with rifle and bayonet, 200 rounds of ammunition, Mills bombs or grenades, pistols and flares, and a pack weighing an incredibly heavy 60 lbs (27 kilograms) or more, containing gas mask, water canteen and rations for two days, plus entrenching tool or spade and hessian sacks. Unbelievably, some were even further handicapped by rolls of barbed wire or pigeon cages (pigeons were carried in order to send messages back to HQ). Machine-gunners carried heavy Lewis guns, weighing over 88 lbs (40 kilograms), or heavy tripods and boxes of ammunition, and were festooned with bandoliers and mills bombs. On the other hand, the officers, in their best uniforms and highly polished boots, in most cases carried only revolvers. Some even wielded swords!

As the infantry advanced and the initial smokescreen cleared, they were mown down in their thousands by the German Maxim machine guns firing 600 rounds per minute. With a range of more than a mile, it would have been impossible for these guns to miss any target. Nevertheless, the heroic lines never faltered, even though very few ever reached the German lines. As each row of men was decimated, their places were instantly taken by new waves, only to succumb to the murderous fire. Some continued to advance doggedly, unaware that they had lost an arm, that half their faces were shot away, or that they had sustained a gaping abdominal wound, trailing loops of bloody intestines like grotesque streamers. Others stumbled around, sightless or stunned and disoriented, not knowing which way to go, until they too were cut down by machine-gun fire.

To add to Haig's errors of judgement, he had assured his troops that the five massive barbed-wire barricades guarding the German lines would be totally destroyed, affording easy access to the enemy trenches. However, due to gross inefficiency, miscalculation and bungled orders, as well as a large number of dud shells that failed to explode, vast stretches remained intact. The few men who managed to reach the barricades were trapped and massacred as they tried desperately to sever the wire with wire cutters, and any gaps along the 16-mile (26-kilometre) barricade quickly became choked with piles of dead bodies. Desperate to gain ascendancy, Haig flung a further ten British divisions, comprising 40 000 men, into the fray resulting in further horrendous losses.

The endless day wore on. The sun blazed down mercilessly, searing the pale skin of the wounded, and clouds of voracious blue-black flies, spawned in the overflowing latrines, descended to feast on the fresh blood and to deposit their maggots in the wounds of the dead and injured. The wounded were unable to drive the flies away, or to crawl back to their own lines, fearful of the machine-gun fire that periodically raked anything that moved.

At long last darkness descended and the guns mercifully fell silent, one by one, but along the endless stretches of no-man's-land could be heard an indescribable sound, bone-chilling in its horror: the sound of tens of thousands of parched throats crying out in agony; of men screaming hoarsely as, with shattered or severed limbs, they attempted to drag themselves out of shell holes or from under corpses in a last supreme effort to return to their lines and to safety. Thousands cried out for water, unable to move, while others attempted to drag their useless limbs back to the trenches. Some called on God, others called faintly for help, or pitifully for their mothers, a stretcher or a priest. Many prayed or sang hymns, cursed or sobbed aloud, and others babbled deliriously and monotonously, on and on. The very earth seemed to cry out in hopeless anguish.

The stretcher-bearers and first-aid orderlies, appalled at the hopeless task before them, stumbled around with hurricane lanterns and torches, trying to avoid stepping on the wounded and the corpses as they attended to the most serious cases, but the sheer volume of dead and dying defeated them almost before they began. Chaplains moved among the heaps of bodies, trying to comfort the dying, administering extreme unction and giving sips of water where they could.

So overwhelmed were the dressing stations with casualties, they were only able to deal with a tiny fraction of those likely to live. It was a slaughterhouse, a scene straight from hell, where, under acetylene lamps and hurricane lanterns, limbs with quite trivial wounds were roughly amputated. It was quicker to do so than deal with splintered bone and gas gangrene or tetanus infections from deep-bullet trauma. The exhausted doctors worked like automatons—cutting, sawing and stitching, their gowns turning from white to crimson and then to an ugly reddish brown as they were repeatedly drenched, striving desperately to stem the arterial blood which sprayed and spurted from innumerable wounds. The severed limbs were thrown on the ground to be carted away by orderlies to a growing mountain of spare parts at the rear of the field, or into a handy shell hole. Hundreds who might have been saved died from loss of blood as they waited for attention, and hundreds more died of shock from the crude surgery.

By daybreak the following morning, 19 000 men (some estimate 21 000), the flower of Britain, lay slaughtered on the field. The tragic reckoning for that one terrible July day was a staggering 57 470 dead and injured, for the gain of not one single foot of territory! When the casualty lists were published, the entire British nation went into mourning for the catastrophic loss of their finest and best young men. Even the enemy, who suffered considerably fewer casualties, called this battle 'The Bath of Blood'. It must surely rank as one of the most tragic, bloody and criminally pointless battles in British history; cold-blooded murder on a scale so enormous it seems impossible to encompass. In its wake came rumours that at least two high-ranking British officers had committed suicide, although the ultimate responsibility for its orchestration certainly rested with General Sir Douglas Haig, a man later dubbed the 'Butcher of the Somme'.

The campaign had been doomed to failure from the outset because the Germans had occupied their position for nearly a year, giving them ample time to build deep and impregnable fortifications and sophisticated communication networks, unlike Haig's troops who, recently arrived, had had no time to become established. Although the artillery had performed well, the battle was also lost because they were equipped mainly with 18- and 19-pounders, which could not breach the enemy's well-fortified trenches, and too few of the more powerful 15-inch howitzers. (These terrible weapons, which spewed out wholesale death, often claimed the lives of their own gunners by rupturing and bursting their lungs and eardrums.)

Following the opening offensive by British troops, the 5th Australian and 61st British divisions were ordered to march to Fromelles, to make a feint attack in support of the continuing Somme offensive. Following fierce fighting, lasting throughout the night of 19 July, thousands of wounded again lay out in no-man's-land, beyond the front lines, crying out and writhing in agony. Chaplain Maxted moved among the men giving what aid he could, until he was killed, and the Reverend J.J. Kennedy, of Myrtleford, also worked courageously, giving comfort to the dying while the enemy artillery crashed onto the Anzac lines.

By midday of 20 July there was an eerie lull by both exhausted armies, and at the sight of so many men lying helpless and in pain, tortured by swarms of midsummer flies, many others ventured forth to rescue them. Dodging from shell hole to shell hole, Private Miles of

Victoria was hailed by a compassionate Bavarian officer, who told him to go back to his lines and bring back an officer to parley (the Bavarians were far less ruthless than the Prussians). Major Murdoch returned with Miles and, watched by hundreds of soldiers lining the parapets on both sides, asked if a truce could be arranged. The German Command agreed that the Anzac stretcher-bearers could collect the wounded from their section of no-man's-land but the offer was refused by British GHQ, who issued an order that no negotiations of any kind were to be entered into with the enemy. However, in the true Anzac spirit of mateship, single men and parties ventured out to bring in the wounded, and on one single night more than 300 men were rescued, brought in on the backs of their mates. (This action recently inspired a sculpture which has been erected on the battlefield of Fromelles, depicting an Anzac Digger carrying a wounded mate on his back.) The battle had ended in disaster, resulting in the loss of many lives, including those of 5533 Australians. So heavy were the casualties, it would be some time before the 5th Australian Division was ready for battle again.

Through witnessing such carnage, James and his mates quickly learned the lessons of survival—their lives depended upon it. In fact, statistics showed that experienced troops lasted approximately six times as long as new recruits. It was, literally, a case of the quick or the dead.

They learned that the most intensive German shelling was aimed at the rear of the field, in order to destroy the guns, ammunition dumps and stores necessary to sustain an army. It was also where the artillery trenches were situated. These huge shells each wrought untold damage. Even miles from an explosion, showers of earth fell from the roof and walls of the trenches, causing candles to glitter and die, while a direct hit could obliterate several trenches full of men, leaving only fragments of flesh and splintered bone. Even distant shells could cause death and serious injury from flying debris and shrapnel. Infection and death usually followed from the gas gangrene and tetanus spores inhabiting the horse manure with which the battlefield was covered. These organisms were almost impossible to eliminate unless soiled instruments were boiled for at least twenty minutes, which was rarely possible at the overcrowded dressing stations.

The constant shelling inevitably wore down the men's nerves, and some were driven insane, unable to tolerate the incessant tension. Others would escape into a cataleptic trance, eyes fixed and staring in a chalky face, unable to move; or shrieking unintelligible, animal sounds, unresponsive to voices. After a time, even the most experienced became jumpy, hands trembling uncontrollably, afraid to sleep lest they never awoke. Most were superstitious and refused to play card games, fearing to be dealt the ace of spades—the death card.

They learned to keep their heads down at all times; to instinctively throw themselves to the ground an instant before their brains registered a shell blast; to take refuge in a crater or dugout, following a gas attack, but only if they wore a gas mask. (The gas, being heavier than air, lingered for some time in hollows.) They learned to identify weapons and missiles: the murderous dumdum bullets, used by both sides though forbidden by the Geneva Convention, which caused horrific injuries; the .303s with which they were issued; daisy cutters—shells of smaller calibre than the 18-pound ones, but which caused far more casualties, splintering and disseminating death in a wide arc upon impact. They soon learned to recognise the shell sounds: the whistle of the daisy cutter, the thunderous roar and scream of the howitzers and coal boxes, the clatter of a machine gun, the hiss and whine of the smaller-calibre shells. Trench mortars created huge craters and often blew the clothes completely off their victims.

Grenades could be primed to burst above ground, causing maximum injury, and could be hurled for 65 yards (59 metres). The men learned to be wary of the ready-primed grenades left by retreating enemy troops. A bombardment diverted from the front trenches to the rear usually meant that an infantry attack was imminent, and they learned to hold their fire until the enemy was within 54 yards (49 metres). Above all, they listened for the soft thud of a gas shell and the rattle of a gas alarm.

They found that although most of the young officers were relatively inexperienced, they could usually rely upon the judgment of the non-commissioned officers, particularly the Sergeants, some of whom had seen action in Gallipoli and the Boer War. Although there were still some British officers attached to Anzac units in 1916, they soon found that the Diggers could not be treated like their highly disciplined and more subservient Tommy counterparts and that they had litttle respect for authority, unless it was based on knowledge and experience.

Despite so much death and fear, spirits were still high as the Anzacs travelled to and from the Front, through fields of golden wheat and barley, bordered with red poppies and blue cornflowers, singing 'Pack up your troubles', 'There's a long, long trail awinding' and 'Armentières' along roads clogged by civilians fleeing their devastated farms and villages. Some drove dilapidated carts, drawn by bony nags or mules too ancient to be requisitioned by the army, overflowing with household goods—chairs, tables, feather mattresses, pots, pans, crockery and chamber pots, surmounted by young children clutching a cat or a birdcage. Usually there was a cow or a goat tethered to the tailboard to be milked at intervals, with a dog plodding along behind. Others wheeled handcarts, wheelbarrows or perambulators piled high with their pathetic belongings, and dragged tired, whining children. For the main, the refugees ignored the soldiers, a look of indifference and silent resignation on each face. The 'Boche' or the 'Anglais' had driven them from their homes, as they had done in the past and doubtless would do again, and when it was all over they would return to their ruined farms and villages and start afresh.

Occasionally a German Taube would fly low, machine-gunning the troops and the civilians with equal impartiality. When the plane had departed, the French would climb out of the drainage channels where they had taken refuge, collect their dead and wounded and continue on their way. James never ceased to marvel at their dull acceptance of the war that ravished their beautiful country, nor the spirit that inspired them to rebuild their shattered lives when they had lost everything, even their relatives and friends. But then, he supposed, there was little alternative.

# ✦ Baptism by Fire ✦

*F*OLLOWING THE DISASTROUS opening battles of the Somme Offensive, Haig decided to send in the 1st Australian Division to spearhead a fresh assault at a place called Pozières, a tiny village comprising a church, a cluster of cottages, an inn and a windmill, situated on rising ground in the otherwise flat Somme Valley. It was held by the Germans, who regarded their position as virtually unassailable. On no less than four occasions the British had attacked the enemy at Pozières and had been repulsed. Haig was convinced that the heavily fortified ridge known as Hill 160 held the key to ultimate domination of the Somme.

Haig abhorred the 'colonials', as he slightingly referred to them, claiming that they were insolent, arrogant and undisciplined, which was probably true. He also resented the fact that, unlike Canada and New Zealand, the Australian War Office had insisted on appointing most of their own officers. This was a wise decision on Australia's part, because the Australians troops would certainly not have tolerated officers chosen under the British system which, in the early years of the war, awarded rank almost exclusively through family influence to the sons of gentlemen, or those with a public school background, regardless of ability or experience. Most of the men whom these officers commanded had been in the trenches for months or even years and knew far more about trench warfare than the officers were ever likely to.

However, recognising the Australians' initiative and daring, Haig was quick to assign them to the worst and most difficult, even hopeless, areas of conflict throughout the war, and frequently used them as a vanguard to sever the barbed-wire entanglements before the British went into action. To do Haig justice, his was not an easy task. He was under constant pressure from the French to deploy his armies and attack the enemy in areas that guaranteed enormous casualties in order to relieve pressure on the French troops. It must have been irresistibly tempting for Haig to employ the high-spirited, courageous young Anzacs in the most dangerous areas, instead of his battle-weary British units.

For two days, the Australian artillery blasted Hill 160 to cut the maze of barbed-wire entanglements and to destroy the 5-feet (1.5-metre) thick fortifications. Then, the moment the guns ceased, just after midnight on 23 July, the troops leaped from their trenches and charged, advancing swiftly to take Pozières and killing and capturing Germans as they went. This was the only advance made on the entire Front at that time.

The Germans, determined to regain Pozières, were quick to counterattack with a furious bombardment which rained ceaselessly down on the Australians for three days. So concentrated was the shelling that the ominous thunder was heard clearly in the southern counties of England.

Now began for the Anzacs their true baptism by fire, a holocaust the like of which had never before been seen on a battlefield, and has perhaps never been witnessed since. One veteran was later to remark that Gallipoli had been a pleasant Sunday School picnic compared to the fiery bloodbath of Pozières.

To James and his mates, it seemed impossible that any human being could survive the avalanche of death that spewed out incessantly from the great German howitzers, and the dense fusillade of machine-gun fire that never ceased for an instant, day or night. It was as though the entire earth rocked and swayed on its axis, lifting and shuddering in a crazy, cataclysmic nightmare of swirling dust and smoke, blinding explosions, deadly flying debris and ear-shattering concussion. To add to the danger and confusion, the poor demented horses harnessed to the gun carriages reared and screamed in terror, lashing out with their massive hooves as the gunners struggled to manoeuvre the 18-pounders between the shell holes.

*Load, fire, recoil!* Day and night the gunners laboured to feed the gun's insatiable maw. Like automatons they worked, sometimes asleep on their feet, deafened by the bombardment, half blinded by the dust, smoke and incessant explosions, eating at their posts when there was anything to eat or drink. Sometimes an entire gun crew suffered a direct hit and men, horses and gun vanished instantly into a yawning, smoking crater.

Relief came only when there were reinforcements to spare, and many of these newly-arrived recruits were worse than useless, so petrified were they with fear. Demoralised out of their wits, many of the young soldiers trapped in this terrifying inferno often broke down, weeping hopelessly and infecting others with their blind panic. Some even bolted mindlessly across no-man's-land, frothing at the mouth and shrieking insanely, until they were gunned down by the enemy or their own officers. Others were so terrified that they refused to leave the trenches, paralysed with fear, eyes staring unfocused in blanched faces. Some cried uncontrollably, others vomited or wet and soiled their trousers.

Soon the battlefield resembled a vast graveyard, the surface pitted with shell craters and littered with broken weaponry and the bloated dead, decaying in the warm midsummer heat and stinking abominably. Tattered clothing, newspapers, documents and pathetic letters and photographs blew about in no-man's-land.

The wounded were sent to the first-aid stations at the rear of the trenches, where they were frequently shelled, and only the very serious cases were relayed to the base hospitals. The stretcher-bearers, many of whom were conscientious objectors, daily risked their lives, and many died heroically trying to save the wounded. (One Australian stretcher-bearer, Private E.A. Corey, was awarded the Military Medal with three bars, believed to be the only such award made.)

Even at the dressing stations the casualties lay in the sun or rain for hours, even days, waiting for attention, which, all too often, came too late. There was little to ease their pain, except for aspirin and morphine and its derivatives, and their wounds were always flyblown by the time they were treated, although this was thought to help fight infection, because the maggots consumed the pus. Dysentery also killed thousands.

At first, the dead bodies were transported to the rear of the field for burial, with the chaplain reading the service and the traditional shot being fired over the grave, but as the death toll rose higher and higher, the bodies were flung into a shell hole, layer upon layer. 'Missing believed dead' would be their bleak obituary, of little comfort to their grieving relatives who would never know the small consolation of mourning at their graves.

*Load, fire, recoil!* There was no time to wonder, as each shell shrieked overhead, where it would land. One quickly became fatalistic. Now, you no longer ducked and held your breath; whatever would be would be, and there was absolutely nothing you could do about it, except, perhaps, pray. You saw a horse, a few feet away, disembowelled by shrapnel. You watched as innumerable lengths of glistening pink entrails fell from the gaping wound, even as the poor beast reared and screamed, madly trying to escape its harness, before someone shot it through the head. You smelt the indescribably foul stench of its burst gut. You witnessed a man running a few steps on the stumps of his legs, unaware that both limbs had been blasted away. You saw the officer who had checked your gun elevation just minutes before, still standing with his head blown off, the artery in his neck pumping out a fountain of scarlet spray like a geyser, drenching his uniform even before he fell.

If you didn't cop it today, there was always tomorrow. Sooner or later there would be a shell, or a bullet, or a grenade, with your name on it, and then it would all be over.

The dead, scantily covered with soil, were frequently resurrected a few days later by a second shell. They lay grinning hideously, seething with great, fat maggots and mantled with shining, blue-black blowflies, smelling atrociously in the midsummer heat. The surrounding area and the barbed-wire barricades would be festooned with hundreds of grisly body parts—arms, legs, heads, torsos and yard upon yard of intestines, shrivelled and burned black in the merciless sun. The stench of decay was perpetually in one's nostrils, and the taste of death never departed; but terror was the overriding, overwhelming sense that blotted everything else out.

*Load, fire, recoil!* Incredibly, wild geese flew in a straight line over that terrible, blasted landscape, never deviating from their course, and larks still sang through the shot and shell as they soared into the blue skies and swooped to feast on the worms that proliferated among the corpses—1916 was a very good year for bird life, and for the bloated rodents that bred in their myriads in no-man's-land.

After a time, James became numbed, inured to the mutilation and death of his fellow man, but he never failed to be moved to anger and sadness by the suffering of a dumb creature. He had always loved animals and it grieved him to see the great, gentle Clydesdales maimed and in agony, and in spite of shocking injuries gallantly struggling to carry on. When it was necessary to put one out of its misery, he would stroke its nose and ears whenever possible, whispering words of encouragement to let the horse know that he was loved, and not alone.

By the end of the second week at Pozières, the Anzacs (by now the 2nd Australian Division had replaced the 1st) had pushed the Germans back even further. The loss of the ridge was a crushing defeat for the enemy, and the Prussian General von Bulow was so incensed he threatened his officers with court martial should they fail to retake the plateau. In a desperate bid to succeed, the great howitzers lobbed more than four shells per minute on the south side of the old Roman road where the Anzacs were dug in. The huge shells wrought untold devastation, day after horrific day, ploughing craters 20 to 30 feet (6 to 9 metres) deep and collapsing earthworks onto thousands of men, burying them alive. Their mates worked frantically to disinter them, using their bare hands or buckets lest they decapitate the victims with their spades, but most were beyond help, suffocated by the heavy loam, and the murderous shelling went on and on, destroying section after section of the maze of dugouts. Most bodies were never recovered, the rescuers unable even to locate where the trenches had been. The death toll was so high—10 000 in all—that the road became known as 'Dead Man's Road'.

James Carthew neither saw nor heard the shell that entombed him in his dugout as he slept, exhausted, along with the rest of his detail. Only just in time he was exhumed, barely alive and suffering from the effects of inhalation pneumonia.

No. 1 Couve Depot. France.
8.8.16

DEAR MOTHER,

*Just a line to say that I am here recovering from the effects of being buried by a shell some three weeks ago. We had a hard time but suppose you have saw by the papers that we kept up our reputation, I am just about feeling myself again and before this reaches you I expect to be back in the firing line. We are getting treated tip top here, plenty of good food and amusements.*

*From here we can see the celebrated white cliffs but suppose that is all I will see of them for the present. I have not had any mail for sometime suppose it will all go astray again, now that I am away from my unit. In this camp I think every unit in the empire is represented. One has a job to tell one from the other.*

*Well Mother we are not allowed to write letters here so you will have to excuse this. Goodbye for the present.*

*Yours Etc. Jim.*

The dislike and distrust the Anzacs had begun to entertain for their British cousins soon turned to contempt during the Pozières Campaign. They found that they could not rely on the British conscripts (who often needed to be led from the rear by the hated military police at the point of a revolver) to give them the support they needed, and they had not forgotten that, despite having travelled 12 000 miles (20 000 kilometres) at considerable sacrifice and cost in response to the mother country's call for aid, the British had charged the Australian Government for all hospitals, camping and training facilities they used.

Furthermore, they regarded Haig and his subordinate, General Gough, as callous murderers, who had orchestrated the needless slaughter at Pozières of 10 000 Australian volunteers, recording the criminal expenditure of human life as 'justifiable wastage'. And as usual, Haig, in his triumphant communiqués to the newspapers, had ascribed the significant victory at Pozières to 'British troops'. (Technically he was correct, because at that time Australians still held British nationality. However, it was clear that he did not wish the 'colonials' to be credited with the many advances and victories to which they were entitled, and the correspondents were forbidden to do so.)

When, eventually, the Anzacs were relieved by Canadian units, observers recorded that 'they strode off, proudly erect, in full view and contemptuous of the German guns, as though they were strolling down Pitt Street. Unlike the British conscripts, who scurried, crouching, from the field.' The Anzacs went with a laugh on their lips and death in their hearts, mourning the 10 000 mates they had left behind forever in the ruins of Pozières.

Gallipoli is a familiar name to every Australian and New Zealander, a name redolent of tragedy and romance; a glorious defeat that inspires enormous national pride in the heroism, gallantry and deathless courage of our young Anzac manhood. In stark contrast, the battle for Pozières, a village in the Somme Valley, is virtually unknown, although there were more men killed in one horrendous week at Pozières than in the entire Gallipoli campaign of eight months. The reason is perhaps not hard to find. Unlike the veterans of Gallipoli, few survivors of the nightmare Somme Offensive ever spoke of their experiences, preferring to blot from their minds such memories as being too agonisingly painful and traumatic to recall—except, perhaps, in their dreams. And yet, as Charles Bean wrote, those few acres of soil are more densely sown with Anzac flesh and bone, more profusely saturated with their lifeblood, than any other spot on earth. (The battlefield has in fact been purchased by the Australian Government and is now officially Australian territory.)

It would be impossible to describe the depths of misery suffered by those men in that hell on earth. No mere words could describe their courage, borne with dignity and humour, the quiet heroism shown day after day in the face of appalling danger and privation. Nor would it be possible to portray the close mateship born of that peril; a new dimension of love that bonded men far closer than brothers.

## IN FLANDERS FIELDS

In Flanders fields the poppies blow
Between the crosses, row on row,
That mark our place; and in the sky
The larks, still bravely singing, fly
Scarce heard amid the guns below.

We are the Dead. Short days ago
We lived, felt dawn, saw sunset glow,
Loved and were loved, and now we lie
In Flanders fields.

Take up our quarrel with the foe:
To you from failing hands we throw
The torch; be yours to hold it high.
If ye break faith with us who die
We shall not sleep, though poppies grow
In Flanders fields.

JOHN McCRAE

# ⇥ Hell on Earth ⇤

AFTER JAMES WAS DISCHARGED from hospital he was sent to a gunnery school near Paris to complete his convalescence. He was then drafted back to the 2nd Field Artillery Battery and posted to the Somme, in the vicinity of Flers.

---

FRANCE
5.9.'16

DEAR ADD,

Am very pleased to say that two of your letters arrived yesterday but did not get Nell's which you said she was writing. I got quite a lot of letters and a parcel or two to make up for lost time, and it was like getting money from home to hear a little news from different parts. Was sorry to hear that Mother was suffering from rheumatics it must be on account of the wet weather; there are a lot of men over here suffering from the same complaint.

I was very glad to hear that I had risen to some extent in the eyes of J. Mac. dont know that I altogether warrant the attention. Well Add have not time to write more this time so will close with love and best wishes to you all.

From your effec Bro Jim.

---

1ST AUST. DIV. BASE DEPOT. FRANCE
17.9.16.

DEAR ADD,

Just a line in answer to yours of June 22nd which reached me a few days ago. It is wonderful where these letters get for such a time,

by the way my letters seem to take just as long to reach home. Well it
is Sunday and I am writing this instead of going to church, so you
see I am not improving in my religious beliefs. I think if a man could
do without it up at the front which he had to do, he should be able to
manage down here, where we are miles away from the front. It is
turning very cold over this way, winter seems to be setting in early as
it should not start till about November. I think there will be some
sickness among our chaps if they are here for the winter. We are
camped right on the sea coast here, and only a few miles from one of
Paris' seaside resorts, it is not very big but very nice, it is connected by
electric tram with the railway that runs through our camp the main
line from Paris, there is something like three hundred trains a day
pass our camp over this line so you can guess what traffic there is. It
is wonderful the progress that has been made since this war started,
almost half of France seems to be made up of hospitals, every
available building having been converted.

The roads are all occupied by motor transports and ambulances,
behind the front I have saw miles of these big motor transports one
behind the other.

Where we were on the Somme was the busyiest place I seen up to
date and was the hottest place I ever want to see. I would like you to
have a look at that battle field after the war, one could never imagine
what it is like unless he was there.

I had a few souvenirs in the form of a german helmet with a spike
and a big brass double eagle, these helmets are made of patient [sic]
leather and look rather gaudy but a bit of shrapnel soon takes the
polish off them. I also had a german rifle which I was going to take
home to do a little sporting as I used to do, but when I came away to
hospital I had to leave them behind, there was plenty of souvenirs of
different kinds laying about but one had more important things to
think about in such a place. 'Add' I have always forgotten to ask you
if Mother is recieving my allotment all right, you have never
mentioned it up to date so I have been wondering. [Margaret saved
all James's allotment for her son's return.]

It was a pity that Jack left it so late to think about the crop, as
I suppose next year we will have to buy chaff, and the ground is

*practically idle. How is Mother keeping hope she is well and got rid of
her rheumatics now that the winter is over. I wish our winter was
over instead of just starting. Well Add this is all this time so will close
with love to all.*

*From your effec. brother Jim.*

---

FRANCE
27.10.'16

MY DEAR MOTHER,

*As this is the Xmas mail I am writing this to you to wish you a
bright and merry Xmas and a happy New Year. There seems to be
little hope of the war being over by this Xmas but I hope that long
before next one arrives we will all be back again in sunny Australia.
Am sending a card to the girls by this mail, also a small parcel to
you, which I hope arrives safely. I am sorry I carnt send you all
something, but I think you understand how we are placed in the
matter of finances, and do not expect too much. I am still in the base
camp but do not expect to be here very much longer so I will probably
spend my Xmas at the front.*

*I am writing this in a YMCA and they are in the midst of
evening service but I am playing a neutral part. We were inspected
at the gun school by the King of Belgium, of coarse we all felt a
little embarrest in the presence of royalty, he is a fine big man and
looks every inch a soldier.*

*Well Mother this is all and I will close wishing you a Merry Xmas.
Your Effec. son Jim.*

There was little prospect of the merry Christmas that her son had
wished Margaret Carthew. If the casualty lists had been frighteningly
long in 1915, they were doubly, triply so as 1916 drew to a close. True,
those from the Middle East were shorter, but France, the place they
called the Western Front, was evidently one vast graveyard of gallant
young Australians. And her James had been buried alive! Margaret
tried not to dwell on the anguish he must have endured, slowly and
agonisingly suffocating, before he was rescued. It simply did not bear
thinking about.

Every day, hundreds more names were printed, and each one represented heartbreak, tragedy and the death of hope for a mother, father, sister, wife or sweetheart. Margaret prayed for these poor souls as she did for herself, but the slaughter went on and on, until it seemed that almost every person one met these days wore a black armband or a mourning veil. She lived for her sons' letters, but she also lived in hourly dread of another telegram from the War Office.

At the beginning of November 1916, in spite of the fact that the winter was proving to be the worst in living memory, General Haig, who had deferred the offensive no less than seven times, finally ordered the Somme campaign to proceed. The Anzac divisions, which had had some respite since the massacres of Pozières and Fromelles, and some British units, were ordered to attack the German line in the vicinity of Gueudecourt and Flers.

En route, through driving rain, they passed through villages shelled and flattened, with the occasional ruined buildings standing starkly, like decayed teeth, in deserted countryside, surrounded by gardens overgrown with riotous briars and creepers and rank weeds. Some of the churchyards had been shelled, and splintered coffins and disinterred skeletons, brown with age, lay scattered far and wide. A large number of starving dogs followed the troops, and were surreptitiously fed titbits from the troops' own sparse rations, and the usual procession of dejected refugees clogged the roads, making progress slow.

Due to the terrible weather, the battlefield quickly turned into a morass of treacherous, stinking mud, up to 15 feet (4.5 metres) deep, the ground so waterlogged that any who were incautious enough to step off the duckboards often drowned before they could be rescued. Both German and Allied armies were so bogged down that any advance was virtually impossible, and shelling the enemy, sniping, trench raids, patrolling and reconnoitring were the only options, when men often needed to be roped together for safety.

---

FRANCE.
22.11.'16

DEAR MOTHER,
*Just a line to say that I am still well and am back at the front*

*again. They have sent me back to the 2nd. Battery which was the one
I was in before going to the trench mortars.*

*It is very hard to take having to start work again after such a long
spell at the base. Things are in an awful state here owing to the wet
weather and heavy traffic and it is almost impossible to walk
anywhere without being bogged. We have only had one fall of snow
here up to date, and I wouldnt mind if it was the last, as it is very
hard on the poor horses.*

*I had a letter from young Fred, it being the first news I have heard
from him.*

*We are back in the old dugout life again, it is wonderful where a
man makes himself at home on active service, if we get back home I
think we will be building houses in the ground.*

*I have had no mail from home for ages, I suppose harvesting is in
full swing by this time. Sorry I carnt go and lend a hand.*

*Well Mum there is little I can write about so I will have to close,
with love and kind regards to all.*

*From your loving son Jim.*

The troops were rotated to do forty-eight hour stints in the listening
posts in no-man's-land, which they reached by a sallyport, or tunnel,
under their own wire barricade, crawling through the mud so that they
were invariably soaked for the duration of the duty. If there were insufficient numbers of men, or if the relieving squad were killed or
wounded, they would remain at their post perhaps for days, existing
on their iron rations and often hungry.

One wonders whether Haig ever ventured within a score of miles of
the Front. Had it not been so tragic, it would be laughable to reflect that
he ordered his infantry and artillery, incredibly followed by the cavalry, to
advance across that vast sea of mud—a quagmire pitted with thousands
of treacherously deep shell holes, deceptively masked with muddy water,
into which hundreds of men vanished without a trace; a limitless, viscous
bog into which whole teams of horses, guns and men were swallowed.
James and the other gunners would have to shoot the poor, terrified
horses as, with eyes wildly distended and neck sinews standing out like
ropes as they struggled, they sank out of sight into the deadly mire.

It was not only the animals that received the merciful coup de grâce. Sometimes, when there was no possibility of rescue, the men were forced to shoot a mate who was drowning in the murderous bog. And then to live, forever after, with the soul-destroying memory of the look in their comrade's eyes as they aimed the gun. Small wonder that many of these men lost their minds and retreated into limbo, rather than face up to bitter reality. (On a lighter note, some were pulled from the mud minus their boots and trousers, occasioning much ribald laughter and derogatory comments of a very personal nature.)

Because the water table was a scant 18 inches (45 centimetres) below the surface, the trenches were mostly waist-deep in freezing ice and water. At first, the men had devised a method of scooping out shelves in the trench walls on which to sleep, but the incessant rain and sleet often caused the walls to collapse, entombing the unlucky occupants, and this was subsequently forbidden. Apart from the ever present danger of shrapnel during shelling, the troops were often half buried in torrents of mud which rained down on them, the clods of frozen earth every bit as lethal as the shrapnel.

If Pozières in midsummer was a recurring nightmare, the Somme Valley in the depths of that terrible winter must have been hell on earth. In spite of this, letters to home were almost invariably cheerful, making light of the dangers and dreadful conditions.

## The Letter

With B.E.F. Jun 10. Dear Wife,
(Oh blast this pencil. 'Ere Bill, lend's a knife.)
I'm in the pink at present, dear,
I think the war will end this year.
We don't see much of them square-'eaded 'Uns.
We're out of harm's way, not bad fed.
I'm just longing for a taste of your old buns.
(Say, Jimmie, spare's a bite of bread.)
There don't seem much to say just now.
(Yer what? Then don't, yer ruddy cow!
And give us back me cigarette!)

I'll soon be 'ome. You mustn't fret.
My feet's improvin', as I told you of.
We're out in the rest now. Never fear.
(VRACH! By crumbs, but that was near.)
Mother might spare you half a sov.
Kiss Nell and Bert. When me and you—
(Eh? What the 'ell! Stand to? Stand to!
Jim, give's a hand with pack on, lad.
Guh! Christ! I'm hit. Take 'old. Aye, bad.
No, damn your iodine. Jim? 'Ere!
Write my old girl, Jim, there's a dear.)

WILFRED OWEN

November and December 1916 were perhaps the nadir for the Anzacs on the Somme, but in spite of the incredible hardship and misery, spirits were never low. Their humour was, at times, macabre, for how could it not be, surrounded by death as they were? Sometimes they would bicker amicably over who would inherit the best pair of boots in the trench, should the present owner have no further use for them, ignoring the wearer's indignant protests that he had other plans for his boots. Target practice was also popular, using German corpses hanging on the barbed wire. One they called Dougie came in for special attention (that General Haig's Christian name happened to be Douglas was no coincidence), and they'd yell with glee when they scored a bullseye, hitting his steel helmet with a satisfying clang.

The men were garrisoned in the front trenches for several days at a stretch, standing to arms with bayonets fixed for an hour at dawn and at dusk, which were the usual times they could expect an attack. Two sentries would stand on the fire step observing no-man's-land through a periscope, and the remaining five or six men would doze until their turn for sentry duty, twice each night. After this they carried out support duty for some time, depending on the availability of reinforcements, before being placed 'on reserve' for the next three days in a muddy, open drain which was virtually as hazardous as the front trenches. It was common to see men standing knee-deep in mud, leaning against a wall and shaking violently with cold, dead asleep.

Often it was necessary to dig a man free of the mud that had frozen as he slept.

Even at rest camp there was little respite to be had. Regular duties included clearing out the miles of communication trenches that had been shelled, emptying latrine buckets and attempting to dig fresh holes in the iron-hard earth. When they could, they spread lime over dugout floors thickly splattered with blood, guts or brain matter following a shell burst, and filled sandbags with any available matter, including spare body parts not attached to a corpse.

The men spent much of their leisure time picking lice from their clothing—an endless task because the pests bred in their millions. Delousing stations supplied fresh underwear occasionally, but the only way to destroy the vermin was to boil the uniforms when going on leave, and even then the men quickly became lousy, the nits in body hair hatching almost before they left the station.

Poor diet and little rest, coupled with the strain of constant danger and the almost nightly trench raids by the enemy, soon exhausted the men, who bore little resemblance to the bronzed, fit Anzacs of a few months before. They were sometimes unable to even wash their faces for weeks at a time, and their nostrils were invariably red raw and constantly running, which caused icicles to form perpetually on the tips of their noses. Heavy snowfalls blanketed horses, guns and the pitiful corpses with a dazzling white shroud. The Australians, accustomed to the warm climate of home and tropical Egypt, found the bitter cold much harder to bear than the British and New Zealanders.

On rare occasions, when at rest camp and conditions permitted, the men visited the tiny estaminet (café) at Maricourt. It was unimaginable bliss to forget the horrors of the field, soaking up the warmth of the stuffy little room and thawing out their frozen feet as they sipped the rough red of the establishment. Incredibly, the café was less than 800 metres from the front line, and the shriek of shells and the thunder of the big guns went on unabated.

In spite of the danger from snipers, the men often walked briskly up and down the open duckboards, stamping their feet and waving their arms to try to keep warm and restore the circulation to their numbed limbs. At rest camp, when they were able to procure any whale oil, they rubbed their feet with the oil and wrapped them in hessian sandbags. Almost all suffered from painful chilblains on hands, feet and ears, the blood and pus sticking to their gloves and socks when they tried to remove the garments.

As time went by, the roads along which ammunition and stores were transported became increasingly impassable. Alerted by their observation planes, the Germans routinely shelled the lorries carrying supplies, and food became even more scarce. Sometimes the men made a sort of porridge from the hard, cement-like issue biscuits by crushing them using an empty shell case and mixing the crumbs with water. Occasionally, if they were lucky, warm tea, sickly sweet with condensed milk, was delivered in petrol cans, but the drink tasted so strongly of petrol or kerosene that the men joked that they were afraid to light a cigarette in case they exploded! However, even this was preferable to the tea made from boiled shell-hole water, the dark brown colour of which owed more to copious amounts of putrescent blood than to the natural colour of the earth. It also tasted indescribably foul.

Even when plentiful, the quality of the food was abysmal, with bread and jam being the staple diet. The bread was always stale and frequently mouldy. Potatoes and eggs were a luxury, but they were often rotten, and bacon was usually rancid. No fires were permitted in the front lines, and even when food arrived it was invariably icy-cold and maggoty. The enemy was no better off; their main diet of turnips and barley was even more sparse.

It is quite impossible for anyone who did not live through the endless hell that was the Somme offensive to comprehend the depths of misery suffered by the Allied forces during that terrible winter of 1916. By day, the only signs of life in that desolate, white, snow-covered 'moonscape' were the hawks that hovered overhead, and the carrion crows alighting to gorge on the many corpses. And at dusk, hordes of sleek rats, which had proliferated in their billions during the warmer months, materialised stealthily for their dreadful feast of the cadavers in no-man's-land, soon reducing the more recent bodies to khaki-clad skeletons within hours of their death. Even more terrible to imagine, many wounded were even attacked by the rodents as they lay dying, too weak to fend them off.

At night, when not standing-to, the men honed their marksmanship on the rats, which became so bold that they would even filch the food from the packs under the heads of sleeping men. The only place food was safe from the predatory rodents was in a wooden ammo box. Some of the men optimistically suspended their rations from the trench ceiling in bags, but the wily scavengers would scale the walls and leap, swinging on the bags while they gnawed holes in them, until the contents fell onto the floor. Following heavy snowfalls, when the cadavers in no-man's-land were covered in more than a foot of snow and there was nothing else to eat, the voracious rodents turned their undivided attention to the trenches, attacking the men as they slept, gnawing at their fingers, noses, lips and ears so that wearing their gas masks was the only option to protect their faces from the ravenous vermin.

Some men died in the trenches of exposure. Frostbite, gangrene and trench foot were so prevalent that often the victims made the terrible journey through bloodstained snow to the dressing stations, crawling long distances on their hands and knees, reluctant to avail themselves of the sledges, which, dragged by three horses, carried the most severely wounded. Even the stretchers required six to eight bearers to struggle—sometimes for many hours—over the treacherous terrain, so pitted with shell holes that duckboards were virtually useless. Wounded men in no-man's-land died by the hundreds, frozen solid before they could be rescued.

More traumatic than the bodily injuries caused by shot and shell were those of the mind; searing, indelible wounds that not even an entire lifetime would ever truly erase. In time one became inured even to the death of one's mates: the decapitated, the disembowelled, the dismembered. It was the comrades who one moment had been lively, laughing, able-bodied men, and the very next instant the living dead, that the mind could not accept. (That was another reason the men carried stolen German revolvers.) Shockingly maimed, limbless, faceless, breathing objects that strained to see out of empty, bloody eye sockets; that pleaded voicelessly to die, from throats or faces no longer there. Some cracked under the intolerable strain and shot themselves.

## S.I.W. (EXTRACT)

One dawn, our wire patrol
Carried him. This time, Death had not missed.
We could do nothing but wipe his bleeding cough.
Could it be accident? Rifles go off ...
Not sniped? No. (Later they found the English ball.)

It was the reasoned crisis of his soul
Against more days of inescapable thrall,
Against infrangibly wired and blind trench wall
Curtained with fire, roofed in with creeping fire,
Slow grazing fire, that would not burn him whole
But kept him for death's promises and scoff,
And life's half-promising, and both their riling.

With him they buried the muzzle his teeth had kissed,
And truthfully wrote the Mother, 'Tim died smiling'.[1]

WILFRED OWEN

[1][A gunshot in the mouth often causes a 'grin'.]

And there were some, without apparent wounds, who simply died.

## THE DEAD-BEAT

He dropped, more sullenly than wearily,
Lay stupid like a cod, heavy like meat,
And none of us could kick him to his feet;
Just blinked at my revolver, blearily;
Didn't appear to know a war was on,
Or see the blasted trench at which he stared.
'I'll do 'em in,' he whined. 'If this hand's spared,
I'll murder them, I will.' A low voice said,
'It's Blighty, p'raps, he sees; his pluck's all gone,
Dreaming of all the valiant, that aren't dead:
Bold uncles, smiling ministerially;

Maybe his brave young wife, getting her fun
In some new home, improved materially.
It's not these stiffs have crazed him; nor the Hun.'

We sent him down at last, out of the way.
Unwounded; stout lad, too, before that strafe.
Malingering? Stretcher-bearers winked, 'Not half!'

Next day, I heard the Doc.'s well-whiskied laugh:
'That scum you sent last night soon died. Hooray!'

WILFRED OWEN

With thousands of men killed each day, death was ever present and, because the earth was frozen iron-hard, it was impossible to bury the dead. The entire battlefield, for a score of miles behind the lines, was littered with putrid, rotting corpses, alive with fat, writhing maggots, and the dugouts were made intolerable with the dreadful stench of decayed human flesh and the excrement of past and present occupants. In time, one became accustomed to trying to drive a team of balky horses, mad with terror, over a carpet of thousands of corpses and disconnected body parts; over the grossly distended carcasses of animals, which, crushed by the gun carriage wheels, emitted unspeakably foul odours as the accumulated gases escaped from the bodies.

Sometimes, during a lull in activities, working parties 'on reserve' would venture out into no-man's-land to try to retrieve the identification disks from the dead lying close to the trenches (so that relatives could be notified), and enemy patrols would be observed doing likewise; a sort of tacit armistice. All too often the bodies would be badly decayed and the men would wear gloves and gas masks for the revolting task, or wrap their hands in rags. Many corpses were so grossly swollen with gas they had even burst from their uniforms, and others so macerated it was almost impossible to remove their clothing to find the dog tag. Occasionally a plump rat would be encountered, resident in the abdominal cavity, having consumed the vicera and become too bloated to make its escape. Invariably, the stench was so overpowering that the men would vomit into their masks.

Lacking a body to which to belong, many spare parts were used as sandbag filling, or to shore up parapets blown flat by shell blasts. It was all too common to see rotting feet, robbed of their precious boots, protruding from earthworks, or skeletal hands reaching out from the trench walls in mute supplication.

When General Birdwood visited the Front at the end of November he was appalled by the conditions his troops were forced to endure. Sickness was rife; blood poisoning, gangrene, frostbite, meningitis, scarlet fever, bronchitis and pneumonia, typhus, tetanus and measles were decimating the ranks. Because water in canteens was invariably frozen, typhoid and dysentery were endemic, caused by drinking water from the shell holes impregnated with urine, faeces, blood, manure and the decayed flesh of animals and humans.

The General lectured his officers sternly on the necessity of caring for the men under their command, and ordered stalls serving coffee and cocoa in jam tins to be set up on duckboards for the exhausted troops coming out of the firing line, and for those going in. He even arranged for a concert party from the Australian Comforts Fund to perform in a barn at Maricourt, and for a one-page newspaper called *The Rising Sun*, containing very welcome news from home, to be distributed to the Australians.

Although it was impossible for either army to advance, due to the appalling weather conditions, patrols and scouting parties ventured out almost nightly to bomb the enemy trenches, or to take a prisoner. The men would reconnitre the enemy from a listening post in no-man's-land and, if the coast was clear, make a sortie. Occasionally, when it was very dark or raining heavily, they would blunder into an enemy scouting party doing likewise, and a fierce hand to hand battle would ensue.

The patrols needed to be stealthy even when returning to their own lines. Should they bump into the barricades and set the tin cans tied to the barbed wire jangling, the sentries, often half asleep from exhaustion, usually shot first and asked questions later. There were certainly many Diggers 'Killed in Action' who died from friendly fire.

Even though there was very little activity on the Somme, except for the shelling, there was little opportunity for James to write home, and in any case there was little he would have been permitted to say, lest the truth about conditions discouraged volunteers. (The AIF was the only army on either side consisting entirely of volunteers, and there were significantly fewer enlistments as the appalling lists of casualties were published.) Besides, Margaret would have been devastated to hear that James's dugout, in which he was supposed to sleep, was sometimes waist-deep in icy water and mud. Neither did he wish to tell her that often his sustenance for the day was half a slice of mouldy bread (which, the Diggers joked, consisted of half sawdust and half weevil-ridden flour) and a spoonful of condensed milk, washed down with shell-hole water containing flotsam on which it was best not to speculate. Nor could he tell her that he could barely remember the last time he had had a bath, or even a good wash, and that he and his mates spent much of their leisure time squashing lice between their thumbnails. Even if James had wanted to tell Margaret any of this, the censor would have destroyed his letters. So in fact, there was really nothing he could write home about at all.

Anyway, one was fully occupied listening tensely for the drone of a 12-inch shell, the whistle as it passed overhead and the 'crump' as it landed. And, most of all, they listened for the deadly, soft thud of a gas shell and the metallic rattle of the gas alarm. The Germans often sent gas over at night to disable the enemy before an attack, so it was prudent to wear a gas mask, but most found sleep almost impossible in its stifling confinement and, in spite of exhaustion, they seldom slept heavily. Instead, they cat-napped, always alert for danger.

At night, to an onlooker, it might have been a pretty sight to watch the red glow fanning across the snow in no-man's-land, like the Aurora Australis, as the great guns sent glowing balls of fire arching across the dark sky. From time to time, rockets firing red, green, blue and yellow star shells exposed the landscape as bright as day, followed by the rattle of machine guns, or the whine of low-calibre bullets if they located a target. And in the early dawn, the earth would be swathed in an eerie white mist in which disembodied, phantom heads seemed to float on a ghostly lake.

# → A Blast to Blighty ←

*E*NGAGED IN MANOEUVRING his 18-pounder into position, James was unaware of an approaching shell until it had landed directly in front of his three horses, killing them instantly. The blast ruptured his eardrums and blew him high into the air as a piece of shrapnel pierced his shoulder deeply, and he was tossed to the ground, unconscious.

Once again, Jack was the harbinger of bad news at Happy Valley. He arrived at his mother's farm one morning bearing the telegram from the War Office Margaret had been dreading.

---

*Regret to inform you that your brother Gunner J.H. Carthew has been seriously wounded. Further particulars received will be at once communicated to you.*
   *Col. Hawker Victoria Barracks.*

---

There was no celebration that Christmas of 1916. Margaret and the girls waited as the long, hot hours passed as if on leaden feet. Was she to lose two of her sons to this terrible war? Then, at last, a cable arrived from England, which Margaret opened with trembling hands. She read the message unsteadily before bursting into tears.

---

*Getting on well. Feeling tiptop. Love, Jim*
   *P.S Do not change the address as they all come to London first.*
*J.H.C.*

3rd. Western Gen. Hospital
Oxford England
16.12.'16

Dear Mother,

I hope you recieved the cable I sent you a few days ago saying that I was getting on well. I hope it did not cause you any uneasiness when you recieved word from the authorities as I suppose you did.

Mother it was really nothing to worry about, as I will probably be up and able to deal with Xmas dinner in style as in days of old. We are all to get a general good time on that day if we are to believe what we hear.

I went through a good deal of pain during the first couple of weeks while I was in the hospital in Rouen in France during which time I had to go through two operations to have the bits of shell taken out, it caught me right where the arm joins the shoulder. It was not such a close call as the last one I had but it was close enough for me, if it had not been for three horses which were killed in front of me I suppose I should have gone.

Mother, I happened to get a glance at the name of the hospital ship as they were taking me on board at Le Havre, and it was no other than the old Warilda which you came across to the West on that time little did I think when I met you at Fremantle that I was going to be carried on board her in France. I was glad when they told me that I was going to be sent to England to recover as I will have an opportunity of having a look at the British Isles, that is providing Jack cables me the necessary which I am going to call on him to do, as soon as I am able to get about.

We are granted fourteen days furlough when we come out of hospital, and if I can manage it am going to have a run over the three. I dont think I shall bother our relatives, as one would have to chance his reception, and thats no good to me.

I looked a dream when I came into the hospital, was flying about a months beard and hair about a foot long padded together with mud — had not had a wash for about a fourtnight, had a look at myself in the glass and nearly took fright.

You cannot imagine what the mud is like in the vicinity of the *line, there are horses laying bogged all over the place with their saddles and harness still on, they just shoot them and leave them where they are.*

*All the ammunition for the batteries has to be taken up to the guns on pack horses, from the railway dumps, also all the rashions for the men in the trenches so you can imagine what things are like. I have not had a letter since leaving the base but I recieved a parcel from Nell the day before I left the line and unfortunately did not have an opportunity to make use of the good things it contained, but they will not go to waste as my mates will make use of them.*

*Well Mum I have written 2 long letters — am taking advantage of them not being scensered [sic], or I hope not, and only having one arm am a little tired. Hoping you are all well and in good health I will close with love to you all.*

*From Your Effec son Jim.*

The festive season on the Somme of 1916, like that of 1915, was vastly different from the first Christmas of the war. This time, the British High Command issued orders that the artillery intensify its fire, targeting areas where it was thought the Germans would gather for Christmas dinner, and again on New Year's Eve as the hour of Berlin's New Year approached, which is earlier than that of Greenwich Mean Time.

---

3RD. AUSTRALIAN AUXILLARY HOSPITAL, DARTFORD
3RD FEB. 1917

DEAR MOTHER,

*Just a line to say that I have been shifted from Oxford to the above hospital which is situated about fifteen miles from London. I had an opportunity of seeing a bit of the latter place on the way through. We got off the train at Paddington and were taken by motor ambulance to Victoria St. Station passing enroute through Hyde Park and Buckingham Palace, at which I was rather disappointed as I expected to see a much finer building than it really is, everything was all covered with snow, and hyde park looked rather nice. While we were waiting for the train a couple of us had a walk down the strand, also had a look at trafalgar square, which is very fine, and I am*

looking forward to having a good look when I get my furlough, which
will not be for a while yet.

This is an Australian hospital, and contains only our own nurses
and patients, it is quite a change after the Tommy hospital where I
was in arguments with the Tommies half the time, one only has to
mention some brave deed that our chaps have never done and he
would have about six tommies after his scalp. But none of us could
growl at the way we were treated there as all hands were treated
splendidly especially by the nurses, who were all very nice indeed. I
had a bundle of letters, 14 a few days ago, which have been travelling
around the world for months, some of them were written last June,
and both sides of them were covered with — try here and try there,
I cannot understand how they reached me at all with the add. that
were on them.

It seems to be far colder here than it was at Oxford but there is
far more snow laying about than there was up there. I was taken
through several of the Colleges at Oxford before coming away, was
very interested with some of the ancient relics, there is some beautiful
carving and architecture to be seen, especially in the chappel, which
every college has attached to it.

In Christchurch cathedral there some old tombs about five
hundred years old. At the museum there are a lot of old relics to be
seen, there are some jewels out of King Alfred's Crown, a pair of
Queen Elizabeth's boots and hundreds of different other things to
numerous to mention. This is a rather rotten place to be in compared
with Oxford, we are about three miles away from the town and
railway, and we are only allowed out from 1 pm to 4 pm so there is
not much time to go that far.

I sent Jack a cable yesterday for a bit of Oscar Ashe, so as to have
a bit of cash when I get my holidays, I hope he sends it along,
otherwise I will not be able to go anywhere much.

My shoulder is healing up splendidly and will not be long before it is
right and as good as it was before. I had a letter from Dave Williams
last week, he is also in England, acting as orderly in one of the hospitals
at Brighton, I think he came across here sick. How are things
progressing in the old place, I suppose its the same old thing, it would

*be a good job if you could get rid of it, as it is really a waste of one's life stopping there year after year, but I suppose there places a lot worse after all, and there are times when I have wished myself there instead of this side of the globe. There is plenty of skating on the ice going on over here and when I get right I am going to try my hand at it.*

*Well Mother think this is all this time so will close with love and kindest regards to you all. From your Effec son Jim.*

*Many happy returns of the 17th of March next.*

---

MONTE VIDEO CAMP, WEYMOUTH
4.3.1917

DEAR MOTHER,

*Just a line to say that I am still alive and well, and trust this finds you in the same condition.*

*I received a parcel of letters yesterday which included three from Add and two from Nell also from Babs and Emm, and W.A. was also represented. I recieved a parcel from Kalgoorlie* [from Nellie] *being the first since leaving the trenches, it contained a knitted cardigan with my colours worked in, also a pr of socks, which also had the colours on, the boys all say I am too beastly flash with my colours on everything.*

*They must have been rather a decent pair of socks that brought ten pounds, she is always doing something for the red cross.* [A pair of socks knitted by Nellie had been raffled for ten pounds. They had the German flag under the heel, and the crossed British and Australian flags around the top.]

*Tell Jack the twenty pounds has arrived safely in London, and is there ready for me when I go on furlough, thank him very much on my behalf. Fred was saying that you have been worrying about me being wounded, now there was really no need for this as I sent you a cable to say I was alright, shortly after arriving at Oxford.*

*I was pleased to hear that Fred had recieved another stripe, he is getting on well. A Sgt. Major and myself were up before the Commandant the other morning it being my first crime since leaving Aust, and was a very serious one, being caught in bed ten minutes after reveille had gone, we were both dismissed but the funy part of it is all leave was stopped for all hands in the hut for seven days, you can just imagine the abuse we have to put up with, getting out of it ourselves and getting them in it.*

*It is disgraceful to see some of the men they have here doing C.B. men with crutches, some with one arm and so on, the heads dont seem to have any regard for a man crippled or otherwise. The weather is keeping very cold here again, that cold that I am afraid almost to go outside the door. I think that the wind that blows off the channel here must come direct from the north pole.*

*Tell Add my German souvenirs that she wanted me to bring home all came to grief, when I came away all the property I had when I landed in England was a suit of pyjamas and they did not belong to me so I will have to get a fresh collection when I return. Fancy the weather being so wet over there for this time of the year, it is very remarkable. Well Mother this is all this time so I will close with love to all.*

*From your loving son Jim.*

While in Blighty (as Britain was known to the troops), James wore the regulation hospital light blue suit with red lapels, but having lost all his clothes at the Front he had a uniform tailored in Savile Row (where the tailors were certainly more accustomed to stitching officers' uniforms than privates'). He also saw a number of musical comedies, including *Chu Chin Chow* and *The Maid of the Mountains.*

---

MONTE VIDEO CAMP, WEYMOUTH
21.3.'17

MY DEAR MOTHER,

*I recieve Nell's letter of the 1st Jan yesterday, was sorry to hear that you have been worrying about me, you know I told you, you was not to do it, and on the first opportunity you go and disobey orders, if it occurs again you will be brought before the orderley room to answer the charge. Well Mother we kept up your birthday here by holding a sports meeting in the camp here, which was fairly well patronised by a lot of the towns people.*

*I expect to be going on furlough about Saturday next as my wound is completely healed up at last, so it will not be long*

*before I am returning across the channel, but we are forming
another division over here out of the details from hospitals etc,
so it is possible that I will be drafted into this, if so it will
probably be a month or two before they are sent over. There is
some talk of them marching through London on Anzac day. I
recieved the photos safely which Nell enclosed, they are not too
bad, considering the photographer who took them, tell Babs she
will have to improve before she gets the honour of taking mine
again. I am going to make straight for Glasgow and
Edinborough as soon as I get leave and from then I don't know
where. I heard the other day that one of the young O'Grady's
was in this camp but I have not saw him yet. I have just scalded
my mouth with hot soup, which we get at 8 pm every night so
you can guess that I am not in the best of temper.*

*Well Mother this is all this time so will close with love and best
wishes to you all from your loving son Jim.*

---

KING GEORGE AND QUEEN MARY VICTORIA LEAGUE CLUB
RAMSAY LODGE, THE MOUND, EDINBURGH
4.4.'17

DEAR MOTHER,

*Just a line to say that I am having the time of my life, landed here
four days ago and am still going strong. I have just finished wrapping
up a small parcel for you so hope it arrives safely, am sending the
Girl a small one by same mail. There are some lovely sights to be seen
here, but the weather is rotten six inches of snow all over the place.
There are quite a lot of our chaps here on leave I think they nearly all
come up here, instead of staying in London. Well Mother my mate is
waiting for me, so will close with love and best wishes to you all.*

*From your Effec son Jim. Excuse short note more later.*

---

AUSTRALIAN BASE CAMP, MONTE VIDEO, WEYMOUTH
11.4.'17

DEAR MOTHER,

*Just a line to say that I have returned off furlough last Saturday
after having the time of my life, you can guess how discontented I am*

feeling now that I have to settle down to camp life once more, I can tell you that it is very hard to take, but suppose one will have to make up his mind and settle down to military life once more. There is one consolation in knowing that I still have four days leave to come before returning to France, for which time I am afraid I will not have very long to wait. I spent the most of my time in Edinburg, and enjoyed myself immensely looking through the old ancient castles and palaces. It is a very fine city as you will see by some of the views I sent along while up there. Edinburg castle is a wonderful structure, it is built up on the rocks hundreds of feet above the town all the old cannon are still in position on the castle walls, one of them is fired every day at 1 o'clock as a time signal, and it shakes the whole town. I thought I was back at the front again the first day I heard it. It is very interesting to see all the old weapons of war which are stowed there for exhibition. The gun carriage is also there which conveyed Victoria to her last resting place. We also went through Holyrood Palace which is also very interesting, the apartments of Mary Queen of Scots are there just as in olden days. The chapel is a total wreck, being destroyed by Oliver Cromwell all that remains are the tombs on the floor of the ancient Lords.

I was unfortunate in not seeing the fleet in while I was there, I wanted to go aboard the Australia which is included in the grand fleet, while they are in port all of us chaps get a harty welcome on board to spend the day. The Melbourne and Sydney are up there also. I had a few days in London as well but do not like it so well as Scotland, the people seem altogether different, of coarse there are a lot of fine sights to be seen. I had a run through the tower and Westminster Abby and a few other places, but I will see more of them when on final leave. The underground railways are a wonderful thing, one can travel to any part of London from one end to the other underground in some places they run under the Thames, and they travel at such a terific rate. There are lifts and revolving stairways to get up and down. One has to have all his wits about him while travelling or he will find himself hopelessly lost.

Well Mother I have been picked out in a draft to rejoin my unit which I think is on Salisbury plains and from there I will return to the hell on earth.

*I sent you a small parcel and a short note from Scotland hope they arrive saftely.*

*I have had two letters from Babs one from Emm and several from the girl since returning but not one from home, dont know where they can be going.*

*I was surprised to hear that Jack's wedding is to take place this month he is making it a welter, I thought I would have been off before him. Convey my heartiest congratulations. Babs was saying that you were keeping splendid, which I was very glad to hear, hope I find you the same on my return. Hope Add and Nell are also keeping well. Well dear Mother this is all the news this time so I will close with love and kind regards to you all.*

*From your Effec son Jim*

---

[Beginning of letter missing]

*We have lovely green fields to do our training on, quite a contrast to the mud of France. There are several big aerodromes situated all around here and every day there are hundreds of planes in training to make good the losses in France.*

*Fancy Harry and Family anticipating a visit in your direction, it will be quite a change for them from the fields. I have not heard from him for goodness knows when. I hope you all enjoyed the four cockies and twenty four parrots, which Nell was roasting at the time of writing, I can assure you that my mouth watered a trifle when I thought of them and looked at my slice of half stale bread which was to be my tea.*

*I suppose by this time Emm will be home with you again. Nell was saying she was returning for Easter.*

*Well Mother this is all this time so will close with love and kind regards to all. From your loving son Jim*

---

WEYMOUTH
6.6.17

DEAR MOTHER,

*Just a line to say I am still alive and well, also that I am having* the time of my life since returning from the plains, the weather is absolutely glorious, quite a pleasure to be alive to enjoy it. I have been doing a good deal of boating lately and have threw out quite a number of challenges to race, but up to date they have not been accepted owing I suppose to our superiority. We journyied to Portland [Portsmouth?] on sunday last and had a good time looking over the ports and citadel which are suppose to be among the strongest in England, they are built right up on the cliffs on a narrow point running out into the channel, it takes some climbing to get to the top but one is rewarded by the sights that are to be seen when one gets up.

Nothing of the citidel can be seen from without, the enterence to it is across a drawbridge and through a tunnel which opens out into a big courtyard which is surrounded by the many buildings which used to be the garrison quarters but is now turned into a camp for our men who are waiting the boat to go home. There is a secret underground chamber which is the hiding place of the king in times of trouble, and has provisions enough stowed away to last two years. Recieved my photos the other day which turned out to be absolutely rotten am going to destroy them and have some more taken.

We went out to the Upway wishing well last night and had a wish, only hope it comes true. It is a wonderful spring and our old King George the third is supposed used the water from it, you have to drink some of the water and throw the rest over your left shoulder, there is an old lady looks after it and supplies all information. I have had no letters from you for goodness knows when.

Well this is all this time so will close with love and kind regards to you all.

From your loving son Jim.

---

LARK HILL, SALISBURY PLAIN
17.7.17

MY DEAR MOTHER,

Just a line to say that I recieved three letters from the girls at home, one from each, was glad to hear that all is well, with the exception of the colds which you were getting over. Well Jack is an old maried man, have been wondering how he is taking it, he seems to be getting along well in the dealing line, especially with stock up to such a price, it is very hard to hear of these things and to think that we have to stay over here in this murderous affair. This war is going to be the ruination of 90 per cent of the men who have left Australia the way that some of our chaps carry on over here, almost makes one ashamed of the fact that he is an Aust. lads that never knew what it was before think of nothing else now but gambling and drinking, there will be more rogues and thieves in the world after this war than ever there was before. Fancy old John Holman being on holidays again really I don't know what I have done to have gone up to such an extent in his estimation. There is a chap called Reid in this hut he comes from Kiewa, suppose you have heard of them, he knows the McLeods very well [Margaret's mother was Christine McLeod], and was telling me that two of the boys have been killed in France one of them was Bert who used to be in the bank at Bright. I also met one of the Gunsons from Myrtleford a few nights ago, was saying he had seen a good few of the boys from there in France — Bob Withers and Bushy Fern and a lot of others, I have never saw him in my life before, and he said he thought I was a Carthew when he saw me in Weymouth about a month ago. I fail to see where the likeness comes in.

I was rather surprised when I heard Jack's wedding was so quiet, I really thought it would be the event of the season, Young Gunson was saying that Agen Hewit got the shock of his life when he heard that she had turned him down, anyway tell him he might have given me an invitation to the wedding.

Well we are getting well trimmed up here, with the gun drill, they are driving me back to France fast, and this is the last resource. Four of my mates got ten days in clink this morning for being off parade, and I missed by the skin of my teeth, was off parade but used a little strategy in evading the officer and was not caught, we have to be on parade at 5.30 am so you can imagine us being off parade at every opportunity. I sent Nell a few more P. cards yesterday hope they land safely. Emm was saying that she was thinking of going back to town with Babs, so suppose she is on the move again by this. We are having some sports here tomorrow, but it is raining now and it will *spoil them. The sports ground is alongside the Stonehenge, the picture of which used to be in the old history book. Well Mother this is all this time so will close with fond love to you all.*

*From your loving son Jim.*

While James convalesced in England and enjoyed some sightseeing, the battlefields he had temporarily escaped could never have been far from his mind. Spring came early to the Somme in 1917, perhaps to compensate for the savagely cruel winter—the most severe in living memory. Grass sprouted from the tops of the clay-filled sandbags crowning the trench parapets, and infinitesimal green shoots ventured timidly forth from the blackened stumps of the trees and shrubs in no-man's-land. Field flowers began to push through the wet, stinking soil, fertile with the putrid, rotting carrion, and butterflies hovered above the budding poppies and daisies. Heedless of shot and shell, birds optimistically built nests on anything remotely resembling a tree, greedily fossicking around the disintegrating corpses for the worms that proliferated among the whitening bones.

As the rain and sleet eased and the snow melted, the drier conditions hatched plagues of fleas and lice, which tormented the men and made life in the trenches even more miserable. Worst of all, now that the overflowing latrines had thawed, clouds of blue-black flies mantled everything in a metallic pall, so that food was invariably flyblown long before it reached the troops, and the men no longer bothered to pick out the maggots from their bully beef.

Paradoxically, now that the weather was milder, there was even more sickness in the lines, due to poor diet, exhaustion and lowered resistance. Frostbite, gangrene, infectious diseases, pneumonia and septicaemia all took their toll, and many died before they reached hospital.

When the murky ice melted, the many bodies floating in the shell holes became visible in all their horror, their tragic, grey, upturned faces still frozen in a rictus of agony and terror, as at the moment of death. While the earth was frozen iron-hard it had been impossible to bury the dead, except in shell holes. Working parties did what they could to collect the bodies and transport them to the rear of the battlefield, but now that the snow had melted, thousands of corpses and body parts littered no-man's-land, and hung in grotesque attitudes on the wire. The entire battlefield reeked like a gigantic charnel house.

It was during this period that the German High Command (having made peace overtures in December which were rejected by the Allies, who demanded nothing less than unconditional surrender) made a reluctant decision to withdraw. Under cover of darkness, and undetected by the British at first, thousands of troops made a stealthy retreat, razing every village, orchard and woodland in their wake that might give cover to the Allies, in a 10-mile (16-kilometre) swathe. While it galled the Prussian generals to do so, the advantages of withdrawing were obvious. The new battle front, to be known as the Hindenburg Line, stretched for 45 miles (72 kilometres) and was far shorter than the old front, allowing a much greater concentration of troops. It consisted of three distinct lines of trenches, between which were barbed-wire entanglements 50 feet (15 metres) deep, and immensely thick gun emplacements connected by a network of railways. The pursuing Allies, arriving late on the scene, would have no such advantage.

Also unfortunate for the Allies was the fact that the vast Russian Empire, rotten to the core, had collapsed like a house of cards during the revolution engineered by the Red Russian faction early in 1917, and Tsar Nicholas was forced to sue for peace with Germany. This allowed the Germans to transfer thirty-five divisions, comprising 140 000 troops, to the Hindenburg Line. The new Front was designed to buy time for the Germans, who hoped the devastating U-boat attacks on British shipping would weaken British defences and destroy their morale.

After the Somme debacle, the British High Command, undeterred by the horrific casualties suffered by the Allies (almost twice those of the German army) and heartened by the entry of the Americans into the war, decided to make 1917 a year of even greater offensives. Their ultimate objective was to break through the German Line to the Belgian coast and capture the U-boat bases between Nieuport and Zeebrugge. Following the successful assault on Arras and Vimy Ridge by the British and Candians on 9 April, Haig and his subordinate Gough decided to order the Anzac Corps to attack the enemy at Bullecourt, a vital point of the line, never dreaming that they might succeed. Like the Germans themselves, Haig believed the Hindenburg Line to be impregnable, but he had no scruples about sacrificing the Australians and New Zealanders to a hopeless cause, in spite of Birdwood's protests. Because Haig's communiqués to the newspapers never credited the Anzacs with the significant victories they had achieved, the Germans had no idea of the calibre of the men ordered to spearhead the assault at Bullecourt on 11 April.

The bad weather had returned to the Front and the Anzacs huddled in their trenches in a blizzard, many dying of exposure, waiting for the tanks promised by the British, which were to mow down the wire barricades prior to the infantry attack. However, these failed to reach the wire before the infantry, who were trapped in a deadly barrage of gunfire and flame-throwers. Facing the certain prospect of being massacred whilst retreating to their trenches, they advanced boldly and, led by Major Percy Black, a Western Australian prospector, slashed a path through the wire and broke through the line. However, they paid a heavy price for victory. Of 3000 men, 2340 were killed, wounded or captured. Had the British artillery given the support promised, casualties would have been far fewer.

The Germans then courageously counterattacked, some even reaching the Anzac trenches to die in fierce hand-to-hand fighting. This victory of the First Battle of Bullecourt was regarded by General Haig as almost impossible, and he referred to it as 'one of the great British deeds of the war'.

In a desperate bid to regain lost ground, the Germans increased their artillery shelling, and Haig issued an order of the day: 'There is no other course but to fight it out with our backs to the wall, and each position held till the last man. The future of mankind and our homes depend on the conduct of our Armies.' So great was the hatred and bitterness of the Australians for Haig, who invariably sent the Anzacs into the worst and most impenetrable sections of the line, the order was openly changed to 'till the last Australian'.

On 15 April, the Germans launched a counterattack near the village of Lagnicourt. Four Australian battalions, a total of 4000 men, put up such strong resistance against the force of 16 000 enemy troops that the Germans were driven back out of the village.

In early May, Haig again ordered the Anzacs to attack at Bullecourt. Birdwood protested, arguing that his men had had little respite from action, and were exhausted, while the British Guards and the British 11th Division were still out after more than seven weeks rest. The Australians were so incensed that two units went on strike. However, the Second Battle of Bullecourt resulted in a stunning victory for the Anzacs against the finest Prussian troops in the German army. Again, the cost was tragically high, resulting in over 7000 casualties from a total of four divisions (16 000 men). This battle marked the end of the disastrous Somme Offensive.

Haig had chosen to believe that the Germans had suffered even greater casualties than the Allies during this campaign, and claimed in his dispatches that 'the enemy losses exceeded the British not improbably by 100 per cent'. However, official statistics subsequently revealed that while Allied casualties totalled a staggering 481 842, or almost half a million, the Germans lost only 236 194 men, or less than a quarter of a million. (The figures for the subsequent Third Battle of Ypres showed virtually the same ratio.) In fact, Haig frequently lied in his communiqués, making much of the Allied advances but never mentioning their reverses. No doubt he believed that this was permissable in order to maintain morale. (For some time, both Lloyd George and Winston Churchill had wished to get rid of Field Marshal Haig, but neither could agree on his replacement. Churchill favoured General John Monash, recognising his brilliance as a strategist and leader, but Lloyd George refused to consider the Australian, objecting that the man was 'not only a Jew and the son of a German immigrant, but he was a Colonial, and an Australian at that'.)

Many historians have labelled Haig as a callous murderer, incompetent, arrogant, vain and pompous, achieving his high office chiefly by virtue of his birth and influence. He has few apologists for the wholesale massacres for which he was responsible, irrationally against the advice of many of his military advisers, which were to virtually wipe out an entire generation of men during four bloody years of conflict; although there were some, like Haig himself, who argued that the end justified the means.

The Battle of the Somme alone squandered almost half a million Allied casualties—for little, if any, gain. It was typical of the man that when a group of concerned men, including Sir Arthur Conan Doyle, devised a bullet-proof vest that successfully repelled most bullets, Haig refused to consider equipping the troops with these, 'because only cowards would want to use it'. We can only conjecture how many thousands of lives it might have saved.

One wonders if, in later years, fêted and lauded as the architect of the hollow victory, he suffered from insomnia. Did he resort to counting sheep? Or did he watch an endless procession of phantom, tattered, khaki-clad, mudstained, bloodstained, maimed, blinded and limbless figures, whom he'd sent to their deaths with a careless stroke of his pen? Did he, I wonder, on his own luxurious deathbed, reckon the game was worth the candle?

# ⇢ Bravery in the Field ⇠

*B*Y THE END OF JUNE 1917 the French army was in a state of collapse, worn out by three years of unremitting conflict. Morale was at its absolute nadir. At Verdun alone there had been a catastrophic loss of over 410 000 men. The troops had lost all confidence in their leaders. They fought on without hope and primarily because the only alternative was court martial and death.

In fact, many units had mutinied. In May, following the Aisne defeat, the battle-weary poilus had had enough. Some regiments were ordered straight back into the trenches, while others were favourably treated and continued to remain out of action. The uprising began with a march of protest, and some defected, vanishing into the woods. Several units commandeered a train and, with whistles blowing, drove away from the Front. Aided by civilian pacifists, the mutiny spread, involving at least 100 000 men. Some even paraded through the streets, baaing to imitate sheep being driven to the slaughter. Officers, desperate to quell the uprising, fired shots into the troops, killing a number of soldiers.

Eventually, General Nivelle was replaced by General Pétain who was able to restore order, but not before 400 men were court-martialled and over forty of the ringleaders executed. There were also uprisings in the British and German armies at about this time. The Allied Generals were terrified of a mass mutiny, and it was decided to order wholesale executions as an example to the troops.

One of the great tragedies of this brutal conflict were the criminal court martials and executions, not only of the ringleaders but also of many brave men, their bodies debilitated and worn out after three years of unremitting, savage fighting, lack of rest and poor diet; their spirits broken and minds driven beyond endurance and the brink of sanity by the danger, harsh discipline and the daily stress of witnessing the terrible carnage of their comrades. There was no redress on this account. Some of their executioners who sat in judgment, in their well-tailored uniforms and boots burnished by their batmen, had never fired a shot in action, endured months of terror in icy, water-logged trenches, nor been splattered by the brains and blood of their dearest mates. It did not matter. They were reviled as cowards and any mark of rank torn viciously from their uniforms before they were brutally executed. More than 300 British and Commonwealth soldiers, including New Zealanders, were executed for 'Cowardice in the Face of the Enemy', but not one Australian suffered the same fate.

At this time, Haig was under constant pressure from the French to deploy his troops and attack the enemy in areas that guaranteed enormous casualties, in order to relieve the burden on the French armies. As usual, the French were proving intractable and intransigent on every detail, and in spite of the fact that Britons were spilling their blood, primarily in order to defend French territory, they did not forget to charge both the British and colonial governments an exorbitant sum for every yard of railway, every train, lorry and ambulance, and every hospital or camping facility used.

On the high seas, the German U-boats and mines were creating havoc, sending many Allied troop and supply ships to the bottom, and it was decided, by the British High Command, to try to push through to the Belgian coast and destroy the enemy submarine bases between Nieuport and Zeebrugge.

To this end, British, Canadian and Anzac sappers had for months secretly dug nineteen tunnels deep beneath the German lines on Messines Ridge, south of Ypres, packing almost one million pounds of explosive at strategic points. In fact, both Allied and German armies were constantly engaged in mining beneath no-man's-land to the opposing lines, in order to establish listening posts, monitoring the other's speech and movement with instruments and sometimes acquiring vital information. The sappers, who were mostly miners in peacetime, were paid more highly than the usual army rate because of the extreme danger of their work. It was a risky and exhausting business, often entailing many hours of work in tunnels hardly wider than their bodies, and sometimes they accidentally broke through into the German mines, and vice versa, or were buried by their own or enemy blasting.

Just after 3am on 7 June, to the horror of the German Command, nineteen gigantic, fiery, crimson mushrooms simultaneously rose into the darkness, with a deafening roar, sending hundreds of tons of earth, concrete, timber and bodies sky high, and causing thousands of casualties. On the previous day, the Germans had saturated the Allied lines with more than 13 000 gas shells and 700 gas bombs containing phosgene and chlorine, leaving many dead—including 500 Anzacs—and others suffering cruelly, drowning slowly as their lungs filled with fluid drawn from their own bodies by the chlorine. In spite of this, the British and Anzac troops advanced with great courage as soon as the debris subsided, taking advantage of the enemy's confusion, and captured Messines. The savage fighting on the south-west section by the Anzacs resulted in more than half the 26 000 casualties suffered by the Allies during the course of the battle.

In early August, a flotilla of ships carrying Birdwood's I Anzac Corps of four divisions comprising 16 000 Australian and New Zealand Diggers, sailed from Southampton, en route for Flanders. The German intelligence were well aware of this and hoped to intercept and sink the transports. Had they succeeded, it would have had a disastrous effect on the course of the war.

---

SOUTHAMPTON
7.8.1917

DEAR MOTHER,

*Just a line to say that I am on my way back to France again at last. I left Lark Hill yesterday and went on board the boat here last night for our trip across the channel, but our voyage proved to be very short as on reaching the entrance to the channel we turned around and returned to port at Southampton, the reason we were told was because there were submarines waiting for us. On reaching port we went ashore and were marched out to this camp which is about five* miles, and you should have heard the row that went on while passing through the streets, one would have almost thought the war was over, although it was about one oclock in the morning all hands seemed to be up to see what was going on, they nearly took possession of the town. I don't know how long we are going to be here, but I suppose it will be only a day or so. I had a couple of days in London last week, but had a rotten time as it did not stop raining the whole time I was there, consequently I could not go out as much as I would like to have done. The weather is keeping wet here now so I suppose we will get a taste of it on our arrival in France.

Well Mother I am going back with a good heart, and I am sure that the Germans have not got a shell that was made for me, I have had a remarkably good run over here, it exceeded by far all expectations. This is a rather nice camp we are in but am afraid we will not be here long enough to enjoy it.

Well dear Mother this is all this time so will close with fondest love to you all. From your loving son Jim.

---

FRANCE
15.8.17

MY DEAR MOTHER,

Just a line to say that I have returned back to the roar of the guns again, landed here yesterday, after being almost continually on the move ever since leaving England, and were all glad that the journey was ended. I am now in the 6th battery of the 2nd Brigade so you can address my letters accordingly, goodness knows how long I will have to wait for my mail now after having been transferred from my own unit, but I will have to wait patiently till it turns up.

Things are not nearly in such a bad condition as they were when I came away from the front last, but if the rain continues it will soon be bad enough. We are camped under canvas sheets here and of coarse one is inclined to feel the cold rather keenly after being used to good huts and plenty of blankets which we had in England, but one will soon get back into his old form again. It is a bit of a nuisance having to write letters to pass the scensor one hardly knows what to write about that was the best of the other side you could put almost anything in them.

*I have been wondering how Fred is getting on, as I have heard nothing from him for some considerable time, but all my letters seem to be going astray somewhere. I was telling you in my letter about being sent back to port well we came across the following night, were escorted by several destroyers.*

*Well Mother this is all this time so will close with love to you all. From your loving son Jim.*

During August the rain fell ceaselessly, rendering weapons useless and making it impossible for the British to make any significant gains. On 26 August, I Anzac Corps arrived in Flanders. The Corps, greatly decimated at Bullecourt, was now reinforced by wounded veterans who had been recuperating in Blighty, including James Carthew, and new volunteers, all of whom had been training for three months on Salisbury Plain to a high degree of efficiency.

The vast quagmire of mud which stretched endlessly across the battlefield hampered any movement, and troops wallowing in the mire were picked off in their hundreds by the enemy from the safety of their heavily fortified dugouts. Even those only slightly wounded often drowned, unable to rise from the treacherous, deadly ooze.

In spite of this, morale was high, and under their own Generals, Birdwood and Brigadier Brudnell-White, the confident Anzacs, together with a division of Scots whom they admired and trusted, attacked boldly at Menin Road on 20 September, routing the enemy. A proud General Birdwood reported: 'Our own Artillery barrage was magnificent, the finest I have ever seen, crushing the Boche advance, and blasting a path through their defences for the following Infantry.' Because only a direct hit by an 8-inch shell could breach the enemy's massive 5-feet (1.5-metre) thick pill boxes, the Diggers wriggled through the mud, under intense crossfire from both Germans and Allies, to drop Mills bombs through the loop-holes, killing the machine gun crews.

Victory at Polygon Wood, a wasteland of tree stumps and craters, followed on 26 September, a triumph for the 4th and 5th divisions, and on 4 October General Ludendorff's army was decisively defeated at Broodseinde. Australian General Plumer described the action as the greatest triumph since the Battle of the Marne (when the French smashed the German advance on Paris in 1914). Five days later, Poel Capelle was taken. General John Monash wrote to his wife: 'I count myself the most fortunate of men to be placed at the head of the finest fighting machine the world has ever seen.'

Haig, mistakenly believing that the German Army was about to collapse, decided to press on towards Passchendaele in spite of teeming rain and the approaching winter. Having lived through the fiery hell of Pozières, and the depths of misery in the freezing trenches of the Somme Valley, the Anzacs believed that nothing on earth could be worse than what they had already experienced. They were wrong!

Passchendaele! Even after more than eighty years the very name inspires dread, redolent of memories too terrible to recall by those who endured the nightmare of the Third Battle of Ypres. Even now, the arcane legacy of that terrible campaign occasionally claims a life—millions of unexploded shells still lie dormant in the deadly mud of that accursed battlefield, the graveyard of almost a million men, friend and foe.

On 9 October, two British divisions and the 2nd Australian Division attacked the enormously strong and entrenched German positions at Poelcappelle, without the benefit of any air cover or reconnaissance to report on enemy strength and disposition. Western Australian General Talbot Hobbs angrily protested that his troops had been exploited, as usual, and forced to lead units of untrained, untried, unfit British troops, who gave little support and were of more hindrance than help. Without sufficient support, the whole advance floundered in the mud. On 12 October, two Anzac divisons, together with five British divisions, advanced on Passchendaele. Over the next fifteen days, 3000 Allied guns fired more than four million shells at the enemy, destroying the drainage system of the Flanders lowlands and flooding the battlefield. The recoil of the guns caused them to sink deep into the quagmire, making it impossible to calibrate them on target.

By this time the Anzacs resembled a rabble of beggars rather than soldiers. Most parcels from home had been ransacked of the warm pullovers, balaclavas, scarves, socks and gloves lovingly knitted by their families, long before arriving at the Front, and of the fruitcakes, tinned ham and other delicacies. Clad in a motley array of filthy, unravelled jumpers, cardigans, waistcoats, ragged civilian coats, threadbare trousers and overcoats, they wound strips of cloth and rags around their legs, heads and hands to serve as puttees, scarves, caps and gloves, and used newspaper under their shirts for protection against the Arctic wind. A few lucky ones had filched thigh-high rubber boots from enemy corpses, stuffing the toes with paper to make them fit.

The Diggers struggled grimly through a sea of sometimes waist-deep mud—diluted with excreta from overflowing latrines and fragments of rotting bodies, pitted with thousands of shell holes—attempting to lay telegraph and telephone cables, dragging up guns and artillery shells, inundated by torrential rain and a merciless hail of murderous shellfire which never ceased, night or day. Duckboards were quite useless and simply vanished into the morass.

So sodden were the men's clothes and so stiff were they with ice, that they weighed up to 50 lbs (23 kilograms) more than when dry. The men were further burdened with their heavy packs containing ground-sheet and waterlogged blanket, rifle and bandolier, grenades, entrenching tool or spade, their rations and waterbottle.

At each laboured, hazardous step, they sank deep into the icy, sucking mire, often losing their precious boots, which were irreplaceable. Should they inadvertently step into a shell hole, indistinguishable in that swamped terrain, they had no chance at all, and simply sank out of sight within seconds, with only the echoes of their hoarse, frantic cries, and a brief flurry of air bubbles to mark their agonised demise. James and his team strove to find a path through the maze of shell holes, in order to drag up their gun, sometimes almost out of sight in the mud, using as many as thirty men and more than a dozen baulky, terrified horses, many of whom frequently became hopelessly bogged and had to be shot.

Haig had ordered the troops to advance one and a quarter miles (2 kilometres) in twenty-four hours, but by the end of that time, with superhuman effort, only one-quarter of a mile (400 metres) had been achieved. There followed four weeks of heroic, gruelling combat in the freezing, waist-deep mud of the trenches, the troops availing themselves when possible, as they advanced, of the German dugouts. When they were fortunate enough to capture one of these, they slept six or eight together, curled like spoons, unable to move or turn or to scratch the lice which tormented them. The stench of bodies unwashed for many weeks was overpowering, but a small price to pay for the warmth they engendered. Unfortunately, the doors and windows faced the retreating German army, which meant the Allies were still very vulnerable.

After fierce hand-to-hand fighting, some Allied troops finally reached the outskirts of Passchendaele in early November, but, completely exhausted, were forced to withdraw. It was left to the Canadians to finally take what was left of Passchendaele, which concluded the Third Battle of Ypres at the terrible cost of an estimated 448 614 Allied soldiers, including 12 000 Australians. It is little wonder that this campaign has been known as 'Tragic Passchendaele'. A pyrrhic victory indeed, for the gain of 3 or 4 miles (6 or 7 kilometres); far short of Haig's ultimate goal of winning through to the Belgian coast and capturing the vital German U-boat bases.

---

FRANCE
23.10.'17

MY DEAR MOTHER,

*Just a line to say that I am practically well with the exception of being almost without my voice owing to the effects of gas which the huns issue at intervals for our benefit, some of our chaps are almost blind as a result.*

*At present I am out from the guns having a much needed few days rest, after having three weeks rotten time, practically on the go night and day taking part in the offensive that has been going on for sometime.*

*We had a terrible job getting our guns into position on the last occasion, at times they were almost out of sight in the mud and the horses that were trying to pull them were almost as bad. It is almost impossible to find a patch of ground without a shell hole, in fact it has been turned over and over, and as soon as a drop of rain comes it is turned into one huge bog. We used to have twelve horses and about thirty men pulling on ropes, it may have been interesting for some of you but not for us, especially when a 5.9 lobs a few yards away and covers you with mud.* [Even less interesting for the men were the not infrequent occasions when a shell landed on the latrines and showered everyone within a kilometre or so with faeces.]

*You will probably notice some pictures of us in the papers as there was an Aust. photographer taking photos of our battery and one was taken at night of our gun just as it fired, you may notice it.*

*Well I have just been looking around this home of ours and I have come to the conclusion that I would sooner have lived in the pig stys we used to have at home than in a hole like this. I was only wondering the other day what sort of men we will be in a few years time even if we are lucky enough to come through.*

*We are getting that way now that we take as much notice of men and horses getting knocked as we do of having our dinner.*

*We never miss the opportunity of making use of one of the German concrete dugouts whenever an opportunity arrives, they are about the only places in which a man seems to feel safe, although even in these one is in danger, some of them have walls and roof about five feet thick of solid concrete, but the windows and doors are all facing the german guns.*

*The other night he put one right through the window killing six and severely wounding the other three, among them was a corporal and two gnrs. of our battery.*

*Well Mother by rights I should not be telling you all this as it does not do you much good in knowing what is going on over here and besides if the scensor opens it he will probably destroy it.*

*Well by the way how did you enjoy your sojurn in town, I here you went very gay down there, it must have been a nice change after being up home for so long without a break. If I was in your place I would be down there every weekend. Babs was very jubilent at having you down there with her, suppose if she had her way you would be remaining in the city.*

*I had a letter from Fred the other day, he seems to be getting along in the same old way, they have the dust to contend with instead of mud. Oh I forgot to tell you that I saw Thornie a few weeks back, passed him on the road as we were coming out of action, he had just returned from England on leave, was only talking to him for a few minutes as we were both on the move.*

*The weather is very miserable and cold, raining most of the time. I suppose we have practically saw the last of the sunshine for this year.*

*I am afraid I will not be able to send you any Xmas greetings this year as I will not be able to get out to obtain any I may send something later if possible.*

*Well Mother, I think I have made up for lost time on this occassion, so I will close with fondest love and best wishes to all.*

*From Your Affec son Jim*

---

FLANDERS
17.11.'17

DEAREST JEAN [BABS],

*(Before I go any further I hope you will excuse the liberty, I think its the first time I've addressed you so.)*

*I've just been reading our Routine Orders of the Division and discovered Jim's name in the list of decorations, and I see he has been awarded the Military Medal. I'm awfully glad to see his name and I want to congratulate you as well as him. I happen to know what he got the medal for, and I will tell you because no doubt he will make light about the matter (perhaps making very little about it.)*

*To start from the beginning — I was in a party that was sent up to his battery on fatigues!!! trench mortars again!!! That was about three weeks ago. (N.B. During the Passchendaele Campaign). We used to go up every day (reveille 2 a.m.!!!) and back to camp each evening.*

*One night Fritz* [the Germans] *set alight to his (Jim's) gun pit with an incendiary shell, setting alight to the ammunition, Jim and the rest of his detachment putting out the fire which under the conditions was a very game thing to do.*

*Its hardly possible for you to realise the conditions they were under, but anyone who knows can appreciate what they had to do. He told me about it next morning when I was up there, and so I was very pleased to see his name in the awards tonight. I am sure you will feel proud of him, as you have good cause to be. I was lucky knowing him up there, (don't think me greedy). He gave me a big feed of army stew !!! and I can tell you I appreciated it. The rest of the party only had bread and jam to do a pretty solid day's work on, so you can imagine how I appreciated the stew!!!!! I haven't seen Jim since but I am writing him a letter of congrats. Thanks very much*

*old Girl for your letter dated 18.9.'17 and also the Xmas card I
received O.K., its awfully good of you to keep writing to me and I can
assure you I appreciate it very much.*

*I'm damn glad to see that the Government has taken such a firm
hand with the strikers [waterside workers] at last. There's no doubt
that they came a terrible cropper this time. It's to be hoped that this
will teach them a lesson — that is if they have any sense at all. Its a
pity that some of them couldn't be transferred here for a short time, I
guess they would only be too glad to get back to peace and quietness.*

*Glad to hear that you got my P.C. from Blighty, the trip over there
just seems like a pleasant dream. I'm glad to know that Fred is
alright, they seem to be stirring things up in Palestine, according to
the papers they have been doing great work.*

*It will be just about Xmas by the time this reaches you so I'll take
the opportunity to wish you all a very Merry Xmas and a Bright and
Prosperous New Year. I wonder where we'll be this time next year,
back in Aus. I hope. Well dear Girl I must say au revoir with all
sorts of good wishes and best love from your old pal Eric Smith.*

*P.S. I hope you get this alright because I'd like you to know how
Jim won his M.M. and I'm sure he won't have much to say about
it himself.*

[Included in the letter is the following poem:]

SIX DAY'S LEAVE
Of many joys the poets sing
And round them myriad tributes bring,
and fancies weave,
They might their choicest terms employ,
Yet never could express the joy,
From all the moil of shots and shell,
From all that makes this life a hell,
I knew not that the World could hold
such bliss as six day's leave.

James thought little of his decoration 'For Bravery in the Field' (one of
the highest honours for valour available to the rank and file soldier).

War, and its associated peril, brings out the very best and the very worst in men, and he'd seen it all—the craven cowardice, the sexual perversion, the dishonesty, the hatred, brutality, greed and envy, and, in shining contrast, the courage, love and self-sacrifice of the vast majority of his comrades. He felt that, having witnessed countless acts of heroism and bravery on the battlefield go unrecognised, he had no more right to the decoration than many thousands of others.

To James and his fellow Anzacs, mateship was far more important and meaningful than it was to the British and French soldiers, who were able to receive frequent letters, parcels and newspapers from home, only a day or two old, and even to spend short leaves with their families. Twelve thousand miles (20 000 kilometres) or more from home, the Australians and New Zealanders had no such way of boosting their morale, and unless severely wounded and unfit for further service, had no prospect of being repatriated until the war's end.

Longed-for letters from home often took six or even nine months to arrive, if indeed they arrived at all, since many ended up at the bottom of the sea. Sometimes a precious parcel was stolen by a corrupt base official, or those behind the lines, or if they did arrive the contents were often mouldy and inedible after a voyage of many months duration. Any newspapers that were available rarely mentioned Australia at all.

Completely isolated from all they held dear, with home a distant, impossible dream, the men relied totally on their mates, bonding far closer than brothers, in a climate of terrifying uncertainty, fear and mortality. Together they sang the sentimental songs that reminded them of home—'There's a long, long trail awinding', 'Little Grey Home in the West', 'Roses in Picardy', 'Rose of No Man's Land' or 'Gundagai'—to the accompaniment of a mouth organ, tin whistle or even a comb and cigarette paper. Ivor Novello's poignant song perhaps epitomises more than any other their painful longing for home.

Keep the home fires burning, while your hearts are yearning,
Tho' the lads are far away they dream of home.
There's a silver lining thru the dark cloud shining,
Turn the dark cloud inside out till the boys come home.

Then there were other songs which they sang with wry humour, usually untouched by bitterness. Officers and NCOs were treated with legendary disrespect:

> If the Sergeant steals your rum, never mind.
> If the Sergeant steals your rum, never mind.
> He's just a bloody sot
> He can take the bloody lot
> If the Sergeant steals your rum, never mind.

More cynical was 'Hangin' on the old barbed wire'.

> We know where the Infantry is,
> Hangin' on the old barbed wire.
> We know where the Sar. Major is,
> Hiding 'neath the dugout floor.
> If you want to see the Generals, I know where they are,
> Theyre miles and miles behind the lines,
> But if you want to find the infantry, I know where they are,
> They're hangin' on the old barbed wire.

Sometimes, cruelly, a postcard from 'a kind, concerned friend' would arrive, telling of a wife's infidelity, or a letter from a fiancée or sweetheart tired of waiting, spelling the end of their hopes and dreams of home and blissful happiness. Many of these men no longer cared if they lived or died, and it was only their mates who pulled them through. Some men even returned early from leave, preferring to be with their cobbers at the Front, feeling guilty that they were not sharing the danger with them.

James Carthew and three of his friends had, early in 1916, made a pact to refuse promotion or a commission in order to stay together. One man accepted a stripe soon after, but in spite of two or three times being offered a commission, James honoured his commitment and remained a private. There were, in fact, many like James who elected to stay with their friends because, inevitably, there was not the same sense of mateship among the commissioned officers.

James never spoke of his despair on losing his two remaining best mates, but his yellow-leafed diary (unfortunately now destroyed) starkly described waking from an exhausted sleep, from which not even a direct shell burst had roused him, to find six of his comrades dead and three severely wounded. All that was left of his two friends was 'a mass of bloody fragments, like cat's meat, their greatcoats looking as though the rats had eaten them'.

After only a few months in the trenches, many Diggers, even those from deeply religious backgrounds, felt they could no longer place their faith in God; a God to whom, they had been told, even a sparrow's fall was important. A God who watched benignly while millions of his beloved creatures maimed, blinded, tortured, dismembered and savagely killed other young innocents with whom they had no quarrel. And yet, when face to face with death, almost all called on the Lord for aid. To these men, the death of one or more of their cobbers was literally the greatest calamity of all; the worst card that a callous fate could deal.

# ⤍ Freedom ⤎

*T*HE WAR DRAGGED ON. Sometimes after a fierce battle a unit would advance and take a few German trenches, only to retreat to their original position, or even further back, the next day, or the next week—costing perhaps thousands of lives, for no conceivable gain.

The gunners' lives were now constantly at risk, not only from the enemy, but from their own field guns. After three years of daily use the barrels were severely worn, sometimes exploding on firing and, all too often, the shells fell short into their own trenches.

Not only was the French army virtually burnt out, but British morale was at an all-time low ebb. After three long years of desperate conflict under appalling stress, poor food and little rest and recreation, the troops had lost any semblance of patriotism, and continued to fight only because they were ordered to do so, sometimes literally at the muzzle of a pistol, and because the alternative was certain death by firing squad.

By this time, many of Britain's volunteer soldiers lay dead on the battlefields of Mons, Ypres, Neuve Chapelle, Loos, Verdun, Pozières, the Somme and Passchendaele. In their places were the conscripts; many from the city slums, factories and mines, puny and narrow-chested, some mentally and physically unfit, and others fresh out of school—enthusiastic, green, unseasoned youths, half trained and sometimes of more trouble than they were worth to the cynical, war-weary veterans.

However, the indomitable Diggers' spirits were still high, and having enlisted to give the Hun a trouncing and win the war, they intended to see it through. Regarded with envy by the Tommies, who labelled them 'undisciplined, uncouth and drunken larrikins' (which some certainly were), the Australians, with the New Zealanders and Canadians, were unquestionably the finest troops in the line. Recognising this, Haig and his subordinate Gough continued to assign the Anzacs (who had been reformed into a single 'Australian Corps' in November) to the most difficult and dangerous sectors of the Front. It was also about this time that the German High Command realised that, in fact, the Anzacs were their most formidable adversaries. (A cartoon published in the Berlin papers depicted Lloyd George climbing laboriously towards Victory over an enormous mountain of Anzac and Canadian corpses.)

The enemy, too, was recruiting unfit men and mere sixteen-year-olds into 'the sausage machine', as the armies on both sides were cynically called, but early in 1918 their forces were considerably strengthened by 35 divisions, each of 4000 men, and 2000 heavy guns from the collapsed Russian Front.

---

BELGIUM
15.1.'18

DEAR MOTHER,

*Am sending along a few views which I have taken on the sly but one must be careful as it is a very serious crime if found out. I am sending this to England by a pal to be posted. Well I think this is all this time so will close with love to you all.*

---

BELGIUM
16.1.'18

MY DEAR MOTHER,

*Just a line to say that I am still alive and well, but have not had any news of you for some time. I suppose the submarines are responsible.*

*We are going through the winter fairly well, we have had a good deal of snow and there is about 4 inches on the ground but it isnt nearly as bad as last winter yet. I had 2 letters from the Girl, she said she had recieved a letter from Nell which travelled by the first Trans Continental train, it must be quite a novelty to see the trains departing for Melbourne.*

*Well I was rather an important individual last Sunday, was presented with my ribbon by General Birdwood and after shaking hands was complimented on what he said was good work.*

*I am sending the piece of ribbon to the Girl, and when I recieve the medal will send it along to you.*

*Things are keeping quiet, no excitement such as we have been used to since coming to France. At present I am down from the guns for a bit of a spell but it will not be long before we are all on the move.*

---

FRANCE
10.3.'18

MY DEAR MOTHER,

*Two letters from Add to hand, glad to hear that you are all well. Well I am writing this outside our gun pit and taking advantage of a bit of sunshine. I think the winter is practically at an end and I am dam glad of it too.*

*I have just recieved a letter from the Girl who is in Bunbury on holidays staying at the Rose Hotel. She seems to be having a gay time of it, with the ex-Premier dining at Gov. House. I am pleased to say I have recieved all the parcels you have sent including the Xmas hamper, it was Tres bon.*

*Was glad to hear you had a decent harvest this year seeing that the crops in general were a failure.*

*There is a very decided smell of gas here, all hands are sneezing and coughing — if it gets any worse I will have to cease writing. We are having a fairly busy time here lately owing to the favourable weather and before long are expecting something big.*

*I would have liked to see conscription passed but as Add said they should not have had a referendum on it.*

*Well Mother will close with love to all*

*From your loving son Jim.*

By 1918, the Allies were bracing themselves for the major offensive which must come soon, if the enemy hoped to snatch victory before the Americans (who had declared war on Germany in April 1917) could make any useful contribution to the action.

Marshal Foch had been appointed Supreme Commander of all Allied forces, even though Petain, who was also a brilliant military strategist, had largely restored order to the battered French Army. However, morale was still low and the British Army was in no better condition. Three years of bitter, unremitting conflict had decimated both armies, and the harsh, often unjust discipline, appalling conditions, poor diet and little rest and recreation had reduced the ranks to a sullen, hopeless state of apathy. Only the spectre of the court martials and the firing squad prevented wholesale revolt.

While the Germans wintered in relative comfort in their deep, massively fortified, safe and well-furnished dugouts, some even furnished with electric light, chairs and beds, the Allies endured unspeakable conditions in their shallow, freezing, mud-filled trenches; filthy, stinking and lice-ridden. Often, with an east wind, they could hear the enemy lustily singing their rousing German songs in their warm, dry refuges. Sometimes the pure, poignant sound of a bugle would be heard on the still, cold air, and even the haunting notes of a violin sonata.

Although the Allied High Command had had prior knowledge of the coming enemy offensive, from their network of listening posts, and from captured prisoners, they were unable to reconnoitre from the air because of constant patrolling by enemy planes, and because all troop movements were made at night. They therefore had little knowledge of the immensity of the opposing forces assembling under cover of darkness. Ranging along the entire Western Front from the British Channel to Rheims were massed 206 German divisions, comprising nearly one million men, of which approximately 63 divisions and 6000 big guns faced Allied forces of a mere 35 divisions and 2000 big guns.

At dawn on 21 March 1918, General Ludendorff unleashed his offensive with a shattering roar, deluging the British sector with a lethal barrage of gas shells capable of reaching more than a score of miles beyond the Front, and simultaneously detonating explosives in saps beneath the British lines. By a bitter stroke of fate, fortune had favoured the enemy, and a dense fog blanketed the battlefield and muffled sound, so that the British were totally unable to see or hear the stealthily approaching army.

While the German field guns bombarded the front lines and machine-gun posts, the huge guns concentrated on the artillery, horse lines and the communication trenches which stretched back miles, along which mule trains carried ammunition, food and supplies. With these reduced to smoking craters, and the deeply laid telephone and electric cables destroyed, the situation was grave.

Unable to retaliate because of poor visibility, the British, and some French units, were overwhelmed by wave after endless wave of superbly trained Prussian storm troopers who attacked with flamethrowers, grenades and machine guns, incinerating, bayoneting and taking prisoners while overhead German planes bombed with impunity.

As the fog cleared in the late afternoon, the British rallied courageously and counterattacked, inflicting severe casualties on the enemy. At day's end, the field was carpeted with khaki and grey-clad corpses and thousands of wounded men, crying out weakly for water and aid. As usual, stretcher-bearers, medical workers and chaplains from both sides, working through the night, ventured out at great risk to their own lives to render aid and bring in the countless casualties.

Once again, Haig issued an order of the day, praising the courage and dedication of the troops, and concluding: 'Every position must be held to the last man. With our backs to the wall and believing in the justice of our cause, each one must fight on until the end. The future of our homes and mankind depends on the conduct of each one of us at this critical moment.' When this order was read out, so great was the prevailing bitterness against Haig that even the officers ignored the derisive and ribald comments of the men who shouted that the officer could 'wipe his effing arse' with the document.

Somehow, as the days passed, the main body of defence held, but the flanks were slowly driven back and the central zone was forced to retreat again and again, to avoid being encircled and captured. Within three weeks the British 5th Army was almost wiped out, and General Gough's 3rd Army driven back nearly 40 miles (65 kilometres).

Although Foch deployed some of his French divisions to reinforce the British line, both armies were deathly weary and hopeless as they fell back, time after time. Most had had no sleep or rest for days, performing like sleepwalkers, scarcely caring whether they lived or died, some no longer even bothering to take shelter from snipers or shells. They had lost more territory in a scant three weeks than they had gained in the previous three years, at the dreadful cost of millions of lives—a staggering average of more than 7000 dead each day.

The Germans, too, were tired, having advanced so rapidly that they had outdistanced their supply units, and short of food, being unable to commandeer any from the already ravished countryside. However, flushed with triumph, they were confident that victory was theirs, if they could continue to keep the Allies on the run and drive them into the sea to ultimate defeat. The Kaiser was so jubilant at the headlong advance of his army that he awarded General Hindenburg the Iron Cross First Class. Curiously, despite the fact that Ludendorff had orchestrated the entire campaign, he was given no award.

By 25 March, no Allied line stood between the Germans and the vital rail junction at Amiens. At this point, the 3rd and 4th Australian divisions, commanded by Monash, were rushed to the Front, stunned to find that Pozières, Mouquet Farm, Baupaume, Hamel and many more villages, and miles of bloodstained territory they had fought and died for, had been reclaimed by the Germans, and that Villers-Bretonneux and Amiens looked certain to fall undefended. British General Congreve was heard to remark: 'Thank heavens the Australians have arrived.'

As they marched, the thousands of refugees who clogged the roads while fleeing from the enemy halted and began to straggle back, overjoyed that 'les Australiens' had arrived, and confident that they would once more halt the disastrous German advance. Retreating Tommies, exhausted and hopeless, jeered tiredly at the Anzacs, shouting that they were going the wrong way and singing 'It's the wrong way to Tipperary ...' Many had fled their units in blind panic in the confusion of the retreat, abandoning their weapons as they ran, and some of these, heartened by the Australian reinforcements, were recruited by Monash to join his Anzac Corps.

On 24 April, in spite of little rest or food after their hasty, forced march, and greatly outnumbered by the crack Prussian troops, two

Australian divisions incredibly stemmed the German juggernaut after several days of desperate, savage fighting near Villers-Bretonneux, saving the town and nearby Amiens from total destruction. It was here that the Red Baron, von Richthofen, was shot down and killed, apparently by an Australian bullet. It was also here that Western Australian Lieutenant Sadlier, with the help of his platoon Sergeant and squad, attacked and destroyed six machine-gun posts, winning himself the Victoria Cross. (To this day, the citizens and schoolchildren of Villers-Bretonneux honour the memory of those Anzacs who made the supreme sacrifice or were wounded while repelling the German advance and preserving the town from virtual annihilation in April 1918. The Mayor's chambers are proudly adorned with the crossed Australian and Tricolor Flags, and the school building was presented to the town by the State of Victoria.)

Determined to reverse the situation, Ludendorff ordered a massive reprisal on the pursuing Anzacs. Trench mortars raked the front lines, field guns directed a concentrated bombardment on the main sector, and the huge howitzers again targeted the artillery, horse lines, field hospitals and supply and ammunition vehicles to the rear with a merciless barrage. The frightful concussion of these murderous missiles alone could burst the lungs and eardrums and cause total blindness by literally tearing the victim's eyeballs from their sockets. Crown Prince Ruprecht's dreadful weapon, the *flammenwerfer*, wrought horrific death and injury, directing a stream of molten tar and petrol at the Anzacs, causing agonising third-degree burns and stripping the roasted flesh from their bones as the tar hardened.

Most terrible of all, more than 20 000 mustard and phosgene gas shells were unleashed to rain ceaselessly on the Allies. As it was almost impossible to work actively while wearing a gas mask, due to lack of oxygen and restricted hearing and vision, there were many thousands of casualties and the battlefield was littered with coughing, vomiting, blinded men staggering helplessly around, to be easily picked off and slaughtered by snipers and machine gunners.

## DULCE ET DECORUM EST

Bent double, like old beggars under sacks,
Knock-kneed, coughing like hags, we cursed through sludge,
Till on the haunting flares we turned our backs
And towards our distant rest began to trudge.
Men marched asleep. Many had lost their boots
But limped on, blood-shod. All went lame; all blind;
Drunk with fatigue; deaf even to the hoots
Of tired, outstripped Five-Nines that dropped behind.

Gas! Gas! Quick, boys! An ecstasy of fumbling,
Fitting the clumsy helmets just in time;
But someone still was yelling out and stumbling
And flound'ring like a man in fire or lime ...
Dim, through the misty panes and thick green light,
As under a green sea, I saw him drowning.

In all my dreams, before my helpless sight,
He plunges at me, guttering, choking, drowning.

If in some smothering dreams you too could pace
Behind the wagon that we flung him in,
And watch the white eyes writhing in his face,
His hanging face, like a devil's sick of sin;
If you could hear, at every jolt, the blood
Come gargling from the froth-corrupted lungs,
Obscene as cancer, bitter as the cud
Of vile, incurable sores on innocent tongues—
My friend, you would not tell with such high zest
To children, ardent for more desperate glory,
The old Lie: Dulce et decorum est
Pro patria mori.[1]

WILFRED OWEN

[1] [How sweet and dutiful it is to die for one's country.]

Because the stretcher-bearers were able to deal with only the most gravely wounded, the gas victims were forced to fend for themselves, and were herded into groups where they sat or lay, their eyes streaming incessantly, coughing away their lives. Some of those less affected would assemble the victims capable of walking into long crocodile queues, each with his left hand holding the shoulder of the man before him and, led by one of the walking wounded, would attempt the long trek back to the dressing stations behind the lines. Many fell by the wayside, unable to summon up the breath to walk, and others quietly died before they could reach the field hospital.

Among these tragic, blinded gas victims was James Carthew. His mother's agony of mind on the receipt of the telegram stating that James had been severely gassed and blinded can only be imagined. No doubt Nellie would also have been officially notified, and the suspense as they waited for news, month after month, must have been dreadful.

Of all the terrible weapons of war, poison gas is the most diabolically cruel. First used by the Germans at Ypres in April 1915, causing huge casualties, the British soon retaliated, but only with limited success because the wind currents were so unreliable. On one occasion, during the Battle of Loos, Haig had ordered gas to be released during a coming action, but when the wind died the Commander refused to release the gas. General Gough, apprised of the situation and told that his own troops would be severely affected, refused to rescind the order and told him to proceed as planned, 'because it would take too long to alter the chain of command.' As a result, nearly 2000 British troops died, needlessly and cruelly. The resulting carnage resembled a slaughterhouse, with the dead and dying lying in piles, and gas settled in the Allied trenches where men vomited and choked to death. These deaths were regarded as mere statistics.

Until gas helmets (the forerunners of the more effective gas mask) were issued, the troops were told to saturate their woollen caps with urine, and hold them over their nose and mouth—a crude and not very efficient method of protection, but probably better than none at all. Unfortunately, fear sometimes made them unable to void, though at other times acute terror often caused incontinence. Subsequently, bombs and shells were used with greater accuracy to disseminate the poison.

Three main types of gas were used: lachrymatory, or tear gas, which caused acute weeping, leaving the victims unable to tolerate a mask; mustard gas, which seared and blistered the skin and eyes, and when inhaled burned away the linings of the lungs and caused liver damage; and phosgene mixed with chlorine, which caused the lungs to fill with water, so that those affected quite literally drowned in their own body fluids.

Although the troops were usually ordered to sleep in their masks, few did so as the insufficient oxygen filtering through engendered a feeling of suffocation. It was common to find a trench full of corpses, their faces darkly cyanosed and eyes dreadfully distended in their last futile struggle with death. Being heavier than air, poison gas would settle in the trenches so that, even if roused by the gas rattle, very often the men had already inhaled the deadly fumes. By the time they were able to don their masks, they found it quite impossible to tolerate the lack of oxygen and would irrationally tear them off again in a mad frenzy as they fought for breath.

A hospital nurse was to write: 'The terrible gas is the worst thing I have ever seen. The intensity of the pain robs a man of all ability to do anything but suffer. The fiery agony eats deeper and deeper into his heart and lungs and a lessening of the terrible fire is all he craves for. It is a nameless horror and the very sight adds ten years to ones life.'

Treatment for those severly gassed included aspiration. Without the benefit of anaesthetic, a long, thick needle was inserted through the chest wall or back muscle into each lung, and fluid and pus pumped out using a primitive rubber pump. In severe cases this agonising procedure was often performed daily for several months.

Even for those who survived a severe gas attack, the prognosis was bleak. The victims faced a lifetime of ill health, tormented by an incessant cough which tore the lining from their lungs, even during sleep. There would be frequent stays in hospital, suffering from bronchitis, pneumonia, pleurisy, influenza, emphysema, tuberculosis and probably cancer. All ended their days prematurely, worn out by the daily struggle for the air which most of us take for granted. (In James's instance, his lungs were further troubled by asthma, making his life, at times, a living hell.)

James spent nearly five months in an English hospital. Apart from being severely gassed, he was blind for a considerable time from mustard-gas burns to his eyes. Once he had recovered somewhat, James rather enjoyed hospital life, having once cherished the ambition to become a doctor. He revered the medicos and simply adored the nurses, making himself useful around the wards and in the kitchens, as soon as he was able.

---

3RD. AUSTRALIAN AUXILLIARY HOSPITAL, DARTFORD
ENGLAND
11.7.'18

DEAR MOTHER,

*You will see by the above that I have been transferred from Croydon — have been here 2 days only and feel like a fish out of water after being at the other hospital so long — they were all sorry to lose me but I think I had a good run, nearly four months, and only for our doctor and sister being away I would have still been there, it was absolutely the best home I have had since I left home, the whole staff would do anything for me, I think I was known throughout the whole division, dont know why.*

*Old Fred arrived just as we were sitting down to tea, the 2 cooks and me and before tea was finished we had his whole experiences since leaving Aust. John Macaulay is not in it with Fred for talking. I dont know what they are going to do with me here but I dont think they will keep me very long as our divisions are all so short of men, we seem to be the only ones that are doing any fighting over there now, and as soon as one is able to get about he is sent back to his unit.*

*On Monday last we went down Petticoat lane to have a look, and its some show, you never saw such a collection of foreigners in all your life. I thought a few bombs amongst them would do a world of good, they absolutely go mad when there is an air raid on — I think they are worse than the gippos. Well the war will soon be going 4 years now and there doesn't seem to be any end in sight yet.*

*It has done nothing but rain since I have been here, and when I was here last year it was snowing. If we are away another year one will not know anyone when we go back.*

*Well Mother will close now with love and best wishes to you all.*
*From your loving son Jim.*

Although it did not seem like it to James, the end of the war was, at last, in sight. The turning point came during the Aisne–Marne Offensive of July and August. Germany had lost half a million troops in the preceding five months (including 30 000 taken prisoner), during which time America finally poured nearly 300 000 men per month into the war effort.

In May 1918, Major General Sir John Monash, who had been knighted on New Year's Day, was given command of the Australian Corps, replacing Birdwood who was put in charge of the 5th British Army. At Hamel in early July, Monash led his army to a stunning victory using tactics that were to become a model for the Allied Offensive. He repeated the manoeuvres in early August in the area of Marcourt Valley, with 20 Allied divisions, capturing a total of 30 000 prisoners. (This was described by Ludendorff as a black day for Germany, and by others as one of the finest feats of the war.) Monash again attacked at Mont St Quentin and Péronne in August and September, capturing more than 13 000 prisoners. More attacks on the Hindenburg Line followed, culminating in a brilliant assault by the 6th Brigade at Montbrehain on 5 October. This was to be the last action fought by Australian infantry, and the men of the Australian Corps were retired for a well-earned rest.

By October, Germany conceded that the war must be ended and began to retire, the troops wreaking pillage, destruction, murder and rape across France and Belgium. Finally, forced by Marshal Foch, Germany sued for unconditional peace. The rumours of defeat sparked a mutiny at Kiel Naval Base, and the collapse of the Austro–Hungarian Empire followed. In spite of this, hostilities continued unabated during negotiations, and many hundreds of men on both sides were killed tragically and unnecessarily, even after the terms of surrender had been accepted. (Among those killed was the poet Wilfred Owen, who died on 4 November, a scant week before the armistice, while obeying orders to needlessly pursue the fleeing Germans across the Belgian canals.) One British general who tried to order his troops into action was pelted with mud and stones by the infuriated soldiers.

MY DEAR MOTHER,

*Just a few lines to say that I am still here, so far we have heard
nothing as regards embarkation and are naturally concerned as so
many things is likely to take place here, so dont be surprised should
you hear that I am sailing for France instead of for home.*

*I had my medal presented to me last week, so it is not worth while
sending it to you now that I have a chance of going home, I felt quite
important for about five minutes.*

*We are having a very decent time here, we are taken on bathing
parade every afternoon — march through the town headed by the
band, it seems to cause quite a deal of excitement among the many
holiday makers that are here.*

*I met Dan Quinlivan in London, he was on leave from France,
I hardly knew him but he knew me, also met a son of Vallance
the policeman who used to be in Bright, he has gone home on the
last boat.*

*I was glad to hear ther was a chance of the old place being sold,
it would be best for all of you to have a change away somewhere.*

*Well Mother this is all so will close with love to you all.*

*From your loving son Jim.*

James did not sail again for France. To his family's great relief, on
23 September 1918 he sailed for Fremantle on a hospital ship, leaving
behind him three terrible, indescribably bloody, soul-destroying years
on the Western Front.

It must have been an emotional moment when James and the
rest of his wounded mates first sighted the shores of Western
Australia. They were up well before dawn, the blind guided and
those unable to walk carried on deck by their cobbers and placed
near the ship's railings, the others standing silently, straining their
eyes to the horizon for the first glimpse of that low, sandy, unim-
pressive but beloved coastline. Then, as the eastern sky paled and
the first vague outline of the hills were viewed, a low, wordless murmur was heard. Somewhere on that packed foredeck someone had

begun to softly play 'Home Sweet Home' on his mouth organ and, suddenly, every eye was blinded by the tears dammed up during the endless, terrible years of their long exile. They were home, they were home!

## EVERYONE SANG

Everyone suddenly burst out singing;
And I was filled with such delight
As prisoned birds must find in freedom,
Winging wildly across the white
Orchards and dark-green fields; on—on—and out of sight.

Everyone's voice was suddenly lifted;
And beauty came like the setting sun:
My heart was shaken with tears; and horror
Drifted away ... O, but Everyone
Was a bird; and the song was wordless; the singing will
never be done.

SIEGFRIED SASSOON

# ⚘ Epilogue ⚘

$A$T PRECISELY THE ELEVENTH HOUR of the eleventh day of the eleventh month of 1918, the guns abruptly fell silent. After more than four dreadful, agonising years of attrition encompassing almost the entire civilised world, the war, for most, was finally over.

One would expect that the news would have been greeted by the troops with triumphant euphoria, rapturous celebration and relief. In fact, this was not so. Brigadier G. Elkington noted: 'There was no cheering or excitement amongst the men. They seemed too exhausted, and no-one seemed to be able to comprehend that it was all over.'

For some, the anguish had just begun; there were many more casualties of this brutal conflict to follow. A large number of men, joyful to be finally home after dreaming for four long years of a blissful reunion, found that their wives or sweethearts, tiring of their grass widowhood, were bestowing their favours elsewhere. There were other wives who could not accept that their virile, handsome, fun-loving young men were now amputees, shell-shocked, gassed, blinded or ill. Many veterans, having found themselves rejected after surviving four years of living hell, took their own lives.

Then there were the bereaved, heartbroken mothers who faded and quietly died because they no longer wished to live, their mainsprings broken. There were some, like Fred's landlady Mrs Forbes, whose one remaining son returned blind, hideously mutilated and half-insane, destroying the harmony of the home and reducing his womenfolk to nervous wrecks.

There was the bitter loneliness of widows and fiancées, like Ethel Seymour, who would never again know the love of a man, for with more than 60 000 males dead there were far too few to go around in post-war Australia, or indeed anywhere else in the world. And there were those who could not forget, remembering endlessly the mates who had died terribly, perhaps visiting the bereaved families to mourn with them. Remembering, too, the eyes of those enemies they had killed: the expression of surprise, dawning horror and disbelief, and the absolute awful finality of blankness in those dead eyes as life was extinguished. Did they have mothers, wives, children, now grieving, as many thousands of Australian families grieved?

Most tragic of all, perhaps, were the shell-shocked and head injured, for whom the war would never end. These poor souls lived in a terrifying world peopled with unimaginable horrors. Some were even unable to recognise their anguished wives and mothers, cowering in terror at their approach. Literally frightened of their own shadows, a loud noise or a banging door would send them diving under the nearest bed, gibbering with fear, sobbing and shaking like an aspen. Some recovered sufficiently to live a more or less normal life; the remainder were relegated to hospitals for the psychiatric care of veterans. Here they roamed the lighted wards night after night, too fearful to lie down because of the inevitable night terrors and the suppressed memories that surfaced in all their ghastly horror when they slept. Most were docile, like robots, staring perpetually into space; others were violent and required heavy sedation, but apart from bromide, morphia, laudanum and other opiates, and aspirin for pain, there were few drugs to help their plight. And for their families there was a long agony, ending only in merciful death.

To the majority of men who returned, trying to get on with their lives again was sometimes difficult. They were expected to be the same young men who had jauntily waved goodbye three or four years ago, but they were as different from those naïve, happy-go-lucky, fun-loving youngsters as night is to day. They were still young in years, but older than Time itself in bitter experience, unable to blot out the scalding, traumatic memories of suffering, tragedy and unbearable loss.

Because most never spoke of their years of hell, their families did not understand their restlessness, their sudden moods, their need to commune with their mates who had gone through the same experiences and suffered the same losses. In fact, they sometimes felt like strangers in the bosom of their loving families, comfortable only with each other.

Inevitably, their values and their whole conception of life were totally changed, having seen the very worst that life—and death—had to offer. They could not comprehend their wives' preoccupation with the most petty, trivial situations, nor tolerate their constant nit-picking, and felt unable to explain this to those who found this inexplicable. And so they suffered in silence, festering inside, and sought more and more the company of mates who understood, and the alcohol which brought temporary oblivion.

Many marriages survived only because there was little alternative, and because men felt obliged to honour their commitments. Divorce in 1919 was still frowned upon by the rigid conventions of the day and could only be obtained where one party was guilty of adultery, or by refusal of conjugal rights. There was no such option as counselling in those days; the returned soldiers were expected to get on with their lives, and in the tough, sanguine pioneer spirit of making the best of things, most did.

Elsewhere, in shattered Europe, things were even more grim. Great Britain emerged from the holocaust victorious in name only, no longer ruling the waves. The dominions of her great Empire were beginning to show signs of independence, her colonies no longer subservient. Her finest youth—the educated middle classes, the nobility, the ordinary people who were the backbone of the land—had been brutally decimated, almost irretrievably, leaving the country weak, uncertain and fearful of the future. Her exchequer had been exhausted, not only by the horrendous cost of the war but by the burden of maintaining a military presence in her rebellious dominions: India, Africa, Northern Ireland and the numerous protectorates and mandates around the globe. Her enormous wealth had melted away, leaving the country bankrupt for at least the next twenty years, as indeed was the rest of Europe.

During the course of the Great War, an estimated eight to ten million troops were killed during the conflict, and more than twenty million were wounded or disabled. In Australia, from a population of almost five million, 417 000 men had volunteered and 330 000 had served overseas.

Approximately 60 000 were killed, of whom 46 000 died on the Western Front, and 156 000 were wounded or taken prisoner. At Gallipoli, 5833 Australians were killed in action, and 1985 died later of wounds. (The Australian Army suffered a 64.8 per cent casualty rate, by far the greatest percentage of any Allied army, which could be partly explained by General Haig's predilection for sending the Anzacs into the worst, most difficult and dangerous areas of the Front. It may also be due to the Anzac spirit of rash bravery, initiative and daring, which made them such superb soldiers.)

During the signing of the Treaty of Versailles in 1919, when delegates of the victorious countries converged on the Palace of Versailles to rearrange the map of Europe, a euphoric American President, Woodrow Wilson, was said to refer to the conflict as 'the war to end all wars'. On the other hand, many observers believed that the terms of the Treaty were unrealistic and too crippling to Germany, which was in any case completely bankrupt already, leaving the way open for grievances to surface. Lloyd George was to remark, prophetically: 'The Treaty was all a great pity. We shall have to do the same thing all over again in twenty-five years time, at three times the cost.' In the same year, Siegfried Sassoon penned this chillingly prescient verse (extract from *Aftermath*):

Do you remember the rats; and the stench
Of corpses rotting in the front of the front-line trench—
And dawn coming, dirty-white, and chill with hopeless rain?
Do you ever stop and ask, 'Is it all going to happen again?'

It is interesting to note that the Australians, unlike the New Zealanders and Canadians, were not required to furnish troops for the Occupation Forces in Germany. Their well-deserved reputation as fun-loving, high-spirited larrikins, and their lack of discipline and riotous behaviour, obviously made them unsuitable candidates for the purpose of maintaining law and order among their former enemy.

In 1919 a mission was sent to the Dardanelles, led by Charles Bean, the official Australian war historian, and General Hughes, the officer commanding the light horse on Gallipoli during the campaign which culminated in the fatal charge on the Nek. It was a sombre group that surveyed the burial grounds and the battle sites of Hill 60, Chunuk Bair, Baby 700, Quinn's Post, Gaba Tepe, Shell Green, Johnston's Jolly and Lone Pine, where the truncated pine tree, a practice target for the troops, still stood. 'Saddest of all,' wrote Bean, 'our unburied dead—the faded red and purple emblems on the uniforms of the 6th Battery, lying where they fell at Lone Pine, the tragic skeletons half clad in rotting uniforms bearing the yellow and black colour patches of the 10th Light Horse and the yellow and green of the 8th lying on an area less than three tennis courts on the Nek, where they died in one of the bravest charges ever made.'

One wonders whether General Hughes felt any guilt or regret for his part in obstinately insisting that the charge go ahead. Or perhaps he shared the view of his British counterpart, General Weston, who was heard to remark, 'Casualties? What do I care for casualties?'

The Anzacs honoured the Turks for their courage, tenacious fighting spirit and fair dealing, and in return the Turks respected the Anzacs as honourable and daring adversaries. Their most formidable opponent was Colonel Mustapha Kemal, who was chiefly responsible for moulding the Turkish Army into an efficient fighting force. In 1934, as President Kemal Attaturk and architect of modern Turkey, he was to write this moving tribute: 'Those heroes that shed their blood and lost their lives ... you are now lying in the soil of a friendly country. Therefore rest in peace. There is no difference between the Johnnies and the Mehmets to us where they lie side by side in this country of ours. You the mothers who sent their sons from far away countries, wipe away your tears. Your sons are now lying in our bosom and are in peace. After having lost their lives on this land they have become our sons as well.'

The narrow passage separating Princess Royal Harbour and King George Sound at Albany in Western Australia, through which sailed the armada bound for Egypt and the Dardanelles, is named Attaturk Entrance in honour of President Attaturk, and the Turks have officially named the beach where the Anzacs landed Anzac Cove. It is a tranquil place today, a shrine for the hundreds of thousands of Australian and New Zealand pilgrims, and others, who are drawn there to pay reverent tribute to the young heroes who were to gain lasting glory and immortality in that famous defeat of 1915. We shall never forget.

—— • ——

Charles Carthew has no known grave. He and the rest of his beloved troop, except for Corporal M.H. Griggs who survived, lay for more than four years unburied, prey to the scavengers which savaged and scattered their bones. In 1920, the burial parties collected their remains for burial in a communal grave, as they would have wished. Their names are inscribed on the monument at Lone Pine which commemorates the 3268 Australians and 456 New Zealanders who have no known graves, and the 960 Australians and 252 New Zealanders who were buried at sea after evacuation, having died due to wounds or disease. It stands over the centre of the Turkish trenches and tunnels which were the scene of heavy fighting during the August offensive.

Charles's fiancée, Ethel Seymour, never married. She remained on the family farm, which was willed to her and her brother, as an unpaid drudge for her brother's wife and family, and was eventually swindled out of her inheritance.

Like many thousands of young women between the wars, Adelaide, Nell and Emily Carthew also remained spinsters, caring for their mother Margaret until her death in 1928. Jane ('Babs') Carthew was almost forty when she married Peter Craig, a farmer, but there were no children. The sisters all lived well into their nineties; Babs was ninety-seven when she died, living independently until the last. It was during these latter years that she talked of her brothers during my visits and gave me the letters and memorabilia on which I have based this book. They had survived for nearly seventy years in an old tin trunk, lovingly preserved with lavender, which luckily repelled the moths and silverfish, and they are still in surprisingly good condition.

Fred Carthew must have been one of Western Australia's first conservationists, unfortunately forty years ahead of his time. On his return from the war, he took up land before accepting a position as Primary Producer's Organiser, travelling the country advising farmers. He tried to persuade them to put back into the soil what they had taken out, and not to denude their properties of trees or use pesticides, which also killed the native wildlife. Unfortunately, most of the cockies, as he called them, regarded him as a harmless eccentric, but I like to think that some of his ideas took root. He corresponded with Lady Eve Balfour, whom he had met in London, and many scientists in Germany and elsewhere, but refused a request by the Country Party to stand for Parliament where he might have made some impact. In 1939 he rejoined the army as an officer, but as he was by then forty-four years old he was not sent into active service. He married at the age of forty, although the marriage ended a few years later. Fred died in his nineties.

James Carthew, my father, never spoke of his experiences at the Western Front, almost as though having once opened the Pandora's box of memories it would be impossible to close the lid on the nightmare of the Great War. Neither did he mention how he won his Military Medal, but would only say, with a grin, that he'd pulled a dead donkey from a shell hole, or saved the Colonel's afternoon tea, or found the medal in a bully beef tin. It was not until I read these letters in 1980 that I learned the story. His official records contain a brief mention: 'On the night of 1st/2nd November 1917 at ANZAC Ridge NE WESTHOEK during an extremely heavy bombardment by gas and HE shells on the battery position, No 2 Gun-pit was hit by a gas shell and the camouflage immediately ignited and ammunition began to explode. These men [Gunner James Holman Carthew and Gunner Nicholas Bannon]—though wearing Box respirators and at great personal risk—extinguished the fire and removed the burning ammunition to a place of safety, thereby saving a considerable amount, and the gun from being destroyed. This act of gallantry was performed whilst shells were falling everywhere and without thought of their own safety.' His medals languished for many years in a box of odds and ends in a kitchen drawer, a repository for old keys, pencil stubs, rubbers, blunt scissors and other useless items.

As a child, I would sometimes spend a wet day looking at the hundreds of postcards my father had sent his sweetheart Nellie, my mother. Some were humorous, but the ones I liked best were those exquisitely embossed or embroidered on satin or organdie, of pansies, violets, roses, forget-me-nots and bluebirds bearing tiny envelopes enclosing messages, each a work of art. When I was about seven, I saw a small Bible in my father's drawer and noticed a reddish-brown flower pressed between the pages. When I asked him what it was he looked at it for a moment and said, 'It's a Flanders Poppy'. Sensing that it was somehow significant I asked if I could have it, and carefully wrapped the crumbling, fragile flower in a piece of silver paper. Regrettably, the poppy and the postcards have been lost, but our family christening robe is still adorned with the beautiful lengths of Brussels lace my father sent my mother from Belgium.

My parents were married in June 1919. My sister Shirley was born in 1920 and I followed in 1922. We were a happy, united little family, shadowed only by my father's ill health, necessitating frequent stays in the Repatriation Hospital, to which he would jokingly refer as his 'Winter Residence'. When he got the stabbing side pains which he knew presaged pneumonia and pleurisy, as happened at least once each winter, he would catch the early train for the four-hour journey from York to Perth, carrying his case up to the Perth Hospital (he would never have considered taking a taxi) where two wards were reserved for the dwindling ranks of old soldiers. There were no miracle drugs in the 1920s and 1930s, but his wonderful constitution always pulled him through. He never complained and I only remember him taking to his bed once.

Unfortunately, he had an extremely low tolerance for alcohol, and on the odd occasions when he indulged in a few drinks with his mates he received a very cool reception from my mother. In spite of this she could do no wrong and he worshipped her until the day he died. He had a fine singing voice and, as Mum accompanied him on the piano, he would sing 'Roses of Picardy', never taking his eyes off her face. I know now that he must have sung this often in the trenches, thinking of her: 'But there's one rose that blooms not in Picardy, it's the rose that I keep in my heart.'

Shortly before he died, my father told me that he never 'went with' another woman after he met my mother, and I know this to be true, even though he must have been sorely tempted during his three years of hell when it seemed unlikely that he would ever return home to his 'girl'.

He was a very fond and tolerant father and had a great sense of humour. It is said that violence begets violence, but, in spite of the fact that James participated for three years in the most violent conflict in history, he never raised his hand or his voice to his daughters or swore in our hearing—'confounded' or 'infernal' were his most extreme expressions, usually when he was wrestling with his white tie prior to going to a ball. Both he and my mother were very fond of dancing, like most of their generation, and I always thought he looked very handsome in his 'tails'.

Only once did he lose his temper with me, and with good reason. I had mischievously pulled his chair from under him as he was about to be seated, so that he sat down heavily on the floor. 'You little Turk!' he roared. 'Go to your room!' Devastated, because I understood Turk was a bad name, I retreated to my bedroom and was sitting disconsolately on the bed when, no more than ten minutes later, he came to bring me back with a hug—suffering, I am sure, more than I.

In 1940 my father announced jauntily that he was going into Perth to enlist. 'They'll want experienced men,' he said confidently. I was horrified when my mother placidly let him go (he was fifty-one years old, although he looked much younger) but she told me not to worry, they would never accept him. She was right. He returned a few hours later considerably deflated.

My father died in 1960, aged seventy-one. I find that I still miss him, even after more than forty years. Now that I have been privileged to read his letters, and those of his two brothers, I have a small inkling of what he and his mates endured, although only those who did endure can truly comprehend that absolute hell. How I wish that I could tell him of the enormous love and pride we, his children, grandchildren and great-grandchildren, all feel for him and his comrades, who fought and died for their country in that Great War that was to end all wars.

## FOR THE FALLEN

They went with songs to the battle, they were young,
Straight of limb, true of eye, steady and aglow.
They were staunch to the end and against odds uncounted,
They fell with their faces to the foe.

They shall grow not old, as we that are left grow old:
Age shall not weary them, nor the years condemn.
At the going down of the sun and in the morning
We will remember them.

As the stars that shall be bright when we are dust,
Moving in marches upon the heavenly plain,
As the stars that are starry in the time of our darkness,
To the end, to the end, they remain.

LAURENCE BINYON